McCormack's Guides, issued annually, are written to make life in Marin, Napa & Sonoma counties easier, happier and understandable. The central theme is useful information, presented in a readable style.

Scholastic Aptitude Test (SAT) scores, rankings for public schools, what to look for in private and public schools, a directory of private schools — they are all inside. The perfect guide for parents or people shopping for homes or apartments in Marin, Napa and Sonoma counties.

"Marin, Napa & Sonoma '92" tells which months have the most rain, which the least, when to expect the summer heat and autumn chill.

Community profiles. Home prices, rents. Housing patterns.

Day-care & hospital services. Directory of day-care providers. Directory of local hospitals and major medical facilities.

Places to visit, things to do. Parks, museums, sports, entertainment.

The commuting scene. Tactics to save time and sanity.

Looking for work? "Marin, Napa & Sonoma '92" tells what jobs are in demand. Salary sampler.

Vital statistics. Population, income. Republicans and Democrats. Crime, ethnic makeup, history.

Don McCormack is a former newspaper reporter, editor and columnist. Cops, courts, planning, schools, politics — he has covered them all.

Publisher and editor Don McCormack formed Donnan Publications in 1984 to publish annual guides to California counties. A graduate of the University of California-Berkeley, McCormack joined the Contra Costa Times in 1969 and covered police, schools, politics, planning, courts and government. Later with the Richmond Independent and Berkeley Gazette, he worked as a reporter, then editor and columnist.

Co-editor and co-publisher Allen Kanda is a resident of San Mateo County. A University of Washington graduate with a degree in chemical engineering, Kanda joined the Richmond Independent in 1973 and worked as a reporter, then editor for the Richmond Independent and Berkeley Gazette.

This book is dedicated to Sean and Cathy Sullivan. Good luck in your new home.

DISCLAIMER

Indexed

ISBN 0-931299-27-6

MARIN, NAPA
& SONOMA '92

Edited by Don McCormack
and Allen Kanda

3211 Elmquist Court, Martinez, CA 94553
Phone: (510) 229-3581 or Fax: (510) 370-7307

We saw the changes coming.

The real estate market is moving in a new direction, and REALTY WORLD® agents are on top of the changes. We have new techniques to give you every possible advantage in today's market.

Our RealAction™ Marketing Plan and RealFax® Home Buyer Plan give REALTY WORLD® agents advanced insight. If you're buying or selling a house, call us today. Look in the White Pages for the REALTY WORLD® office nearest you.

REALTY WORLD
THE RESULTS PEOPLE.

REALTY WORLD-
AHO REALTY
506 S. Main St.
Sebastopol, CA 95472
(707) 823-1790

REALTY WORLD-
AMERICAN REALTY
2200 County Center Drive,
Ste. A & B
Santa Rosa, CA 95403
(707) 528-8587

REALTY WORLD-
BENCHMARK REALTY
977 Slate Drive
Santa Rosa, CA 95405
(707) 545-5352

REALTY WORLD-
O'ROURKE, INC.
4908 Sonoma Hwy.
Santa Rosa, CA 95409
(707) 538-8002

REALTY WORLD-
SANTA ROSA PROP.
301 Farmers Ln., Ste. 103
Santa Rosa, CA 95404
(707) 571-8000

REALTY WORLD-
TERRACE PROP., INC.
518 College Ave.
Santa Rosa, CA 95404
(707) 544-5434

Each office independently owned and operated.

© 1990 Realty World Corporation

EQUAL HOUSING
OPPORTUNITY

Table of Contents

Cover Photo:
St. Helena
Hospital and
Health Center in
Napa County.
See chapter on
hospitals.

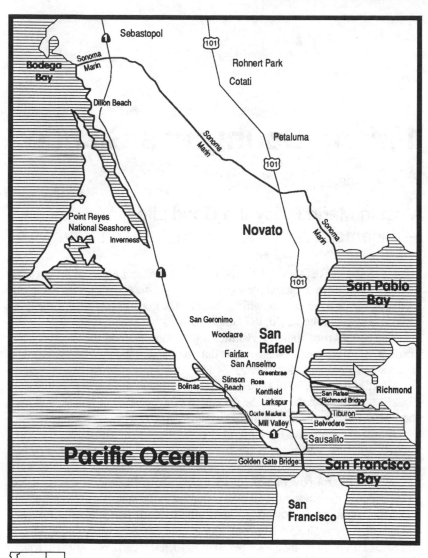

Marin County

1/Marin County at a Glance

Most in Marin Enjoy the Good Life
— Income, School Scores on the High Side

HILLY, BORDERED BY BAY AND PACIFIC, Marin is one of the prettiest counties in California, famed for its views, its style, its eccentricities (exaggerated) and for its southern tip, which holds up the north end of one of the most famous bridges in the world, the Golden Gate.

The county runs roughly 31 miles top to bottom along the Highway 101 corridor, 35 miles east to west, and is dominated near the middle by its single mountain, Tamalpais, elevation 2,571 feet.

West of Tamalpais, in summer, the winds blow, the fogs swirl, the cold nips. East of Tamalpais, with the exception of a few days of bluster and rain, the weather is balmy from January through December.

Marin residents love the west: the Pacific, the waves, the views, the seals, the fish, the flora, the fauna. Aside from a few hardy souls, however, they live east of Mt. Tamalpais. Mountain and hills shelter the east from the elements.

In land, Marin covers 520 square miles, about 12 times the size of San Francisco, but it's among the smallest counties in the state, third from bottom.

Marin is one of the slowest-growing urban counties in California. It started the half century with 85,610 people, jumped to 146,820 within a decade, an increase of 72 percent, then to 208,250 in 1970, another 42 percent. Then slam went the door. The population in the 1970s rose by 7 percent to 222,568 and in the 1980s by 3 percent. About 230,096 (1990 census) now reside in Marin.

Marin Style

"Only in Marin" pigeonholes the county for outsiders who think Marin has attracted an unusually large number of goofs.

Marin residents, or some portion of them, are always searching, searching,

Marin County Population

City or Area	Male	Female	Total	*Total
Belvedere	1,016	1,131	2,147	2,170
Bolinas	550	548	1,098	NA
Corte Madera	3,916	4,356	8,272	8,325
Fairfax	3,345	3,586	6,931	7,025
Inverness	684	738	1,422	NA
Kentfield	2,905	3,125	6,030	NA
Larkspur	4,967	6,103	11,070	11,200
Lucas Valley-Mrnwd	2,883	3,099	5,982	NA
Mill Valley	5,974	7,064	13,038	13,150
Novato	23,123	24,462	47,585	48,100
Ross	1,022	1,101	2,123	2,160
San Anselmo	5,534	6,209	11,743	11,800
San Rafael	23,755	24,649	48,404	49,750
Santa Venetia	1,647	1,715	3,362	NA
Sausalito	3,554	3,598	7,152	7,225
Tiburon	3,555	3,977	7,532	7,675
Woodacre	743	735	1,478	NA
Remainder*	22,748	17,602	30,350	NA
Countywide	114,001	116,095	230,096	233,500.

Source: 1990 Census. Remainder population includes about 5,500 San Quentin inmates. *Population estimates by California Dept. of Finance, Jan. 1, 1991. NA (not available).

for the right therapist or therapy, the special restaurant, the elusive diet, the skilled plastic surgeon — for the anyone and the anything that will enable them to squeeze the maximum out of life.

When they are not searching, many are fretting, fretting, fretting, especially over the environment. Save that tree, preserve that hill, don't you dare build that home or road. None of this is harmful but the wealth of the county makes a great deal of it seem shallow.

Marin is among the richest counties in the state; indeed by one measure, joint income, it is the richest, $55,605 per couple in the 1989 state tax tally. And many of the residents are unabashedly dedicated to living the good life. On any weekend night in Marin, the wine flows by the vat.

The Real Marin

School rankings perhaps give a more accurate picture. They're quite high, which usually means someone at home is pushing the kids to study, that education is prized for itself.

Coming & Going
(Driver License Address Changes)

County	Moved to Marin from	Moved Out of Marin to	Net
Alameda	937	792	145
Alpine	2	0	2
Amador	3	10	-7
Butte	78	129	-51
Calaveras	5	16	-11
Colusa	6	7	-1
Contra Costa	610	784	-174
Del Norte	9	6	3
El Dorado	37	70	-33
Fresno	64	58	6
Glenn	6	1	5
Humboldt	49	59	-10
Imperial	6	2	4
Inyo	4	4	0
Kern	36	33	3
Kings	8	7	1
Lake	42	103	-61
Lassen	8	7	1
Los Angeles	1,145	786	359
Madera	9	16	-7
Mariposa	13	3	10
Mendocino	60	82	-22
Merced	21	24	-3
Modoc	3	7	-4
Mono	6	4	2
Monterey	114	73	41
Napa	112	207	-95
Nevada	36	91	-55
Orange	282	239	43
Placer	69	111	-42
Plumas	6	9	-3
Riverside	76	100	-24
Sacramento	265	414	149
San Benito	3	4	-1
San Bernardino	58	52	6
San Diego	410	438	-28
San Francisco	3,588	2,047	1,541

Coming & Going
(Driver License Address Changes)

County	Moved to Marin from	Moved Out of Marin to	Net
San Joaquin	66	78	-12
San Luis Obispo	67	83	16
San Mateo	664	509	155
Santa Barbara	128	152	-24
Santa Clara	443	395	48
Santa Cruz	126	156	-30
Shasta	23	41	-18
Sierra	0	4	-4
Siskiyou	14	17	-3
Solano	181	395	-214
Sonoma	1,365	2,938	-1,573
Stanislaus	24	34	-5
Sutter	10	15	-5
Tehama	4	10	-6
Trinity	1	3	-2
Tulare	14	14	0
Tuolumne	16	25	-9
Ventura	81	63	18
Yolo	90	135	-45
Yuba	7	12	-5
All Counties	11,515	11,874	-359
Out of State	3,566	2,842	724
Total	15,081	14,716	365

Source: California Department of Finance, 1991. Data covers fiscal year July 1, 1990-June 30, 1991. Out-of-state counts have been adjusted for non-compliers.

Crime, with the exception of a few neighborhoods, is very low.

Towns like Tiburon, Belvedere, Mill Valley and Sausalito — well-to-do or rich — often seem to set the tone for the county. But the most populous towns, San Rafael and Novato, are generally middle-class burgs, with modest homes and many apartments.

Marin is one of the few counties that can aptly be described as cosmopolitan. Many residents are well-traveled and well-educated or bosses or managers. They stage plays, make movies (George Lucas has his studios in Marin), support the arts. Yet Middle America is always popping up. When a Larkspur restaurant placed two nude statues out front, complaints followed and the statues were removed.

Average Household Income

City or Area	1990	1991
Belvedere	$107,900	$112,500
Corte Madera	58,300	60,800
Fairfax	46,500	48,500
Larkspur-Kentfield	72,000	75,100
Mill Valley	65,300	68,100
Novato	62,400	65,100
Ross	118,200	123,300
San Anselmo	54,000	56,300
San Rafael	58,700	61,200
Sausalito-Marin City	68,800	71,800
Tiburon	78,200	81,600
Remainder	˙44,300	46,200
Countywide	62,700	65,400

Source: *Projects '90*, Association of Bay Area Governments, January, 1990; U.S. Bureau of Labor Statistics. Income is stated in constant 1988 dollars, rounded off to the nearest $100. Income for 1991 is an estimate based on 1990 income adjusted by the Bay Area consumer price index for the September, 1990-September, 1991, period. A full-year adjustment may vary.

History

In the beginning, there were Indians, Miwoks, destined for tragedy. They fished, hunted, ground nuts for meal and lived in lodges made of willow.

Sir Francis Drake, of piratical and Armada fame, or a member of his crew may have been the first White to set foot in Marin. In June, 1579, Drake's ship, the Golden Hinde, sailed into either San Francisco Bay or Drakes Bay, off Point Reyes, made contact with the Indians, and soon sailed off.

Many dispute the landing of Sir Francis, but no matter. The buccaneer sailed into local lore.

The Spanish

Although Spanish captains sailed the coast of California in the 1500s, explorers did not arrive in the Bay Area until 1769. Distance and fierce Indians to the Southwest quickly choked the flow of settlers. Fifty years later Spanish-Hispanics in Northern California numbered below 2,000.

Church policy in those days was to bring the Indians to the mission (in San Francisco), and instruct them in the habits of the field and the ways of God. Having no immunity to Western diseases, many contracted small pox or measles and died. On the secular side, the rancheros, needing workers, indentured or enslaved Indians, further depleting their numbers.

Russians and Yankees

The Russians in 1812 built Fort Ross in Sonoma County, worrying the Californios. For this reason and others, they moved north from San Francisco, opened a mission at San Rafael and divided the countryside into rancheros. Some Indians fought back. One band was led by a Chief Marin, defeated in the end but formidable enough for the tribute of naming the county in his honor.

Meanwhile, the United States ventured into the Midwest and trappers were making their way over the mountains, followed a few years later by settlers. The Russians trapped the local otter out of existence, became discouraged and left.

The Yankee story can be summarized: They came, they coveted, they conquered, more by numbers than anything else. Spain and Mexico (which took over from Spain in 1821) never put together a successful plan to colonize California — a great strategic failing.

The Americans shot and snared the grizzly, cut the trees, farmed the land, fished the Bay and Pacific, ignored, swindled or bought the Californios into oblivion and apparently treated the remaining Indians with enough ill will to ensure the extinction of all but a few.

Railroads and Ferries

The arrival of the Yankees coincided historically with two great inventions of the 1800s: trains and steamships. Ferry slips were built at Sausalito and

Marin County Ethnic Makeup

City, Town or Area	White	Black	Hisp.	Asn./PI	N. Am.
Belvedere	2,084	0	40	22	0
Bolinas	1,030	14	30	13	8
Corte Madera	7,407	75	348	421	14
Fairfax	6,336	89	337	134	29
Inverness	1,348	4	44	14	11
Kentfield	5,662	25	165	170	7
Larkspur	10,217	82	432	315	16
Lucas Valley/Mrnwd	5,244	66	279	387	5
Mill Valley	11,953	182	365	485	25
Novato	4,314	1,296	3,460	2,245	207
Ross	2,040	1	45	31	6
San Anselmo	10,762	92	530	301	48
San Rafael	37,402	1,306	6,951	2,542	135
Santa Venitia	2,734	79	334	197	14
Sausalito	6,596	73	225	241	10
Strawberry	3,843	103	162	261	6
Tiburon	6,922	67	256	273	9
Woodacre	1,376	4	69	25	3
Remainder*	31,395	3,971	3,858	987	108
Countywide	194,665	7,529	17,530	9,064	661

Source: 1990 Census. Key: Hisp. (Hispanic); Asn./PI (Asian/Pacific Islander); N. Am. (Native American including American Indian, Eskimo and Aleut). Not included, a small number identified by census as "other race." *Reminder includes 5,500 San Quentin imates.

Tiburon. Rail lines, one even ascending Mt. Tamalpais, snaked up the county.

Train, ship and ferry allowed farmers to supply San Francisco food and fish and, by reducing travel time, opened Marin to excursions from the City.

The population at the turn of the century stood about 15,000.

When the businessman of old and his family wanted relief from the stink, noise and rush of San Francisco, they looked north to Marin. There they found shade of pine and redwood, burble of brook, diversions of hiking and fishing, and when they tired of all that, the pleasures of tippling, dining, carousing.

About the turn of the century, Belvedere Cove was noted for its houseboats, called arks. Men rowed from ark to ark, sampling hospitality and parties. A launch deposited them in the morning at San Francisco and work.

Culture and Conservation

Marin in its formative years had the good fortune to attract the educated, the progressive, the wealthy and the cultivated. They bought land for parks, led the fight to conserve land, funded concerts and other musical events, patronized artists and instilled the idea that support for the arts and for conservation should be routinely enthusiastic, not occasional.

Of special note, William Kent purchased Muir Woods and donated it for a park and led the fight to preserve Mt. Tamalpais. His mother Adaline donated the land for the present College of Marin.

Earthquake, Twenties and Thirties

The earthquake of 1906 leveled San Francisco and implanted in City dwellers an attitude of, "I'm getting outta here." Marin's population grew steadily and by 1930 stood at 41,648.

Unfortunately, the logic behind the move was as faulty as the San Andreas. Marin, like the entire Bay Area, is very much earthquake country. The San Andreas, the biggest fault, runs straight through Tomales Bay and, in fact, created the Bay. Your phone book contains information about how to prepare for and what to do in a big quake — a prudent read.

The Golden Gate Bridge

The idea for spanning the Golden Gate dates back almost to the Forty Niners and retrospectively the bridge was probably inevitable. It opened on May 28, 1937, a feat of grace and engineering.

"Paradise was lost," someone later wrote, a reference to the opening of Marin to great pressures to develop. But it might be argued that instead of lost, paradise was expanded. Tens of thousands now enjoy Marin who otherwise might not have. By 1940, the population had reached 52,907.

World War II

The World War boomed the West Coast, Marin no exception. Sausalito built ships, Novato flew planes (Hamilton Air Force Base). Men and women came from all over the country to work in the new industries. Marin got its first major infusion of Blacks, in a village now called Marin City, located just outside Sausalito.

Highway 101

A logical addition to the Golden Gate Bridge, Highway 101 was started in the '50s and, in Sonoma County, is still being built. As revolutionary as the Golden Gate Bridge was, it could not realize its potential until feeder roads were improved. 101 was one vast road improvement. From 1850 to 1950, Marin grew by 85,000 people. In the 20 years after 1950, it added 123,00 people.

Golden Gate Recreational Area

In the early 1970s, Congressman Phil Burton, a legislative whiz whose

Marin County Voter Registration

City & Area	Demo.	Repub.	Decl.	All
Belvedere	494	938	151	1,605
Corte Madera	2,864	1,573	629	5,194
Fairfax	3,084	800	575	4,622
Greenbrae	903	1,062	186	2,191
Larkspur	3,589	2,877	788	7,384
Lucas Valley	537	443	117	1,106
Mill Valley	5,210	2,349	1,023	8,781
Novato	11,051	9,158	2,788	23,430
Ross	616	797	198	1,640
San Anselmo	4,692	1,914	895	7,707
San Rafael	13,262	9,191	2,838	25,815
Sausalito	2,484	1,463	803	4,862
Tiburon	2,109	2,089	648	4,912
Unincor. Marin	20,057	11,986	4,591	37,487
Countywide	69,512	45,135	15,927	133,439

Source: Marin Registrar of Voters, Sept. 1991. Key: Demo. (Democrat); Repub. (Republican); Decl. (Declined to state political party preference).

idea of exercise was limited to cigar lifting, pushed through one of the largest park purchases in the history of California.

The result, now called the Golden Gate National Recreational Area, includes the Marin headlands and Point Reyes, thousands of acres along the Pacific Coast, Muir Woods, Alcatraz and parts of the San Francisco coast.

The Great Slowdown

After the building boom of the 1960s and 1970s, Marin collectively said "Whoa." Of the county's 11 cities, five declined in population between the 1980 and 1990 census — Belvedere, Fairfax, Ross, San Anselmo and Sausalito. Novato, with space to grow, and San Rafael each took on about 3,700 residents.

Marin is still building: Novato is opening a shopping center and more housing tracts are planned. But in some towns, construction of a house or two is greeted with all the elation medieval Europe accorded the bubonic plague.

If you want to buy in Marin, you must, usually, look to the resale market.

Marin Today

Interesting, always willing to debate, to argue. Perhaps more tuned to the outside world than the backyard. Marin residents are always flying to struggling countries, especially Russia, to offer their help.

To many people, as familiar as an old shoe. Because the population is

Presidential Voting In Marin County

Year	Democrat	D-Votes	Republican	R-Votes
1948	Truman*	12,540	Dewey	18,747
1952	Stevenson	14,236	Eisenhower*	29,574
1956	Stevenson	17,301	Eisenhower*	33,792
1960	Kennedy*	27,888	Nixon	37,620
1964	Johnson*	46,462	Goldwater	28,682
1968	Humphrey	36,278	Nixon*	41,422
1972	McGovern	47,414	Nixon*	54,123
1976	Carter*	43,590	Ford	53,425
1980	Carter	39,231	Reagan*	53,425
1984	Mondale	57,533	Reagan*	56,887
1988	Dukakis	69,394	Bush*	46,885

Source: California Secretary of State's office. * Election winner.

stable, people have had a chance to get to know each other.

About to become grayer. Sonoma and Marin have about the same percentage of residents over 55 years (23.3 percent and 23.5). But in children under age 18, Sonoma counts 23.4 percent of its population and Marin 18.4.

A little more diverse.

More liberal. Nixon and Reagan (in his first race) carried Marin. In the last two elections, Mondale and Dukakis got the nod.

Still devoted to wine, chocolate, cheese and pasta with diversions into tofu — and despite its desire to save much of the world from itself, unapologetic about its pursuit of the sweet life. But then, where is it written that the good life is the dull life?

2/Marin County School Rankings

Elementary, Middle and High, by Districts

ALTHOUGH MANY MARIN and North Bay schools score well over the 50th percentile, the question — how good are the schools — is difficult to answer because scores are greatly influenced by parents and background.

If your mother and father attended college and drummed into you that you should attend college, well, chances are good — many studies strongly indicate — that you're going to score high on tests that try to determine the minimum you should know.

That's what the CAP tests attempted to do: they tested basic knowledge. The children filled in the bubbles. The tests are now history, shot down in the political wars that regularly sweep the state. New tests will be along in a few years.

In the meantime the CAP results are among the best we have for determining roughly how the children are doing academically and how the school is made up demographically. High scores generally identify well-to-do or educated neighborhoods; middling scores, middle-class neighborhoods; low scores, poor neighborhoods. These correlations hold up even when such factors as teacher salaries and per-pupil expenditures are equalized. For more discussion see the chapter on how public schools work.

These rankings, issued by the California Department of Education, are slightly weighted to allow for enrollment differences but are very close to unalloyed percentiles.

What Percentiles Mean

If a school scores in the 91st percentile, it has done better than 91 percent of the other public schools in the state. If it scores in the 51st percentile, it has done better than 51 percent of the others; the 40th rank, better than 40 percent of the others. If a school scores in the first percentile, 99 percent of the other schools have scored higher.

Rankings

These rankings are drawn from state tests given over three years, 1988, 1989, 1990. For the most part, they will follow a pattern. High one year will be high the next, low will be low.

When the numbers fluctuate wildly, the number of children who took the tests will often be low. In a small class, one or two kids having a bad or good day will cause the wide swings. Sometimes the children simply fail to understand instructions and this lowers their grade. Sometimes they just have an off day.

A Cautionary Note

Ranking systems don't recognize overall gains or losses. If every school in California raised raw scores 20 percent, some schools would still be ranked at the bottom, a few at the top. The same if every raw score dropped. A ranking system shows how one school did against all other schools. There is no one perfect method of testing.

BOLINAS-STINSON UNIFIED
District-Wide

Third Grade	1988	1989	1990
Reading	88	95	98
Writing	54	91	93
Math	67	91	75
No. Tested	36	17	16
Sixth Grade	1988	1989	1990
Reading	98	74	99
Writing	87	49	74
Math	91	84	97
No. Tested	21	23	18
Eighth Grade	1988	1989	1990
Reading	97	97	99
Writing	93	—	—
Math	98	90	94
History	99	95	99
Science	96	74	89
No. Tested	17	17	15

Bolinas Elementary, Bolinas

Third Grade	1988	1989	1990
Reading	81	90	96
Writing	55	84	87
Math	63	85	72
No. Tested	36	17	16

Sixth Grade	1988	1989	1990
Reading	97	69	98
Writing	80	48	71
Math	87	77	96
No. Tested	21	23	18
Eighth Grade	1988	1989	1990
Reading	96	95	99
Writing	92	—	—
Math	97	87	93
History	98	93	99
Science	96	75	87
No. Tested	17	17	15

DIXIE ELEMENTARY SCHOOL DISTRICT
District-Wide

Third Grade	1988	1989	1990
Reading	97	98	96
Writing	98	96	97
Math	97	97	96
No. Tested	106	142	149
Sixth Grade	1988	1989	1990
Reading	92	94	98
Writing	95	87	93
Math	97	97	97
No. Tested	137	133	155

DIXIE (Continued)
District-Wide

Eighth Grade	1988	1989	1990
Reading	96	94	89
Writing	98	—	—
Math	93	86	87
History	98	96	96
Science	97	94	92
No. Tested	115	132	145

Dixie Elementary, San Rafael

Third Grade	1988	1989	1990
Reading	96	94	90
Writing	95	86	94
Math	97	89	95
No.Tested	45	74	71

Miller Creek Middle, San Rafael

Sixth Grade	1988	1989	1990
Reading	86	90	96
Writing	91	83	89
Math	93	95	96
No. Tested	137	133	155

Eighth Grade	1988	1989	1990
Reading	95	93	87
Writing	87	—	—
Math	91	83	85
History	97	94	95
Science	97	92	90
No. Tested	115	132	145

Vallecito Elementary,San Rafael

Third Grade	1988	1989	1990
Reading	91	97	92
Writing	94	96	92
Math	90	97	89
No. Tested	61	68	78

KENTFIELD ELEM. DISTRICT
District-Wide

Third Grade	1988	1989	1990
Reading	99	99	98
Writing	93	98	99
Math	98	98	97
No. Tested	91	105	87

Sixth Grade	1988	1989	1990
Reading	98	99	99
Writing	99	98	98
Math	99	97	98
No. Tested	74	69	71

Eighth Grade	1988	1989	1990
Reading	96	96	98
Writing	96	—	—

Eighth Grade	1988	1989	1990
Math	96	96	98
History	94	98	96
Science	94	99	99
No. Tested	67	69	72

Bacich (Anthony G.) Elem., Kentfield

Third Grade	1988	1989	1990
Reading	98	98	96
Writing	88	96	98
Math	96	97	93
No. Tested	91	105	87

Kent (Adaline E.) Middle, Kentfield

Sixth Grade	1988	1989	1990
Reading	97	99	98
Writing	99	96	94
Math	98	96	97
No. Tested	74	69	71

Eighth Grade	1988	1989	1990
Reading	94	95	97
Writing	95	—	—
Math	95	96	98
History	94	97	96
Science	92	99	99
No. Tested	67	69	72

LAGUNA JOINT ELEM. DISTRICT
District-Wide

Third Grade	1988	1989	1990
Reading	79	99	23
Writing	79	81	22
Math	90	94	61
No. Tested	3	3	5

Sixth Grade	1988	1989	1990
Reading	—	—	95
Writing	—	—	89
Math	—	—	65
No. Tested	—	—	4

Laguna Elem., Petaluma

Third Grade	1988	1989	1990
Reading	73	97	28
Writing	74	75	25
Math	84	88	60
No. Tested	3	3	5

Sixth Grade	1988	1989	1990
Reading	—	—	89
Writing	—	—	84
Math	—	—	62
No. Tested	—	—	4

LAGUNITAS ELEM. DISTRICT
District-Wide

Third Grade	1988	1989	1990
Reading	96	96	97
Writing	84	88	87
Math	98	98	95
No. Tested	37	34	35
Sixth Grade	1988	1989	1990
Reading	99	98	98
Writing	98	96	98
Math	99	91	92
No. Tested	37	24	42
Eighth Grade	1988	1989	1990
Reading	97	88	98
Writing	96	—	—
Math	97	77	96
History	94	93	92
Science	92	91	96
No. Tested	26	27	23

Lagunitas Elem., San Geronimo

Third Grade	1988	1989	1990
Reading	93	97	99
Writing	90	90	96
Math	98	97	96
No. Tested	23	14	18
Sixth Grade	1988	1989	1990
Reading	98	97	97
Writing	98	93	97
Math	96	87	91
No. Tested	34	24	35
Eighth Grade	1988	1989	1990
Reading	95	85	97
Writing	95	—	—
Math	96	75	96
History	93	91	90
Science	89	90	96
No. Tested	26	27	23

San Geronimo Vly. Elem., San Geronimo

Third Grade	1988	1989	1990
Reading	80	85	72
Writing	50	74	49
Math	86	81	81
No. Tested	14	20	17
Sixth Grade	1988	1989	1990
Reading	91	—	74
Writing	22	—	87
Math	66	—	46
No. Tested	3	—	7

LARKSPUR ELEM. DISTRICT
District-Wide

Third Grade	1988	1989	1990
Reading	98	99	92
Writing	97	94	82
Math	96	96	78
No. Tested	55	69	86
Sixth Grade	1988	1989	1990
Reading	99	98	98
Writing	99	99	97
Math	99	97	98
No. Tested	76	69	67
Eighth Grade	1988	1989	1990
Reading	99	99	99
Writing	99	—	—
Math	97	97	97
History	98	97	98
Science	99	99	98
No. Tested	69	73	94

Hall Middle, Larkspur

Sixth Grade	1988	1989	1990
Reading	98	97	96
Writing	99	98	93
Math	98	96	97
No. Tested	76	69	67
Eighth Grade	1988	1989	1990
Reading	98	98	98
Writing	98	—	—
Math	96	98	97
History	98	96	98
Science	98	98	97
No. Tested	69	73	94

Neil Cummins Elem., Corte Madera

Third Grade	1988	1989	1990
Reading	97	98	87
Writing	93	89	75
Math	93	92	74
No. Tested	55	69	86

LINCON ELEM. DISTRICT
District-Wide

Third Grade	1988	1989	1990
Reading	32	—	99
Writing	2	—	87
Math	89	—	46
No. Tested	2	—	3

Lincoln Elem.

Third Grade	1988	1989	1990
Reading	34	—	99
Writing	10	—	80

LINCON (Continued)
Lincoln Elem.

Third Grade	1988	1989	1990
Math	82	—	47
No. Tested	2	—	3

MILL VALLEY ELEM. DISTRICT
District-Wide

Third Grade	1988	1989	1990
Reading	99	99	99
Writing	99	99	99
Math	99	99	99
No. Tested	173	160	189
Sixth Grade	1988	1989	1990
Reading	98	99	98
Writing	97	98	94
Math	97	98	97
No. Tested	135	170	161
Eighth Grade	1988	1989	1990
Reading	97	99	98
Writing	98	—	—
Math	99	99	97
History	99	99	98
Science	99	99	99
No. Tested	175	175	141

Mill Valley Middle, Mill Valley

Sixth Grade	1988	1989	1990
Reading	95	98	97
Writing	94	97	90
Math	93	97	96
No. Tested	135	170	161
Eighth Grade	1988	1989	1990
Reading	96	98	97
Writing	97	—	—
Math	98	98	97
History	98	98	98
Science	99	99	98
No. Tested	175	175	141

Old Mill Elem., Mill Valley

Third Grade	1988	1989	1990
Reading	99	99	99
Writing	99	97	99
Math	99	99	99
No. Tested	53	41	53

Park Elem., Mill Valley

Third Grade	1988	1989	1990
Reading	98	99	97
Writing	98	99	99
Math	98	99	98
No. Tested	54	43	43

Strawberry Point Elem., Mill Valley

Third Grade	1988	1989	1990
Reading	98	83	97
Writing	97	80	97
Math	98	81	98
No. Tested	36	32	43

Tamalpais Valley Elem., Mill Valley

Third Grade	1988	1989	1990
Reading	95	99	98
Writing	97	96	98
Math	98	99	98
No. Tested	30	44	50

NICASIO ELEM.DISTRICT
District-Wide

Third Grade	1988	1989	1990
Reading	—	95	50
Writing	—	83	56
Math	—	94	1
No. Tested	—	8	4
Sixth Grade	1988	1989	1990
Reading	'93	98	99
Writing	62	99	83
Math	89	69	87
No. Tested	4	2	3
Eighth Grade	1988	1989	1990
Reading	96	96	99
Writing	92	—	—
Math	99	80	94
History	99	99	99
Science	99	99	99
No. Tested	6	5	5

Nicasio Elem., Nicasio

Third Grade	1988	1989	1990
Reading	—	91	51
Writing	—	77	54
Math	—	88	9
No. Tested	—	8	4
Sixth Grade	1988	1989	1990
Reading	88	97	99
Writing	59	98	78
Math	81	64	83
No. Tested	4	2	3
Eighth Grade	1988	1989	1990
Reading	94	95	99
Writing	89	—	—
Math	99	98	93
History	99	99	99
Science	99	99	99
No. Tested	6	5	5

NOVATO UNIFIED
District-Wide

Third Grade	1988	1989	1990
Reading	94	93	92
Writing	93	94	93
Math	96	91	96
No. Tested	559	596	603
Sixth Grade	1988	1989	1990
Reading	92	96	89
Writing	93	95	91
Math	93	96	90
No. Tested	504	565	557
Eighth Grade	1988	1989	1990
Reading	90	91	87
Writing	84	—	—
Math	91	92	94
History	92	92	86
Science	92	91	92
No. Tested	539	508	485
Twelfth Grade	1988	1989	1990
Reading	91	87	90
Writing	—	88	92
Math	81	93	92
No. Tested	590	543	455

North Marin High, Novato

Twelfth Grade	1988	1989	1990
Reading	34	2	2
Writing	—	—	—
Math	21	49	12
No. Tested	11	8	6

Novato High, Novato

Twelfth Grade	1988	1989	1990
Reading	90	87	87
Writing	—	92	92
Math	74	90	85
No. Tested	296	264	231

San Marin High, Novato

Twelfth Grade	1988	1989	1990
Reading	84	78	90
Writing	—	75	81
Math	84	89	92
No. Tested	283	271	218

Hamilton Elem., Hamilton AFB

Third Grade	1988	1989	1990
Reading	76	78	92
Writing	71	88	95
Math	73	78	98
No. Tested	101	88	87

Sixth Grade	1988	1989	1990
Reading	90	89	91
Writing	83	84	86
Math	91	86	86
No. Tested	73	56	51

Loma Verde Elem., Novato

Third Grade	1988	1989	1990
Reading	59	78	84
Writing	61	60	71
Math	81	69	77
No. Tested	58	73	56
Sixth Grade	1988	1989	1990
Reading	95	—	—
Writing	80	—	—
Math	88	—	—
No. Tested	60	—	—

Lu Sutton Elem., Novato

Third Grade	1988	1989	1990
Reading	76	76	81
Writing	69	80	74
Math	79	65	87
No. Tested	86	59	80
Sixth Grade	1988	1989	1990
Reading	64	69	64
Writing	92	70	73
Math	69	64	63
No. Tested	57	54	29

Lynwood Elem., Novato

Third Grade	1988	1989	1990
Reading	75	85	73
Writing	91	94	92
Math	90	90	91
No. Tested	53	62	58
Sixth Grade	1988	1989	1990
Reading	95	87	63
Writing	94	58	76
Math	99	76	74
No. Tested	59	25	21

Olive Elem., Novato

Third Grade	1988	1989	1990
Reading	93	84	86
Writing	91	85	69
Math	89	74	75
No. Tested	57	60	68
Sixth Grade	1988	1989	1990
Reading	74	95	93
Writing	59	94	81
Math	79	89	78
No. Tested	52	49	50

Pleasant Valley Elem., Novato

Third Grade	1988	1989	1990
Reading	97	93	92
Writing	98	92	95
Math	98	81	95
No. Tested	61	83	84
Sixth Grade	1988	1989	1990
Reading	75	84	76
Writing	75	94	81
Math	78	97	81
No. Tested	58	29	22

Rancho Elem., Novato

Third Grade	1988	1989	1990
Reading	98	95	98
Writing	97	97	98
Math	98	92	98
No. Tested	86	84	88
Sixth Grade	1988	1989	1990
Reading	94	96	98
Writing	95	97	94
Math	92	94	98
No. Tested	85	70	53

San Ramon Elem., Novato

Third Grade	1988	1989	1990
Reading	95	95	65
Writing	94	95	69
Math	98	97	81
No. Tested	57	87	82
Sixth Grade	1988	1989	1990
Reading	80	88	81
Writing	86	76	73
Math	77	74	80
No. Tested	60	30	22

San Jose Middle, Novato

Sixth Grade	1988	1989	1990
Reading	—	83	72
Writing	—	90	82
Math	—	89	74
No. Tested	—	111	140
Eighth Grade	1988	1989	1990
Reading	71	89	85
Writing	62	—	—
Math	80	90	93
History	83	90	79
Science	84	90	93
No. Tested	258	255	247

Sinaloa Middle, Novato

Sixth Grade	1988	1989	1990
Reading	—	96	76

Sixth Grade	1988	1989	1990
Writing	—	96	91
Math	—	97	91
No. Tested	—	141	169
Eighth Grade	1988	1989	1990
Reading	92	88	80
Writing	90	—	—
Math	94	91	94
History	94	90	87
Science	94	88	86
No. Tested	281	253	238

REED UNION ELEM. DISTRICT
District-Wide

Third Grade	1988	1989	1990
Reading	99	99	98
Writing	99	98	98
Math	99	99	99
No. Tested	95	101	83
Sixth Grade	1988	1989	1990
Reading	96	98	98
Writing	91	94	98
Math	95	98	97
No. Tested	90	90	83
Eighth Grade	1988	1989	1990
Reading	99	96	94
Writing	99	—	—
Math	98	98	92
History	98	98	98
Science	98	99	93
No. Tested	103	95	82

Bell Aire Elem., Tiburon

Third Grade	1988	1989	1990
Reading	98	99	97
Writing	98	94	96
Math	99	98	99
No. Tested	95	101	83

Del Mar Middle, Tiburon

Sixth Grade	1988	1989	1990
Reading	92	96	97
Writing	84	90	95
Math	91	97	94
No. Tested	90	90	83
Eighth Grade	1988	1989	1990
Reading	98	95	94
Writing	98	—	—
Math	97	97	89
History	97	97	96
Science	98	98	91
No. Tested	103	95	82

ROSS ELEM. DISTRICT
District-Wide

Third Grade	1988	1989	1990
Reading	99	94	99
Writing	99	96	99
Math	99	99	98
No. Tested	28	31	41

Sixth Grade	1988	1989	1990
Reading	99	99	99
Writing	99	98	98
Math	99	99	99
No. Tested	37	38	28

Eighth Grade	1988	1989	1990
Reading	99	99	93
Writing	99	—	—
Math	99	99	98
History	99	99	99
Science	99	99	98
No. Tested	27	38	32

Ross Elem., Ross

Third Grade	1988	1989	1990
Reading	99	89	98
Writing	98	93	99
Math	98	97	96
No. Tested	28	31	41

Sixth Grade	1988	1989	1990
Reading	99	98	97
Writing	98	95	94
Math	98	99	98
No. Tested	37	38	28

Eighth Grade	1988	1989	1990
Reading	99	99	92
Writing	99	—	—
Math	99	99	99
History	99	99	99
Science	99	97	97
No. Tested	27	38	32

ROSS VALLEY SCHOOL DISTRICT
District-Wide

Third Grade	1988	1989	1990
Reading	93	95	96
Writing	81	96	90
Math	97	98	91
No. Tested	142	147	195

Sixth Grade	1988	1989	1990
Reading	98	98	98
Writing	93	93	95
Math	97	97	97
No. Tested	131	145	167

Eighth Grade	1988	1989	1990
Reading	91	95	98
Writing	83	—	—
Math	93	93	95
History	94	96	98
Science	92	95	98
No. Tested	158	140	143

Manor Elem., Fairfax

Third Grade	1988	1989	1990
Reading	79	88	84
Writing	62	94	89
Math	92	94	84
No. Tested	63	57	65

Sixth Grade	1988	1989	1990
Reading	97	89	85
Writing	79	85	87
Math	95	92	89
No. Tested	48	45	51

Fairfax White Hill, Fairfax

Eighth Grade	1988	1989	1990
Reading	88	94	98
Writing	80	—	—
Math	92	91	94
History	94	94	96
Science	91	95	97
No. Tested	158	140	143

Brookside Elem., San Anselmo

Third Grade	1988	1989	1990
Reading	91	97	97
Writing	75	95	79
Math	92	97	85
No. Tested	45	64	81

Sixth Grade	1988	1989	1990
Reading	91	96	97
Writing	90	92	86
Math	88	90	94
No. Tested	55	55	71

Wade Thomas Elem., San Anselmo

Third Grade	1988	1989	1990
Reading	94	80	85
Writing	91	78	83
Math	96	91	90
No. Tested	34	26	49

Sixth Grade	1988	1989	1990
Reading	99	98	99
Writing	91	90	98
Math	99	96	97
No. Tested	28	45	45

SAN RAFAEL CITY ELEM. DISTRICT
District-Wide

Third Grade	1988	1989	1990
Reading	78	87	86
Writing	81	84	86
Math	88	82	90
No. Tested	253	244	251
Sixth Grade	1988	1989	1990
Reading	75	77	89
Writing	88	93	94
Math	82	84	82
No. Tested	201	231	207
Eighth Grade	1988	1989	1990
Reading	54	89	66
Writing	68	—	—
Math	74	70	64
History	81	90	89
Science	80	62	73
No. Tested	258	222	228

Bahia Vista Elem., San Rafael

Third Grade	1988	1989	1990
Reading	44	28	38
Writing	62	25	36
Math	60	24	42
No. Tested	58	58	54

Coleman Elem., San Rafael

Sixth Grade	1988	1989	1990
Reading	67	80	57
Writing	65	90	56
Math	76	88	71
No. Tested	56	41	39

Gallinas Elem., San Rafael

Third Grade	1988	1989	1990
Reading	76	63	50
Writing	82	56	50
Math	86	50	64
No. Tested	45	46	51

Glenwood Elem., San Rafael

Third Grade	1988	1989	1990
Reading	98	98	96
Writing	96	96	91
Math	97	94	94
No. Tested	43	53	57

Sun Valley Elem., San Rafael

Third Grade	1988	1989	1990
Reading	57	96	99
Writing	65	96	99
Math	64	92	98
No. Tested	51	46	50

James B. Davidson Middle, San Rafael

Sixth Grade	1988	1989	1990
Reading	69	72	83
Writing	82	89	89
Math	74	77	76
No. Tested	201	231	207
Eighth Grade	1988	1989	1990
Reading	54	86	66
Writing	65	—	—
Math	71	68	64
History	79	86	86
Science	78	62	74
No. Tested	258	222	228

SAN RAFAEL CITY HIGH DISTRICT
District-Wide

Twelfth Grade	1988	1989	1990
Reading	77	81	74
Writing	—	89	95
Math	86	84	73
No. Tested	454	440	353

San Rafael High, San Rafael

Twelfth Grade	1988	1989	1990
Reading	68	60	65
Writing	—	67	83
Math	82	71	66
No. Tested	224	229	200

Terra Linda High, San Rafael

Twelfth Grade	1988	1989	1990
Reading	82	93	84
Writing	—	98	97
Math	87	92	83
No. Tested	208	196	146

SAUSALITO ELEM. DISTRICT
District-Wide

Third Grade	1988	1989	1990
Reading	97	50	23
Writing	85	51	23
Math	99	27	22
No. Tested	30	39	38
Sixth Grade	1988	1989	1990
Reading	63	66	55
Writing	52	79	43
Math	85	71	57
No. Tested	42	37	34
Eighth Grade	1988	1989	1990
Reading	77	91	88
Writing	81	—	—
Math	88	73	86
History	93	82	90

Eighth Grade	1988	1989	1990
Science	72	76	78
No. Tested	32	36	44

Bayside Elem., Sausalito

Third Grade	1988	1989	1990
Reading	97	55	24
Writing	86	54	23
Math	99	31	25
No. Tested	24	33	30

Martin Luther King, Sausalito

Sixth Grade	1988	1989	1990
Reading	61	63	48
Writing	57	75	41
Math	80	66	57
No. Tested	37	33	29

Eighth Grade	1988	1989	1990
Reading	80	87	85
Writing	76	—	—
Math	83	74	86
History	90	74	86
Science	71	83	78
No. Tested	27	28	40

North Bay Elem., Sausalito

Third Grade	1988	1989	1990
Reading	45	25	45
Writing	40	39	41
Math	86	29	31
No. Tested	6	6	8

Sixth Grade	1988	1989	1990
Reading	45	58	85
Writing	15	57	51
Math	50	59	51
No. Tested	5	4	5

Eighth Grade	1988	1989	1990
Reading	35	89	86
Writing	81	—	—
Math	82	54	47
History	95	91	96
Science	76	50	73
No. Tested	5	8	4

SHORELINE UNIFIED
District-Wide

Third Grade	1988	1989	1990
Reading	95	73	64
Writing	72	62	64
Math	96	84	80
No. Tested	60	62	66

Sixth Grade	1988	1989	1990
Reading	91	52	76

Sixth Grade	1988	1989	1990
Writing	89	61	83
Math	91	73	41
No. Tested	42	52	57

Eighth Grade	1988	1989	1990
Reading	90	84	98
Writing	91	—	—
Math	67	74	92
History	90	67	93
Science	89	82	98
No. Tested	49	62	43

Twelfth Grade	1988	1989	1990
Reading	96	99	90
Writing	—	57	79
Math	65	59	53
No. Tested	45	41	39

Tomales High, Tomales

Twelfth Grade	1988	1989	1990
Reading	93	97	88
Writing	—	58	78
Math	61	58	54
No. Tested	45	41	39

Bodega Bay Elem., Bodega Bay

Third Grade	1988	1989	1990
Reading	85	49	74
Writing	47	67	77
Math	74	62	95
No. Tested	9	11	5

Inverness Elem., Pt. Reyes Station

Third Grade	1988	1989	1990
Reading	98	44	77
Writing	60	29	78
Math	86	59	79
No. Tested	15	18	19

Tomales Elem., Tomales

Third Grade	1988	1989	1990
Reading	94	94	73
Writing	94	88	73
Math	99	96	63
No. Tested	15	19	21

Sixth Grade	1988	1989	1990
Reading	63	18	62
Writing	61	41	72
Math	68	46	39
No. Tested	18	35	31

Eighth Grade	1988	1989	1990
Reading	72	53	70
Writing	85	—	—
Math	74	63	73

SHORELINE (Continued)
Tomales Elem., Tomales

Eighth Grade	1988	1989	1990
History	66	41	76
Science	88	66	76
No. Tested	26	32	20

West Marin Elem., Pt. Reyes Station

Third Grade	1988	1989	1990
Reading	73	65	36
Writing	48	45	29
Math	74	57	75
No. Tested	21	14	21
Sixth Grade	1988	1989	1990
Reading	94	97	72
Writing	92	90	84
Math	93	93	47
No. Tested	24	17	26
Eighth Grade	1988	1989	1990
Reading	93	95	99
Writing	85	—	—
Math	59	77	97
History	96	83	97
Science	81	90	99
No. Tested	23	30	23

TAMALPAIS UNION HIGH DISTRICT
District-Wide

Twelfth Grade	1988	1989	1990
Reading	97	97	97
Writing	—	97	94
Math	96	97	95
No. Tested	840	769	701

Mewah Mountain High, Larkspur

Twelfth Grade	1988	1989	1990
Reading	50	42	50
Writing	—	13	14
Math	31	63	11
No. Tested	31	34	38

Redwood High, Larkspur

Twelfth Grade	1988	1989	1990
Reading	90	98	97

Twelfth Grade	1988	1989	1990
Writing	—	98	95
Math	97	97	98
No. Tested	327	305	307

Sir Francis Drake High, San Anselmo

Twelfth Grade	1988	1989	1990
Reading	96	94	91
Writing	—	76	67
Math	95	93	87
No. Tested	200	187	134

Tamalpais High, Mill Valley

Twelfth Grade	1988	1989	1990
Reading	97	97	93
Writing	—	97	96
Math	96	95	91
No. Tested	282	243	222

UNION JOINT ELEM. DISTRICT
District-Wide

Third Grade	1988	1989	1990
Reading	43	95	33
Writing	18	90	18
Math	14	60	15
No. Tested	5	2	6
Sixth Grade	1988	1989	1990
Reading	78	36	—
Writing	18	59	—
Math	25	3	—
No. Tested	2	3	—

Union Elem., Petaluma

Third Grade	1988	1989	1990
Reading	44	91	34
Writing	21	84	21
Math	15	58	19
No. Tested	5	2	6
Sixth Grade	1988	1989	1990
Reading	74	39	—
Writing	18	58	—
Math	26	16	—
No. Tested	2	3	—

3/Marin City Profiles

Home Values, Rents from 1990 Census, Towns and Cities on Parade

EVERY YEAR OR SO THE CHRONICLE, the largest-circulation newspaper in Northern California, ranks Bay Area cities to identify the best and worst. Housing, schools, crime, weather, commuting, shopping, dining are some of the attributes used to assess the cities.

The exercise is a bit hokey because no attention is paid to size. Ross, population 2,123, is lumped with San Francisco, 723,959, and never mind that in San Francisco Ross might not even measure up to the status of a neighborhood. Nonetheless, the rankings do serve as a rough indicator of what is considered the good life.

Marin cities dominate the top ten: Palo Alto, number one, was followed by San Rafael, Sausalito, Corte Madera, Mill Valley and Tiburon. Belvedere was tied for 10th, Ross for 12th and San Anselmo came in 16th. Larkspur was 23rd, and San Francisco and Novato were tied for 24th.

The lower the points, the higher the ranking. San Francisco was given one point for commuting (best commute), Novato was penalized 82. Palo Alto was given 6 points in commuting, San Rafael 52.

The old Marin bugaboo: everything is great except the bloody commute.

Services

A word about what does what in Marin (and other counties). Two main agencies, the cities and the county, provide the bulk of government services. What they do not provide, small agencies or private parties do. For example, school districts, separately elected, set policy for local schools. Private firms collect garbage.

If you live in an incorporated city, city hall will fill the potholes, hire the

Number & Value of Owner-Occupied Dwellings in Marin

City or Area	< $100K -199K	$200K -299K	$300K -399K	$400K -499K	$500K -plus
Belvedere	7	8	12	20	646
Bolinas	81	104	44	17	10
Corte Madera	117	536	1,010	373	200
Fairfax	250	729	484	103	51
Inverness	89	136	73	30	22
Kentfield	37	109	233	382	996
Larkspur	130	310	425	518	720
Lucas Valley/Mrnwd	123	489	761	276	93
Mill Valley	156	480	723	644	1,298
Novato	1,542	4,124	2,426	822	631
Ross	8	9	25	45	508
San Anselmo	235	892	1,122	446	331
San Rafael	867	2,359	3,025	1,409	1,378
Santa Venitia	114	527	193	57	23
Sausalito	64	125	234	182	659
Strawberry	21	78	218	151	276
Tiburon	30	74	272	175	1,207
Woodacre	63	166	128	37	17

Source: 1990 Census. The chart shows the number of owner-occupied dwellings within a set price range. Data for some towns or residential areas, like Stinson Beach and Greenbrae, are grouped with those covering a larger geographic area.

cops, determine zoning, build and run the parks and, often, provide water and other services. If you live in unincorporated towns or areas, the board of supervisors and county government will hire sheriff's deputies to patrol the streets, public works people to fix the roads, planners to work out zonings and land use.

Although both cities and county provide municipal services, they differ in important ways. Cities have been strong in parks and rec., counties weak. County governments, in conjunction with the state, provide medical care for the poor and indigent. California cities rarely get involved in medical care.

City council members represent — and are elected by — only the people within the city's borders. County supervisors represent both city and county residents. Where services overlap or run close together, confusion sometimes follows. In some parts, city police will patrol one side of a street, sheriff's deputies the other. For more information, call your local supervisor or city hall.

Belvedere

Small city, an appendage off the Tiburon peninsula. One of wealthiest

Median & Average Prices of Owner-Occupied Homes

City or Area	Units	Median	Average
Belvedere	693	*$500,001	$582,457
Bolinas	256	240,500	253,451
Corte Madera	2,236	346,000	355,873
Fairfax	1,617	279,800	290,458
Inverness	350	266,200	284,579
Kentfield	1,757	*500,001	503,335
Larkspur	2,103	436,000	433,848
Lucas Valley/Mrnwd	1,742	334,000	340,875
Mill Valley	3,301	445,300	444,592
Novato	9,545	279,600	300,776
Ross	595	*500,001	566,597
San Anselmo	3,026	334,400	348,286
San Rafael	9,038	342,700	359,886
Santa Venitia	914	266,700	281,007
Sausalito	1,264	*500,001	474,586
Strawberry	744	436,400	447,006
Tiburon	1,758	*500,001	523,835
Woodacre	411	286,300	300,085

Source: 1990 Census. Asterisk (*) prices were the maximum reported by census. Actual prices may have been higher. Median means half way. In 100 homes, the 50th is the median.

cities in Bay Region. Although connected to the mainland since anyone can remember, Belvedere exudes appearance of an island. It rises abruptly from the water, climbs into a tall hill, then drops off on the other side.

Great views. Belvedere, which translates in Italian to "beautiful view," sticks out far enough to peek around Cavallo Point near Sausalito and glimpse the Golden Gate Bridge. Connected to Tiburon by two roads at either end of the "island." Between the roads shimmers a lagoon with housing.

The state in its 1990 tally counted 1,029 housing units: 839 single family, 45 single-family attached, 145 multiples, zero mobile homes. Census reports 77 percent of housing units are owner-occupied, 23 percent rentals.

Winding roads. No parking on some stretches. Land being scarce, cars are shoehorned into tight spaces. Hedges, walls and fences hide many homes from street. Some are in mansion class; many small or middling. Two-bedroom home, cove view, was going in mid 1991 for $649,000. Homes with Bay or San Francisco view come in often at $2 million plus. Design orients homes toward water, not street. Some residents are pushing for underground utility lines.

Belvedere has own police force, a luxury for a city of about 2,200. Crime not tracked by FBI but very low. In 1991 the town divided, with many arguments, over a proposal to house 35 homeless men in a local church. Ultimately, the idea was killed.

Academic rankings in elementary school among highest in state. Voters in 1990 agreed to raise taxes by $96 a parcel over five years to support schools.

Belvedere and Tiburon going in together for new library. Bel also has community center.

Hoist the Geritol. About 39 percent of Belvedere residents are over age 55.

Bolinas

The bad boy of Marin County, raggle-taggle and unkempt but, by some, secretly admired. About 1,100 residents. Located on coast, off Highway 1, just above Stinson Beach. Hard to find because residents rip up road signs to discourage tourists.

Little or no parking. Small beach that locals use. Handful of stores, a saloon that doubles as town hall, church, built in 1874, marine biology lab.

Wild berries crowd the roadside. Homes along road old and weather-beaten. Few near ocean on pilings. Here and there evidence of paint.

Away from the business strip, a few newer, larger, more expensive homes. Impression of town, especially on a foggy summer day: dreary. Why the fuss?

Others towns talk about conservation and protecting the environment, and some do a fair job. But it's a commitment with certain limits. It's all very nice to love the redwoods and deer but it's much more pleasant to love them if you have a glass of cabernet in hand and if, when inclined, you can stroll to the deli for a smoked turkey sandwich or whiz to San Fran on 101 to a play or movie. Marin owes much of its allure to the way it has mixed city and country.

Comes Bolinas. Its water system can't even support hot tubs. And the town, through its influence over water, has just about killed anything new. General plan opposes streets: "a waste of land and energy."

More than any other town in the county, Bolinas has turned its back on the city and especially on the temptations of the tourist dollar.

Corte Madera

A town of 8,272 residents that straddles Highway 101 just above Mill Valley and extends east to Bay. A shoppers' delight.

Used to be wooded. When Presidio in San Francisco was built, much of the timber came from Corte Madera (cut wood).

Corte Madera has snared the biggest shopping plaza in Marin County (The Village at Corte Madera: Nordstrom, Macy's, about 90 other stores) and right across the freeway is another shopping plaza, Town Center, about 60 shops, restaurants. Many cities these days thrive or decline according to their sales tax base. Corte Madera, in this category, is a winner.

The 1990 state count showed 3,692 housing units, of which 2,444 are single homes, 350 single attached, 898 multiples, and zero mobile homes.

Corte Madera started 1950 with 668 housing units. The next decade it added about 1,300, the following 1,000. In the 1970s, units added dropped to about 300; in the 1980s, it bumped up slightly to 400 new units.

What kind of housing will you find? Generally, tract models popular 1950-70, and this includes housing down on the Bay. All generally well kept. Some lots command views; Corte Madera, for most part, is flat.

Shares police with Larkspur. Police department called "Twin Cities." Crime low; shoplifting at stores pushes up crime rate. Corte Madera made headlines in 1991 when Mitchell brothers, X-rated filmmakers, fell out. Jim was arrested on suspicion of shooting and killing Artie.

Corte Madera shares schools with Larkspur. Academic rankings, with few exceptions, in the 90s, among tops in state.

Eight parks, trails, ecological reserve on Bay, wildlife habitat. Excursions, tap, ballet, gymnastics, soccer, Little League, aerobics, summer program for kids, kids' basketball, adult softball.

By Marin standards, good commute. If freeway goes fast, you'll go fast.

Fairfax

A town of about 7,500 located west of San Anselmo. If you play word association with Fairfax, you might come up with middle-aged hippy.

On the streets of Fairfax, you'll see often enough to be noticed men in their forties with long, often gray, hair and the look that says Berkeley 1968.

Housing units in 1990 totaled 3,508 — single homes 2,338, single attached 238, multiples 932, mobile homes zero. Apartments are near the downtown, along Sir Francis Drake Boulevard.

Many homes are small and old and have one-car garages. About half predate 1950. A lot of fixer uppers. Fairfax also has its newer, more expensive homes but not many. In the 1980s, town added about 130 single homes. Most of its "modern" construction took place in '50s and '60s — about 1,300 units.

Long-established restaurants, good feeling of community. Pleasant place to sip and chat. All towns pride themselves on being friendly but Fairfax is small enough to allow residents to get to know one another.

Fairfax pavilion offers activities from dance to basketball. Annual June Arts and Crafts festival. Easter egg hunt. Many streets meander along canyon floors but Fairfax also rises into the hills. At top of Fairfax-Bolinas Road, a golf course. Three city parks, lot of open space just outside city limits.

The census counted about 450 teenagers in Fairfax. In their leisure moments, many can be found at the new Youth Center, which includes a cafe called "Herb's Hot Oil House." Academic rankings in the 80s and 90s.

Crime not tracked by FBI but probably low. Commute is a little more difficult than for most Marin. Fairfax is about six miles from freeway. Sir Francis Drake Boulevard, at times, can be congested.

Rental Units & Rates in Marin County

City or Area	< $100 –249	$250 –499	$500 –749	$750 –999	$1,000 -plus
Belvedere	0	4	13	34	160
Bolinas	9	34	45	42	29
Corte Madera	15	65	282	243	455
Fairfax	70	137	492	343	159
Inverness	12	43	62	42	25
Kentfield	5	31	199	158	108
Larkspur	22	167	780	1,127	674
Lucas Valley/Mrnwd	4	3	15	71	175
Mill Valley	71	141	605	534	652
Novato	148	615	2,339	1,746	1,134
Ross	0	4	11	8	35
San Anselmo	27	252	633	456	343
San Rafael	290	967	4,384	2,259	1,115
Santa Venitia	32	31	101	64	89
Sausalito	29	145	387	667	818
Strawberry	48	152	387	414	245
Tiburon	39	66	108	287	581
Woodacre	3	27	36	32	41
Countywide	1,322	3,386	11,642	9,293	8,005

Source: 1990 Census. The chart shows the number of rental units counted within a set range of rates. Data for some towns or residential areas, like Stinson Beach and Greenbrae, are grouped with those covering a larger geographic area.

Greenbrae

A neighborhood that newspapers usually mention in a way that suggests it's a town.

A section of Greenbrae was absorbed by Larkspur in 1950 and is still considered "Greenbrae." The remainder extends into unincorporated land governed by the board of supervisors. Approximate location: to the right and left of Sir Francis Drake Boulevard just west of Highway 101.

Middle- to upper middle-class area. Many apartments in the Larkspur section. Single homes, some with great views, in unincorporated area (also Larkspur). Streets rise from Sir Francis Drake Boulevard into hills. Home to Barbara Boxer, congresswoman, and Marin General Hospital.

Right off freeway. Near ferry. Good commute.

Inverness

Hamlet sheltered on the west side of Tomales Bay. Charming if you like

Median & Average Rents of Renter-Occupied Dwellings

City or Area	Units	Median	Average
Belvedere	220	$1,001	$1,133
Bodega Bay	165	703	723
Corte Madera	1,079	923	941
Fairfax	1,227	698	728
Inverness	197	641	682
Kentfield	511	775	829
Larkspur	2,802	842	864
Lucas Valley/Mrnwd	280	1,001	1,091
Mill Valley	2,058	836	863
Novato	6,863	742	792
Ross	75	1,001	1,015
San Anselmo	1,745	719	773
San Rafael	9,181	691	731
Santa Venitia	324	729	777
Sausalito	2,085	923	934
Strawberry	1,263	772	794
Tiburon	1,097	1,001	996
Woodacre	147	777	810
Countywide	35,386	763	806

Source: 1990 Census. Median means half way. In 100 homes, the 50th is the median.

woods, water and seclusion. Noted for restaurants and getting soaked in winter rains. Some flooding in early 1980s. A long drive to San Fran.

Kentfield

Upper middle-class to wealthy neighborhood, located in hills between Larkspur and Ross. Homes set back from roads, among pine, redwoods and manzanita. Low-profile roofs. Designed to blend in. No sidewalks. Meandering streets. Big lots. Many homes have views. Unincorporated.

Because of its location, Kentfield gets more rain than most other Marin towns.

Academic rankings generally in the 90s. Voters in 1991 raised parcel tax from $97 to $167 to help schools. Money to pay for educational program, not construction.

College of Marin is located in Kentfield.

Larkspur

Say "Larkspur" and many people will add "ferry." Although most of the town lies west of Highway 101, a small portion fronts on the Bay and there

Home Price Sampler from Classified Ads

Belvedere

2-bedroom, 1.5-bath, waterfront, large decks, secluded gardens, deep-water boat dock, views of S.F. and Belvedere. $1,350,000.

3-bedroom, 2.5-bath, new paint, carpet, newly remodeled kitchen & bath, garden patio, private rear lane for parking convenience. $699,000.

5-bedroom, 3.5-bath, formal dining, library, maid's quarters, decks, boat docks & 2 hoists. $2,200,000.

Bolinas

2-bedroom, 2-bath, view condo with fireplace, close to good shopping and easy access to 101. $241,000.

3-bedroom, 2.5-bath, exclusive estate on 1.93 acres in Chapman Park with secluded tranquil setting. $749,000.

4-bedroom, 2-bath, remodeled commuter's dream, family room opens to redwood deck with hot tub and private yard, skylighted. $329,000.

Fairfax

3-bedroom, 2.5-bath, large family room, formal dining, fireplace, master bedroom, wood floors, laundry, two large decks, wooded view. $339,950.

3-bedroom, 2.5-bath, creekside setting, completely remodeled, extra large rooms, pool site, walk to town. $499,000.

1-bedroom, 2-bath, hilltop mini-estate, total privacy, dramatic setting, acre of breathtaking landscaped gardens, expansion possibilities. $539,000.

Greenbrae

3-bedroom, 2-bath, small and charming, surprising back yard spa & pool. Private patio, yard, walk to everything. $495,000.

4-bedroom, 2.5-bath, level lot, large library living room combination, pool, great location. $469,000.

Inverness

2-plus-bedroom, near Bear Valley Road. $399,950.

2-bedroom, 1.5-bath, large pool, redwood deck, sunny lot, separate studio. $400,000.

Kentfield

3-bedroom, 2-bath, hardwood floors, formal dining, fireplace in living room, 50 x 150 usable lot. $329,000.

3-bedroom, decks, view, sauna, spacious living room, family, dining rooms, 2 fireplaces. $649,000.

Larkspur

Studio cottage, completely landlocked, very private in serene, woodsy setting, fixerupper. $155,000.

3-bedroom, 2-bath, new, big master suite with walk-in closets & spa tub, hardwood floors in kitchen, vaulted ceilings, deck, fenced. $525,000.

6+-bedroom, 3-bath, a forever view from most rooms, enchanting Victorian, with separate guest house. $875,000.

Lucas Valley-Marinwood

4-bedroom, 2-bath, pool, den, family room, atrium. $470,500.

5-bedroom, 4.5-bath, vaulted ceilings, marble fireplaces, formal dining, family room, 3,600 sq. ft. $769,000.

Mill Valley

5-bedroom, 2-bath, new paint, renewed baths & carpet, master with fireplace, large family room, park-like back yard, hill views. $486,500.

4-bedroom, 2-bath, large lot, open floor plan, vaulted ceiling & fireplace in living room, private, great for entertaining. $494,000.

5-bedroom, 2.5-bath, S.F. view, on prestigious Strawberry Point, quarter-acre, pool, atrium. $795,000.

you'll find Marin's main ferry terminal.

A city of contrasts, Larkspur is modern and open by ferry terminal, and on other side of town reminiscent of forest primeval. Some streets glide back into redwoods that have been allowed to grow where they please, and that includes the streets. North of Corte Madera Creek, in what maps identify as Greenbrae, the land has been given over to apartments.

Although Larkspur has its older homes, most of the housing units were built in the 1960s and 1970s. The town looks new. Construction fell off in the 1980s — about 300 units. According to census, town added just six people in 1980s.

Home Price Sampler from Classified Ads

Nicasio

5-bedroom, 4.5-bath, 4.5 acres, pool, guest cabin. $895,000.

4-bedroom, 3-bath, passive solar home, decks, 3 fireplaces, sauna, hot tub, privacy, views. $740,000.

Novato

3-bedroom, 1.5-bath, lovely landscaping, close to Miwok Park, hiking trails, transportation & shops. $163,000.

3-bedroom, 2-bath, light, bright, completely updated, European-style kitchen, spacious family room with fireplace. $299,000.

Point Reyes

2-bedroom, 1-bath, historic Victorian, remodeled, oak floors, marble fireplace. $219,000.

Ross

4-plus-bedroom, 3-bath, large family room, formal dining, modern kitchen, hardwood floors, 3/4-acre of terraced gardens. $719,000.

3-bedroom, 2-bath, veranda, patio, hot tub, gracious Mediterranean, privacy, sunshine, immaculate, top location. $699,000.

San Anselmo

2-bedroom, 1-bath, oversized level lot, fireplace, hardwood floors, formal dining, 2-car detached garage, large basement. $269,000,

3-bedroom, 2-bath, large solarium patio, terraced lot with sweeping views, new kitchen, top-of-line appliances, immaculate. $359,500.

6-bedroom, 5-bath, almost 1.5 acres, secluded grounds, formal dining, library, dance-music studio, workout room, office, pool, hot tub, sauna, deck, patio, views, sport court. $1,050,000.

San Geronimo

4-bedroom, estate lot, 4,300 sq. ft., adj. to golf course. $549,000.

3-story, contemporary, 2 acres, overlooks golf course. $429,000.

San Rafael

4-bedroom, 2-bath, fireplace, family room, formal dining, den-study, beam ceilings, skylights, patio, $319,500.

4-bedroom, 3.5-bath, 2 years old, family room, charming back yard, pool. $795,000.

Santa Venetia

3-bedroom, 2-bath, fruit trees, walk to water. $295,000.

Sausalito

2-bedroom, 2-bath, loft, 2 large skylights, vaulted ceiling, large living room, south exposure, deck, quiet location. $269,500.

2-bedroom, 2-bath, townhome, marble entry, fireplace, Bay views, courtyard. $278,000.

Stinson Beach

3-bedroom, 2.5-bath, landscaped, large rooms from another era, office, ocean, Mt. Tam views, lots of parking. $630,000.

Tiburon

3-bedroom, 2-bath, spacious decks, level fenced patio area, stunning views, excellent location, walk to town & ferry. $599,000.

4-bedroom, 3-bath, waterfront, deep-water dock, pool, hot tub, desirable neighborhood, ideal for entertaining. $799,000.

Woodacre

2-bedroom, 1.5-bath, fireplace, loft, hardwood floors, vaulted ceilings, decks. $189,000.

2-bedroom, 2-bath, one-car garage, den, country living, potential is in the half-acre double lot. $249,000.

Source: Survey of classified ads, summer and fall, 1991.

Some homes have views. Many apartments do. Town generally well kept. Middle America. In its 1990 count, the state tallied 5,909 housing units, of which 2,087 were single homes, 350 single-family attached, 3,307 multiples, 165 mobile homes.

Downtown, which had a pretty restaurant section, has been made even prettier along Magnolia — street repaved, brick-lined sidewalks.

Crime low. Police department called "Twin Cities." Shared with Corte Madera. Same with schools. Academic rankings in the 90s.

Eight parks, trails. Little League and kids' sports, softball, afterschool activities, adult softball, dance, walking groups, volleyball courts.

Good commute. Quick access to Highway 101. Not too far from San Rafael Bridge. Ferry terminal (parking) in backyard. Town name a mistake. Wife of founding developer thought local flower called lupine was a larkspur.

Recent tempest: restaurant stuck two nude statutes (tame stuff) out front. Raised eyebrows and protests. Cosmo Marin, prudish Marin, inexplicable Marin. Statues were removed.

Marin City

During World War II, Blacks came to Marin County to work in shipyards at Sausalito. After the war, many stayed. They live in eight five-story buildings, public housing, just outside Sausalito called Marin City.

Kids attend Sausalito schools. Community Center. Baseball field. Boys and Girls Club. Seniors Center. Commercial-residential development going up at site formerly used for flea market.

Good commute. Right off 101, near Golden Gate Bridge.

Marin City is unincorporated, which means government by the board of supervisors from San Rafael but local groups wield a lot of influence.

About 30 percent of residents have been in the complex since it was built 30 years ago. Buildings designed by protege of Frank Lloyd Wright.

Marinwood

Located west of Highway 101, between San Rafael and Novato. A subdivision, built over decades after 1950, that blends into Lucas Valley subdivision. Middle class. Mix of housing styles. Condos near freeway. Most just plain suburban tract, 3-4 bedroom, well maintained. Kids educated in San Rafael District schools. To reach, take Miller Creek Road off of 101.

Mill Valley

Pleasant town that comes in for a good bit of kidding because in the 1970s and 1980s it came to symbolize the hot tub values of the county. Located in the shadow of Mt. Tamalpais.

Quaint downtown, restaurants, delis, coffee shops, clothing stores, bookstores, a theater, art gallery, antique stores. Street layout gives a village square feeling, friendly, inviting.

Mill Valley starts down on Richardson Bay, moves west into the valley floor and then rises into redwoods, a nice mix. On summer days, the fog will often break through over the hills.

The state in its 1990 count showed 6,215 housing units, of which 3,925 were single homes, 352 single attached, 1,930 multiples, 8 mobile homes.

Styles vary widely, a reflection of age of the town: cottages, condos, apartments, bungalows, Tudors, gaudy Victorians, small one-story homes in Tamalpais Valley (outside city limits), modern middle-class homes, large homes hidden behind long driveways in the wooded hills.

Some homes just old and plain. But Mill Valley has knockout Victorian and custom homes. It also has knockout fights over views and privacy.

City council limits size of new homes according to size of lot. When property values soared, some people tore down small homes and replaced with giants to increase value of holdings. This upset others who complained new homes were too large for parcels.

Mill Valley got its population spurt in 1950s and 1960s. Many homes will reflect upper-middle styles of those decades. Number of people per household is dropping, an indication of fewer children, more empty nesters and single adults.

Crime low. No homicides in 1990, 1989, 1988. Academic rankings quite high. Strawberry Point School was closed in 1990 and is now occupied by Smith and Hawken, manufacturer of gardening tools. The kids were transferred to Edna Maguire, newly renovated.

Local residents and businesses through a foundation raised well over $100,000 for schools in 1991 — indicating strong community support for education.

Another good sign: Voters recently raised parcel tax from $120 to $155 to help schools.

About a dozen parks. Botanical gardens. Mt. Tam hiking. Community center. Nine-hole golf course. Dog run, trails at Bay Front Park. Bridge club. Seniors center. Afterschool child care, pre- and post-natal classes, aerobics, tennis, softball, soccer, traditional kids' games. Big-time film festival. Plays. Experimental theater. Arts festival. Festival of Wine and Gourmet Food every June. Heavy into arts and outdoors. Big annual footrace: the Dipsea.

Local light: Millie Hughes-Fulford, astronaut. Flew in space shuttle in 1991.

A short hop to Golden Gate Bridge. Typical jams associated with bridge but overall a good commute. Some street congestion and a few residents complain about tourists taking shortcuts through their streets. Money allotted to synchronize traffic lights.

Town was named after lumber mill, recently rebuilt to keep past alive. After 1906 earthquake, Mill Valley redwoods helped rebuild San Francisco.

Little League season kicks off with a parade down Throckmorton Avenue. Supervised kiddie programs in summer.

One mother, full of praise, noted that on rare sunny days at summer camp, sunscreen was applied as soon as kids got off buses.

Nicasio

Hamlet in West Marin. George Lucas, of "Star Wars" fame, lives at and has his headquarters at a ranch near Nicasio.

Many of his film operations are located in buildings at Nicasio and throughout San Rafael. Action scenes from "Star Wars," "Indiana Jones" and

"The Hunt for Red October" were put together at Lucas locations in Marin County.

Town of Nicasio some distance removed. Historic Catholic Church. Popular restaurant. Rolling countryside, gold in summer, green in winter and spring. Estate homes on many ranches.

Novato

After Spanish land grant, Rancho de Novato. Incorporated in 1960. Marin's largest and second most populous city, and having the land to grow, the city most likely to add people in the future.

Recent study revealed that one-third of residents had moved to Novato in last three years.

About to open a big shopping mall, 70-90 stores, just off Highway 101 — Macy's Homestore, Target, Costco, Marshall's in first phase. Called Vintage Oaks Shopping Center.

Good housing mix: upscale Bahia Parks located near the Petaluma River and horse estates out Indian Valley Road.

In and all around town, a lot of middle-class housing, sturdy, suburban and well-cared-for. Many homes on and near San Marin Drive have views.

Townhouses and custom homes are tucked away along Alameda Del Prado, woodsy, deer nibble the lawns day and evening.

If you take Marin Valley Drive, you'll find behind the hills one of the prettiest mobilehome parks in the Bay Area.

Novato is home to Hamilton Air Force Base, deactivated in 1975 but not the housing sections, which extend west down Ignacio Boulevard and provide homes for military personnel and their families. The soldiers and sailors, etc., are stationed about the Bay Area.

When the Gulf War ended, Novato threw a rousing parade for the homecoming troops. Although Novato shares Marin's environmental values, it is more conservative in other matters. Democrats outnumber Republicans but barely.

Crime rate low. No homicides in 1990, two each in 1989 and 1988.

Novato and Marin County have been arguing over Hamilton for years. Many would like to see the airport go civilian and allow big jets into the North Bay. Many more are aghast at the idea.

The latest proposal is to develop 402 of the 1,600 acres into 1,400 townhouses and homes and commercial buildings (1.2 million square feet). Cost about $530 million. Many fights over housing, growth. Other areas of contention: Bahia Point and Black Point, famous for its annual Renaissance Faires. Site has been sold. 152 homes, 18-hole golf course planned.

Housing units in 1990 totaled 18,560 — single family 10,156, single attached 2,784, multiples 5,130, mobile homes, 490.

A dozen parks, tennis courts, golf course, the traditional activities for the

Novato

Where the past and future come together

*N*ovato is the kind of place that makes you want to set down roots - the kind of place that inspires dreams of a bright and promising future. It's the kind of community that takes pride in its traditions and values and sets forth unlimited opportunities.

Set in beautiful Marin County, it provides easy access to San Francisco, the East Bay and all the amenities to be found in a large, metropolitan setting. Yet Novato residents find their community complete unto itself with excellent schools, shopping, businesses, restaurants, recreation - even a private airport.

Come set down roots in Novato - build your traditions and explore the future.

*F*rank Howard Allen is the leading realtor serving Novato and the entire North Bay area. Whether you're searching for a first house or a million dollar estate, Frank Howard Allen can help you find the perfect place to call home. Call us at (415) 897-3000.

FRANK HOWARD
ALLEN
REALTORS

kids, two marinas, two museums, new movie complex, youth center. Summer academics for kids. Farmers' market. Weekly newspaper. Art, Wine, Music Festival. Horse country.

Indian Valley College, a big plus. Community colleges are treasure troves of activities, academic, vocational and physical. Bonds recently passed for street and storm repairs, and for parks.

School rankings generally in the top 30th percentile, many in the 90s. Much community support for schools.

San Ramon Elementary closed temporarily — wood rot, seismic safety.

Bel Marin Keys, a waterfront community, is located just outside city limits, on the Bay. Instead of lawns out back, yachts and boats. More development planned for adjoining land.

New firehouse recently opened to protect east side. In the planning stage, a Center for Research on Aging. County airport north of Novato.

Commute so-so. Better than anything in neighboring Sonoma County but the 28 miles to San Fran are often long miles.

When a sound wall, 14 feet high, was built along Highway 101, residents protested that part of it was too high, and called it the "The Great Wall of Novato." Cal Trans agreed to knock off two feet.

Point Reyes Station

Small town at south end of Tomales Bay. Diner fries its potatoes in an unusually tasty way, worth a visit from hamburger crowd. Book store, small shops. Town paper years ago won a Pulitzer for its reporting on a controversial mind-straightening program. Just outside city limits, sheep graze.

Ross

Rich, wooded, small, quiet, hilly. Tennis courts in back yards. Nannies and mothers stroll the streets with kiddies. Golf course.

Started the 1980s with 954 housing units, finished with 970 (single homes 882, multiples 88). Lost about one-fourth of its population, from 2,801 to 2,123.

Boom town Ross ain't. Nice it is. Some homes fall into middle-class but Ross has a lot of big new and old stuff that without quibbling can be described as opulent. Art and Garden Center, two other parks. Lagunitas Country Club.

Crime not tracked by FBI but rich towns almost invariably are very low in crime (otherwise rich would move). Kids attend local elementary school. Academic rankings among tops in state. Child Magazine in 1991 named Ross School one of top ten schools in nation.

Town took name from railroad station. Widow of local land baron deeded station land to railroad with understanding it would be named after departed hubby.

Ross straddles Sir Francis Drake Boulevard, next to San Anselmo and San Rafael, and ascends into hills. Narrow streets, walls and gates protect privacy.

Commute not great but not bad either. Drake congests during peak hours but the distance to the freeway is just a few miles. The rest depends on how fast 101 is moving.

San Anselmo

When you enter San Anselmo from Ross, you find sidewalks, older, smaller, homes and kids (not many) playing in the streets. San Anselmo comes across as a town that years ago used to be blue collar but as demographics changed evolved into middle-class professional.

A town with a center. Shops, delis, cafes along San Anselmo Avenue. People munch their sandwiches in Creek Park, which has picnic tables. Sunday jazz at coffee shop. No parking meters. Traffic along Sir Francis Drake Boulevard and Red Hill Avenue jars nerves but pace in neighborhoods much slower. About 130 antique stores. Calls itself antique capital of Northern California.

A total of 5,485 housing units, the state reported in 1990, of which 4,124 were single homes, 110 single-family attached, 1,251 multiples, zero mobile homes.

Housing styles a mix. A little over 50 percent of San Anselmo's housing stock predates 1950. About a third was built between 1950 and 1970.

Butterfield Road, which crosses into unincorporated San Anselmo, illustrates the common pattern. Near Sir Francis Drake Boulevard, the homes are small and pre-World War II. As Butterfield rises into the hills, the homes get bigger and newer but not uniformly, older mixed with newer. At the top is a well-kept tract, a mix of three and four bedrooms, its style about 1960.

Hidden behind these are a few streets with 1980s eye stoppers: three-car garages, two stories, square footage over 3,000. When Marin and Bay Area home values took off in the 1980s, many people took their equity and went shopping for the much bigger and better.

San Anselmo in 1976 gave the go-ahead to granny units — cottages or small apartments tucked behind homes — but to encourage affordable housing attached rent controls to the structures.

Five parks, library. Tennis, baseball, softball, soccer, arts and crafts. Playing fields at the schools. Public swimming in summer at Drake High School. Summer wine and food festival. Teens hang out at Youth Center in nearby Fairfax. San Anselmo donated money to fund the center.

Academic rankings in the 90s but voters in Ross school district, which also serves Fairfax, recently turned down an $8.2 million bond to rebuild schools.

Crime low. Zero homicides in 1990, 1989, 1988.

Commute typical mid-Marin. Peak hours, it's going to take 10-15 minutes to reach freeway, then it's up to 101. Buses available. Park-and-Ride lot.

One striking site: a seminary with stone buildings that draw their inspiration from the Middle Ages.

San Geronimo

Hamlet in Western Marin, off Sir Francis Drake Boulevard. Single-family homes built in hills. Older ones small, newer big. Golf course. School district runs Montessori classes. Cultural center.

San Rafael

Oldest city in county and most populous. Bisected by Highway 101. Diverse neighborhoods, including one that brings San Rafael into contact with the new demographics of California: poor and multicultural.

Pretty town, mix of quaint and snazzy, many middle-class neighborhoods, some poor, and the God knows what, a.k.a. the county administrative complex, designed by Frank Lloyd Wright. Dominican College, historic and charming. Victorians in the downtown. Falkirk Mansion, a 17-room Victorian, serves as cultural center.

In 1990 housing units totaled 21,036 — single homes 9,845, single attached 1,645, multiples 9,142, mobile homes 404. The neighborhoods:

• Downtown and environs. Older homes, many pre-World War II. One-car garages. Many homes show care and attention. Some views from the hills. Narrow streets in hills, a common pattern. Mix of sizes.

Multitude of shops along main drags. Streets crowded on Saturdays. Neighborhood is right off the freeway, which helps generate customers. Like most downtowns, it loses a lot to the shopping malls but seems to be holding its own. Restaurants, Victorians, city buildings, library. Pleasant place to stroll.

• Dominican College. Located east of Highway 101, north of Third Street. Sets tone for neighborhood, which has a tweedy, "Goodbye, Mr. Chips" flavor. Homes are big, woodsy, quietly impressive, nice, expensive. College is a town institution, beloved even by Protestants and pagans, a rich source of culture.

• Peacock Gap. Just east of 101, a mid-sized shopping mall and San Rafael High School. Further out along Pt. San Pedro Road, Peacock Gap, a country club subdivision: townhouses, upper-middle homes and some knock-your-eye-out custom homes. Nearby, McNear Beach, one of the most popular parks in the county.

• Canal neighborhood. East of Highway 101, just south of San Rafael Canal. Mostly apartments. Informal labor pool. On almost any morning you can hire someone off a street corner.

One of Marin's few hot spots in crime. Prostitution, stabbings, occasional homicide, drugs. One ice-cream vendor was busted for selling cocaine from his cart. Local business people and residents upset. Want city hall to assign more cops and in late 1991, more cops were sent to neighborhood.

Many law-abiding residents in section, which attracts poor and recent immigrants. Belvedere Street seems to have most problems.

• Terra Linda. Divided by a ridge from the downtown. Just west of the freeway, Northgate Mall (Sears, Mervyn's, Emporium), a hotel, new office buildings and atop one hill, an imposing apartment complex with commanding views of the Bay and countryside.

Traveling west, Terra Linda proper, basically middle-class housing, typical suburban of 1960s, nothing flashy, many three-bedroom, two-bath, lawns mowed, shrubs trimmed, middle America.

• Lucas Valley. Moving north from Terra Linda, the terrain rises and over the crest lies Lucas Valley Road, which ties into Marinwood further north. These neighborhoods are often spoken of as if they were separate towns.

For the most part, they are unincorporated subdivisions governed from San Rafael by board of supervisors. To complicate matters, parts of Lucas Valley are within the city limits of San Rafael.

Kids attend San Rafael district schools. Academic rankings in these neighborhoods are generally high.

Lucas Valley starts out near the freeway as a middle class subdivision, the housing styles reminiscent of the 1950s to 1970s. The homes are generally well maintained, the trees and shrubs have had a chance to grow and cast some shade. Near the freeway is a community center.

Homes are still being built, some in estate class. Older homes in Lucas Valley smaller, sell for much less.

• County Administration Complex. Designed by Wright. Includes 2,000-seat theater, exhibition hall, freeway, lagoon. Attracts visitors from all over planet. What the master (Wright) wrought. Good place to sell car. Weekends, parking lots are used to move cars offered by private parties.

Some housing going in nearby. Also planned, a new jail but Marin has been fighting this project for years.

San Rafael had one homicide in 1990, one each in 1989 and 1988. Except for Canal neighborhood, San Rafael crime is low and even Canal, compared to parts of Richmond and Oakland, comes off not that bad. Those communities lack resources to deal with many of their problems. San Rafael has more to offer.

School rankings range from 50th to 90th percentile. An integrated school district and likely to become more so.

Three regional parks, including China Camp down on Bay, neighborhood parks, 20 parks in all, public pools, tennis courts. Sailing, fishing, biking, hiking, tennis, typical kid and adult team sports. Farmers Market at Marin Center, opera, ballet, Marin Symphony. Shakespeare at Dominican College.

Commute better than most. From home to freeway, for many people, is just a matter of blocks. Straight shot via San Rafael Bridge to East Bay. Park and Ride lot. Ferry in nearby Larkspur.

If you work for the county government, a major employer, a short hop up the road. Chamber of commerce says about 35 percent of local work force lives in San Rafael.

San Quentin prison is located just outside city limits, near San Rafael

Bridge. Another big employer, about 1,500 people. When executions are scheduled, protesters arrive.

If a cat lover, steer clear of Civic Center North, a housing development. The salt marsh harvest mouse, a rarity, lives in the neighborhood. No cats allowed, decreed government.

Santa Venetia

Unincorporated neighborhood, mostly middle-class tract homes, located east of the Marin Civic Center. Kids attend school in San Rafael district.

Marin Community Jewish Center: swimming pools, fitness room, spa, basketball courts, aerobics and dance studio, library, 350-seat theater, Jewish cultural, religious programs. Non-Jews welcome.

National Guard armory in Santa Venetia has been used for winter shelter for homeless.

McInnes Park, 440 acres, to be overhauled, possibly made into something that would attract more people, make money. Among suggestions: video arcade, kiddie rides, miniature golf course, batting cages. Some people, naturally, say no, no, no. Concerns about traffic.

Sausalito

Residential-tourist town located just around the corner from the Golden Gate. Streets wind through hills, great views of Bay and bridge to Oakland and, for some, Angel Island.

Discovered by explorer Juan de Ayala, who apparently spotted a "little willow" (Saucelito) on the site.

A lovely burg but there must be times when the permanent residents wish the tourists would leave them in peace. Then again, maybe not. Tourists keep Sausalito in sales tax revenues and this helps run city.

Homes a mix: many well over 50 years old, but here and there some spanking new ones. Large, small and tiny homes. Apartments near water. Townhouses near south entrance from freeway. Houseboats, about 350 of them, from junks to floating mansions.

On the steeper hills, you park below and walk up, or you park above and walk down. Some homeowners have formed a taxing district to bury utility lines. Improves views, appearance of streets.

State in 1990 counted 4,547 housing units in Sausalito, 1,644 of them single homes, 386 single attached, 2,421 multiples, 96 mobile homes. Many empty nesters, few children. About 19 percent of the county's population is under age 18. But in Sausalito, kids tally about 9 percent.

Integrated school district. Sausalito kids attend same schools as Marin City kids. School rankings above the 50th percentile.

Commute excellent, a few minutes drive to Golden Gate. Ferries work the commute times weekdays, serve tourists at other hours.

On summer mornings, the fog often creeps over the hills and down into neighborhoods but by mid-day it fades under the sunlight.

Crime not tracked by FBI, but given demographics (upper middle class) should be low. Where shops and tourists come together, thefts are often plentiful.

In parks, Sausalito is not overloaded. Steep terrain makes parks expensive. But in activities — shopping, fishing, boating, arts and crafts — a lot to offer. Nice town to stroll. If you have bucks, great restaurants. Annual arts festival.

Famed for enforcing parking meters, at expense of tourists. Feed those coins, 75 cents an hour, raised recently from 50 cents.

Stinson Beach

Small beach town on Highway 1, the yin to Bolinas yang. Stinson likes tourists. Couple dozen businesses, library, bookstore cater to beach crowd. Flowers blooming their heads off in painted tubs. No sidewalks, little parking.

Away from the business section and the beach, older homes set on unpaved streets. New homes in the expensive and guarded Seadrift.

Stinson exists solely for the lovely beach, which is well-kept, clean and accessible. No charge for admission, day use only, crowded on good weather days, somewhat crowded even in bad. Picnic tables, snack shop, lifeguards, signs warning you swim at own risk. Occasional shark warnings, often ignored.

Strawberry Point

Neighborhood on Richardson Bay, near Tiburon. Upscale. Site of Golden Gate Baptist Theological Seminary. Some construction. Much arguing over building of docks for homes.

Tiburon

One of richest towns in Bay Region. Located on a hilly peninsula jutting into San Francisco Bay. Great views.

Crime not measured by FBI but predictably low. Tiburon has own police force. Academic rankings among highest in state. Voters in 1990 agreed to raise taxes by $96 a parcel over five years to support school programs.

Served by Tiburon Boulevard, which runs along shore from Highway 101. Most homes are located on steep streets that ascend from the boulevard and look south toward Richardson Bay. At the tip of the peninsula, some homes line the shore.

The city in 1990 counted 3,626 residential units: single homes 1,988, single attached 656, multiples 979. Multiples include apartment complex of 102 units, and some housing for elderly.

Commute fairly good. Highway 101 just down the road. Red and White runs morning and evening ferries to the City from Tiburon.

Sister city to Belvedere, a south side appendage, also rich. Both share a small downtown: bookstores, supermarkets, beauty salons, clothing stores, banks, realtors, about a dozen restaurants and cafes. New town hall, library on way. Also new fire house, designed to look like a home, a trend in suburbia. Local newspaper serves both Bel and Tib.

Tennis clubs, yacht clubs, several parks, wildlife sanctuary. Angel Island across Raccoon Strait. Money enough for recreation at home. Wine festival in spring.

Blackie's pasture, near water and Tiburon Boulevard, to be turned into trails, salt marsh and viewpoints. The late Blackie was a horse.

Utility lines in Hill Haven neighborhood to be buried, at residents' expense. Improves looks, property values, goes the reasoning.

Used to be railroad, working-class town. Ferries lugged trains down to San Francisco. Spanish called the peninsula "Punta de Tiburon (Shark Point).

Tomales

Historic small town in northwest Marin, population about 500. Many homes restored. Farm country. Sheep graze in nearby fields

Country town; a long commute. Residents have said goodbye to city and value rural obscurity. General store, Lady of Assumption Church built in 1860. Coffee house, deli. Nice town to visit.

Woodacre

Hamlet in West Marin, off of Sir Francis Drake Boulevard. Summer cottages. Small, old, remodeled and expanded into year-round homes. Newer homes blended in.

Popular with people ready to settle down. Of town's 1,478 residents, about 47 percent are between ages 30 and 50, and kids under 19 make up another 23 percent.

Rural. Mix of blue collar and professionals. Dogs and horses. Woodacre Improvement Club brings people together for swimming and fun. Fourth of July parade. Redwoods on edge of town. Small market.

Napa County

4/Napa County at a Glance

Population, Stats of a Pretty, Hospitable Area Famous for Its Wines, Vineyards and Vistas

FAMOUS FOR ITS WINES and vineyards, Napa County starts almost at San Pablo Bay, near Vallejo, and moves north in a rectangular lump that widens at the city of Napa until it hits Lake County, a distance of about 35 miles.

It is, in all seasons, a pretty and hospitable county. The Napa Valley, drained by a river, runs up and down its east side, miles and miles of neatly kept vineyards and wineries, many open for a tasting.

Ridges rise to the west, then sweep down to the Sonoma Valley, another wine region.

To the east, the Napa Valley ascends into terrain that falls and rises and here and there levels out into wine and ranch country until it reaches a man-made lake, Berryessa, near the eastern border. Grand vistas. In the fall, after a few rains, the countryside, almost overnight, turns green.

Where the Wineries and People Are

Although wineries thrive in the hills, the great majority are located in Napa Valley, along with most of the county's towns and residents.

The 1990 census counted 110,765 residents in Napa County, and of these at least 74 percent, or 82,265, live in the five towns that run up the valley: American Canyon, City of Napa, Yountville, St. Helena and Calistoga. When you throw in the hamlets, the number is probably over 80 percent.

Crime is low, school rankings, generally, middling to high. The commute to job centers, particularly in the East Bay, is not the greatest in the western hemisphere but many would find the tradeoff — a nice home in a lovely area — worth an extra half hour on the road.

In the last 20 years or so, suburbia has crept into valley, to the consternation

Napa County Population

City or Area	Male	Female	Total	*Total
American Canyon	3,775	3,931	7,706	NA
Angwin	1,722	1,781	3,503	NA
Calistoga	2,115	2,353	4,468	4,500
Deer Park	863	962	1,825	NA
Napa	29,993	31,849	61,842	63,000
St. Helena	2,323	2,667	4,990	5,000
Yountville	2,040	1,219	3,259	3,330
Remainder	12,061	11,111	23,172	NA
Countywide	54,892	55,873	110,765	112,700

Source: 1990 Census. *Population estimates by California Department of Finance, Jan. 1, 1991.

of many who think the region should be preserved for wine growing.

But not a lot of suburbia. The City of Napa and American Canyon, near Vallejo and outside of the wine-growing region, account for almost all the growth. If you are looking to settle in Napa, they are the towns in which to start your search.

Coming & Going
(Driver License Address Changes)

County	Moved to Napa from	Moved Out of Napa to	Net
Alameda	318	177	141
Alpine	1	1	0
Amador	4	13	-9
Butte	70	78	-8
Calaveras	6	6	0
Colusa	5	3	2
Contra Costa	389	210	179
Del Norte	2	6	-4
El Dorado	41	46	-5
Fresno	48	67	-19
Glenn	4	9	-5
Humboldt	31	42	-11
Imperial	6	6	0
Inyo	0	6	-6
Kern	45	37	8
Kings	6	13	-7
Lake	109	144	-35
Lassen	2	5	-3
Los Angeles	422	180	242
Madera	11	8	3
Marin	207	112	95
Mariposa	12	1	11
Mendocino	35	51	-16
Merced	17	12	5
Modoc	4	0	4
Mono	5	0	5
Monterey	66	41	25
Nevada	27	22	5
Orange	123	93	30
Placer	37	47	-10
Plumas	8	10	-2
Riverside	57	45	12
Sacramento	187	321	-134
San Benito	7	4	3
San Bernardino	74	79	-5
San Diego	141	127	14
San Francisco	301	199	102
San Joaquin	63	73	-10

Coming & Going
(Driver License Address Changes)

County	Moved to Napa from	Moved Out of Napa to	Net
San Luis Obispo	40	52	-12
San Mateo	251	84	167
Santa Barbara	50	37	13
Santa Clara	223	152	71
Santa Cruz	33	31	2
Shasta	24	59	-35
Sierra	2	1	1
Siskiyou	7	16	-9
Solano	1,113	1,016	97
Sonoma	469	533	-64
Stanislaus	43	39	4
Sutter	8	10	-2
Tehama	11	16	-5
Trinity	6	6	0
Tulare	25	19	6
Tuolumne	9	15	-6
Ventura	69	35	34
Yolo	73	81	-8
Yuba	11	15	-4
All Counties	5,358	4,511	847
Out of State	1,071	1,090	-19
Total	6,429	5,601	828

Source: California Department of Finance, 1991. Data covers fiscal year July 1, 1990-June 30, 1991. Out-of-state counts have been adjusted for non-compliers.

History

Napa was on the fringe of the Spanish-Mexican conquest. In the 1800s the Californios gradually moved north of San Francisco. What befell the Indians of Marin and Sonoma also destroyed the tribes of Napa. By the mid-1800s, the land was firmly in hands of settlers, the Indians almost all destroyed or scattered (See Sonoma).

1830s. Mexicans, led by Mariano Vallejo, defeat the Wappo Indians in several battles. Smallpox sweeps the tribes, killing thousands.

1836. First land grant made in the Napa Valley, to George Yount, a mountain man and trapper who had fought with General Jackson at the Battle of New Orleans. Arriving in Sonoma in the 1830s, he endeared himself to Vallejo and upon embracing Catholicism was granted 11,814 acres.

Average Household Income

City or Area	1990	1991
American Canyon	$38,200	$39,800
Calistoga	39,800	41,500
Napa	38,700	40,400
St. Helena	33,500	34,900
Yountville	31,900	33,300
Remainder	49,100	51,200
Countywide	40,200	41,900

Source: *Projects '90*, Association of Bay Area Governments, January, 1990; U.S. Bureau of Labor Statistics. Income is stated in constant 1988 dollars, rounded off to the nearest $100. Income for 1991 is an estimate based on 1990 income adjusted by the Bay Area consumer price index for the September, 1990-September, 1991, period.

Other land grants followed.

Yount built a sawmill, ran his grant as a rancho and established a reputation for hospitality and in the 1840s welcomed American immigrants.

1846. Bear Flag Revolt. Yankees seize Vallejo at Sonoma. Mexican-American War breaks out, leading to defeat of Mexico and the absorption of California into the Union.

1848-49. Gold discovered in Sierra. Invasion of the Forty Niners. Demand for wheat and flour increased. Napa Valley prospered.

Wheat was the major crop in the late 19th century. Napa also was famous for its apples, peaches, olives and prunes.

1850. Napa County, one of the original 27, holds its first election.

Dawning of Modern Wine Industry

1858. Although Mariano Vallejo had produced a crude wine that was fermented in cow skins, historians date the beginning of the modern wine industry in the Napa Valley with Charles Krug, a Prussian immigrant. In 1858, using a cider press, he produced 1,200 gallons of wine from grapes grown near Napa City.

Krug apparently was influenced by Count Agoston Haraszthy, who did much to introduce and encourage wine production in the North Bay, especially in the nearby Sonoma Valley.

Wine production greatly expanded in the 1860s,1870s and 1880s, spurred by a plant disease, phylloxera, that destroyed many French vineyards and weakened French competition.

Phylloxera devastated Northern California vineyards in 1890s and forced growers to rethink their methods, to the benefit of the industry. A vine, native

Voter Registration

City	Demo.	Repub.	Decl.	All
American Canyon	2,416	1,168	436	4,125
Calistoga	827	1,091	148	2,114
Napa City	16,840	11,888	2,538	32,212
St. Helena	1,195	1,276	233	2,797
Yountville	1,118	690	134	1,988
County	29,063	22,671	4,847	58,257

Source: Napa County Registrar of Voters, October, 1991. Key: Demo. (Democrat), Repub. (Republican), Decl. (Decline to state preference), NA (not available).

Presidential Voting in Napa County

Year	Democrat	Votes	Republican	Votes
1956	Stevenson	10,623	Eisenhower*	13,610
1960	Kennedy*	13,499	Nixon	15,125
1964	Johnson*	19,580	Goldwater	11,567
1968	Humphrey	14,762	Nixon*	14,270
1972	McGovern	14,529	Nixon*	23,403
1976	Carter*	18,048	Ford	20,839
1980	Carter	14,898	Reagan*	23,632
1984	Mondale	18,599	Reagan*	26,322
1988	Dukakis	22,283	Bush*	23,235

Source: California Secretary of State's office. * Election winner.

to Eastern United States and hearty enough to resist the disease, was introduced.

1864. Construction begins on Napa Valley Railroad, from City of Napa to Calistoga, a popular resort. At Napa City, travelers take steamboat.

1876. Napa State Asylum, cost $1.5 million, 600 patients. Hailed as one of the most progressive institutions in country. Becomes major employer, about 2,500 people near turn of century.

The 20th Century and Prohibition

1900. Napa starts the century with a population of 16,451.

1920. Prohibition starts, a great blow to the valley. Many wineries fail. Some survived by concentrating on wine for medicinal or religious reasons — exempted from law — and by selling grapes so individuals could make wine. Law allowed each person to produce 200 gallons a year.

1933. Prohibition repealed. Wine industry starts to revive but is kept small

Napa County Ethnic Makeup

City, Town or Area	White	Black	Hisp.	Asn./PI	N. Am.
American Canyon	5,251	450	781	1,155	56
Angwin	2,638	89	353	372	13
Calistoga	3,297	12	1,098	13	6
Deer Park	1,532	14	218	54	7
Napa City	50,550	214	9,425	1,204	404
St. Helena	3,847	22	1,034	71	10
Yountville	2,817	56	326	42	18
Remainder	19,521	310	2,706	458	158
Countywide	89,453	1,167	15,941	3,391	687

Source: 1990 Census. Key: Hisp. (Hispanic); Asn./PI (Asian/Pacific Islander); N. Am. (Native American including American Indian, Eskimo and Aleut). Not included, a small number identified by census as "other race."

by Depression. People don't have money to buy wine.

1941. World War II boomed the population of the county, many of the new residents going to work at naval yards in Vallejo. As part of war effort, Highway 29 was upgraded, which helped usher in suburbia after war.

Modern Times

1945. The end of World War II began a period of great prosperity in the United States. America discovers and rediscovers the joys of wine.

Many people take to visiting the Valley to sample wines. Wineries open tasting rooms. Tourism becomes a big business in the valley.

1950s. To secure water supply, Berryessa Valley was dammed, creating a large lake now popular as a recreation spot.

1968. Napa County Board of Supervisors restricts subdivisions to protect vineyards from encroaching suburbia. Protection remains a sensitive issue. Many fear car pollution and construction threaten vineyards.

5/Napa County School Rankings

Elementary, Middle and High, by Districts

THESE RANKINGS ARE drawn from state tests given over three years, 1988, 1989, 1990. For the most part, they will follow a pattern. High one year will be high the next, low will be low.

When the numbers fluctuate wildly, the number of children who took the tests will often be low. In a small class, one or two kids having a bad or good day will cause wide swings. Sometimes the children fail to understand instructions and this lowers their grade. Sometimes they just have an off day.

A Cautionary Note

Ranking systems don't recognize overall gains or losses. If every school in California raised raw scores 20 percent, some schools would still be ranked at the bottom, a few at the top. The same if every raw score dropped. A ranking system shows how one school did against all other schools. There is no one perfect method of testing.

Family background, particularly education of parents, greatly influences how children will score in schools. See introduction to Marin scores (Chapter 2) and chapter on How Public Schools Work.

CALISTOGA JOINT UNIFIED SCHOOL DISTRICT
District-Wide

Third Grade	1988	1989	1990
Reading	50	50	44
Writing	42	71	54
Math	33	48	21
No. Tested	39	30	43

Sixth Grade	1988	1989	1990
Reading	78	31	47
Writing	68	45	60
Math	56	51	49
No. Tested	51	58	48

Eighth Grade	1988	1989	1990
Reading	60	22	93
Writing	—	—	—

CALISTOGA UNIFIED (Continued)
District-Wide

Eighth Grade	1988	1989	1990
Math	64	50	91
History	82	40	85
Science	89	70	72
No. Tested	49	41	44

Twelfth Grade	1988	1989	1990
Reading	53	26	15
Writing	—	69	28
Math	71	43	2
No.Tested	43	50	35

Calistoga Elementary

Third Grade	1988	1989	1990
Reading	50	50	45
Writing	42	68	53
Math	35	49	25
No. Tested	39	30	43

Sixth Grade	1988	1989	1990
Reading	73	32	47
Writing	65	46	60
Math	55	53	48
No. Tested	51	58	48

Calistoga Junior-Senior High

Eighth Grade	1988	1989	1990
Reading	56	25	92
Writing	—	—	—
Math	66	50	88
History	79	39	82
Science	87	70	74
No. Tested	49	41	44

Twelfth Grade	1988	1989	1990
Reading	52	32	22
Writing	—	68	29
Math	70	46	10
No.Tested	42	43	30

HOWELL MOUNTAIN ELEMENTARY SCHOOL DISTRICT
District Wide

Third Grade	1988	1989	1990
Reading	43	58	46
Writing	2	52	15
Math	14	37	85
No. Tested	18	17	9

Sixth Grade	1988	1989	1990
Reading	26	60	65
Writing	39	74	66
Math	71	93	70
No. Tested	13	22	21

Eighth Grade	1988	1989	1990
Reading	96	98	89
Writing	—	—	—
Math	91	78	77
History	92	95	91
Science	89	93	66
No. Tested	10	18	17

Howell Mountain Elementary

Third Grade	1988	1989	1990
Reading	44	58	47
Writing	11	54	19
Math	15	39	78
No. Tested	18	17	9

Sixth Grade	1988	1989	1990
Reading	28	57	59
Writing	38	69	65
Math	64	89	67
No. Tested	13	22	21

Eighth Grade	1988	1989	1990
Reading	94	97	86
Writing	—	—	—
Math	89	75	76
History	89	93	90
Science	87	91	68
No. Tested	10	18	17

NAPA VALLEY UNIFIED DISTRICT
District-Wide

Third Grade	1988	1989	1990
Reading	92	87	78
Writing	90	80	71
Math	88	85	74
No. Tested	867	997	1,063

Sixth Grade	1988	1989	1990
Reading	84	89	83
Writing	80	77	78
Math	83	84	82
No. Tested	758	824	904

Eighth Grade	1988	1989	1990
Reading	69	78	76
Writing	—	—	—
Math	83	85	82
History	73	75	74
Science	77	81	76
No. Tested	763	760	782

Twelfth Grade	1988	1989	1990
Reading	79	62	75
Writing	—	59	79
Math	80	61	74
No.Tested	641	699	572

Alta Heights Elementary

Third Grade	1988	1989	1990
Reading	87	95	95
Writing	85	85	95
Math	76	95	90
No. Tested	80	74	77
Sixth Grade	1988	1989	1990
Reading	91	98	92
Writing	81	85	91
Math	66	93	88
No. Tested	41	51	59

Bel Aire Park Elementary

Third Grade	1988	1989	1990
Reading	89	66	47
Writing	84	60	41
Math	88	59	27
No. Tested	45	32	63
Sixth Grade	1988	1989	1990
Reading	59	94	77
Writing	71	79	84
Math	74	88	80
No. Tested	45	35	39

Browns Valley Elementary

Third Grade	1988	1989	1990
Reading	97	98	88
Writing	98	97	84
Math	85	96	86
No. Tested	76	95	97
Sixth Grade	1988	1989	1990
Reading	95	97	95
Writing	90	84	89
Math	84	96	89
No. Tested	87	77	76

Capell Elementary

Third Grade	1988	1989	1990
Reading	21	81	75
Writing	35	55	77
Math	77	76	60
No. Tested	3	5	7
Sixth Grade	1988	1989	1990
Reading	88	55	90
Writing	81	78	35
Math	51	87	44
No. Tested	3	2	2

Carneros Elementary

Third Grade	1988	1989	1990
Reading	38	40	46
Writing	30	30	56
Math	27	58	48
No. Tested	13	12	8

Sixth Grade	1988	1989	1990
Reading	66	98	90
Writing	89	85	53
Math	76	71	76
No. Tested	11	12	15

Donaldson Way Elementary

Third Grade	1988	1989	1990
Reading	84	73	72
Writing	83	56	59
Math	80	80	72
No. Tested	26	35	42
Sixth Grade	1988	1989	1990
Reading	35	41	50
Writing	57	53	38
Math	51	37	83
No.Tested	33	32	32

El Centro Elementary

Third Grade	1988	1989	1990
Reading	91	82	87
Writing	91	73	88
Math	85	86	79
No. Tested	32	44	44
Sixth Grade	1988	1989	1990
Reading	98	72	94
Writing	89	69	89
Math	96	82	82
No. Tested	33	46	41

McPherson Elementary

Third Grade	1988	1989	1990
Reading	61	38	64
Writing	42	41	67
Math	44	13	56
No. Tested	75	55	82
Sixth Grade	1988	1989	1990
Reading	66	44	29
Writing	28	25	40
Math	36	22	54
No. Tested	49	64	59

Mt. George Elementary

Third Grade	1988	1989	1990
Reading	97	95	97
Writing	94	94	97
Math	97	91	97
No. Tested	27	38	32
Sixth Grade	1988	1989	1990
Reading	96	96	97
Writing	87	95	96
Math	94	98	96
No. Tested	31	31	43

Napa High

Twelfth Grade	1988	1989	1990
Reading	75	63	72
Writing	—	51	68
Math	82	55	78
No. Tested	322	327	271

Napa Junction Elementary

Third Grade	1988	1989	1990
Reading	65	51	34
Writing	77	38	27
Math	69	60	34
No. Tested	56	75	62
Sixth Grade	1988	1989	1990
Reading	17	34	76
Writing	36	56	50
Math	23	32	52
No. Tested	52	58	68

Northwood Elementary

Third Grade	1988	1989	1990
Reading	99	94	88
Writing	99	95	88
Math	95	94	82
No. Tested	78	92	81
Sixth Grade	1988	1989	1990
Reading	95	96	93
Writing	97	97	93
Math	98	94	88
No. Tested	67	71	63

Phillips Elementary

Third Grade	1988	1989	1990
Reading	80	82	82
Writing	68	81	77
Math	64	71	85
No. Tested	52	47	60
Sixth Grade	1988	1989	1990
Reading	47	63	54
Writing	51	39	71
Math	48	71	68
No. Tested	38	45	74

Redwood Middle School

Eighth Grade	1988	1989	1990
Reading	64	78	77
Writing	—	—	—
Math	76	78	76
History	76	79	78
Science	76	85	83
No. Tested	374	389	410

Salvador Elementary

Third Grade	1988	1989	1990
Reading	92	83	62
Writing	89	84	80
Math	75	91	82
No. Tested	18	30	27
Sixth Grade	1988	1989	1990
Reading	94	91	45
Writing	78	88	85
Math	86	94	88
No. Tested	18	33	21

Shearer Elementary

Third Grade	1988	1989	1990
Reading	62	43	37
Writing	50	37	27
Math	45	27	38
No. Tested	59	93	101
Sixth Grade	1988	1989	1990
Reading	35	62	52
Writing	47	41	30
Math	49	36	39
No. Tested	65	66	76

Silverado Middle School

Eighth Grade	1988	1989	1990
Reading	67	75	73
Writing	—	—	—
Math	82	84	82
History	66	68	65
Science	75	77	69
No. Tested	389	371	372

Snow Elementary

Third Grade	1988	1989	1990
Reading	76	89	59
Writing	67	78	40
Math	35	68	48
No. Tested	27	36	36
Sixth Grade	1988	1989	1990
Reading	95	43	72
Writing	52	48	71
Math	64	49	63
No. Tested	30	26	31

Vichy Elementary

Third Grade	1988	1989	1990
Reading	99	98	96
Writing	98	98	93
Math	98	99	95
No. Tested	44	58	62
Sixth Grade	1988	1989	1990
Reading	82	97	97

Sixth Grade	1988	1989	1990
Writing	93	95	84
Math	90	98	91
No. Tested	44	47	44

Vintage High

Twelfth Grade	1988	1989	1990
Reading	82	69	74
Writing	—	78	86
Math	76	71	68
No. Tested	304	341	301

West Park Elementary

Third Grade	1988	1989	1990
Reading	88	44	74
Writing	78	50	54
Math	89	66	64
No. Tested	28	34	40

Sixth Grade	1988	1989	1990
Reading	81	98	69
Writing	59	91	66
Math	92	96	65
No. Tested	32	29	23

Westwood Elementary

Third Grade	1988	1989	1990
Reading	61	57	43
Writing	55	38	39
Math	83	45	53
No. Tested	52	58	57

Sixth Grade	1988	1989	1990
Reading	76	26	38
Writing	55	32	44
Math	77	15	44
No. Tested	40	48	61

Wooden Valley Elementary

Third Grade	1988	1989	1990
Reading	78	62	68
Writing	60	80	63
Math	49	57	29
No. Tested	5	9	8

Sixth Grade	1988	1989	1990
Reading	88	80	83
Writing	45	52	24
Math	75	64	66
No. Tested	4	5	6

Yountville Elementary

Third Grade	1988	1989	1990
Reading	23	43	45
Writing	37	41	23
Math	40	71	54
No. Tested	16	23	21

Sixth Grade	1988	1989	1990
Reading	53	88	28
Writing	57	71	64
Math	77	76	50
No. Tested	14	12	18

ST. HELENA UNIFIED SCHOOL DISTRICT
District Wide

Third Grade	1988	1989	1990
Reading	56	60	81
Writing	50	48	64
Math	70	48	58
No. Tested	87	84	86

Sixth Grade	1988	1989	1990
Reading	89	92	78
Writing	84	80	50
Math	91	80	75
No. Tested	87	93	96

Eighth Grade	1988	1989	1990
Reading	94	80	72
Writing	—	—	—
Math	85	88	76
History	94	93	94
Science	88	66	80
No. Tested	81	102	86

Twelfth Grade	1988	1989	1990
Reading	93	61	80
Writing	43	70	—
Math	69	59	92
No.Tested	118	112	101

Monticello Elementary

Third Grade	1988	1989	1990
Reading	75	99	80
Writing	69	84	89
Math	53	82	68
No. Tested	3	3	5

St. Helena Elementary

Third Grade	1988	1989	1990
Reading	51	60	76
Writing	50	45	60
Math	65	49	57
No. Tested	84	83	81

Stevenson Middle

Sixth Grade	1988	1989	1990
Reading	82	87	70
Writing	77	74	51
Math	84	75	69
No. Tested	87	93	96

ST. HELENA UNIFIED (Continued)

Stevenson Middle

Eighth Grade	1988	1989	1990
Reading	92	78	72
Writing	—	—	—
Math	80	85	75
History	93	91	94
Science	86	66	79

Eighth Grade	1988	1989	1990
No. Tested	81	102	86

St. Helena High

Twelfth Grade	1988	1989	1990
Reading	92	61	77
Writing	—	47	66
Math	71	57	88
No. Tested	114	108	101

6/Napa City Profiles

Census Reports on Home Values, Rents — Picturesque Living in a Valley of Vintners

FOR A BRIEF DISCUSSION of the roles of local governments, see the beginning of Marin City Profiles, Chapter 3.

American Canyon

Napa County's newest city, residents voting to incorporate in November 1991. Located just north of Vallejo and very much within the Vallejo orbit, even though Vallejo is located in Solano County.

As you drive north on Highway 29, American Canyon is the first Napa town to greet you but if it weren't for the road signs you would think you were in Vallejo. In the 1970s and 1980s, developers discovered Vallejo, added subdivision after subdivision and when they got to the county line, they didn't stop. The two cities flow into one another.

American Canyon, which extends down to the Napa River, has a lot of new housing. What it doesn't have is stores and shopping. But no problem. Drive a few blocks and you'll run into Vallejo's newest additions, a Walmart, and a giant supermarket. Drive a few blocks more and you'll hit Marine World and the county fairgrounds — first class recreation.

Population 7,706, according to census. About 25 percent under age 18, about 25 percent over 55. Mobile homes are part of the scene.

Total housing units about 2,725, of which 88 percent are owner-occupied (census), a good sign of social stability.

The best San Fran or East Bay commute in Napa County. Straight shot to the Crockett Bridge and down I-80 to Oakland and East Bay. BART stations along way, at Richmond and El Cerrito.

American Canyon is served by Napa Valley Unified School District. Two

---

Home Price Sampler from Classified Ads

American Canyon

2-bedroom, 2-bath, $81,000.

3-bedroom, 2-bath, 2-car garage, 1,318 sq. ft. $159,000.

Calistoga

2-bedroom, 2-bath, 1.33-acre lot, mature trees, creek, fireplace, kitchen w/large dining area. $330,000

3-bedroom, 2.5-bath, small office, 2 fireplaces, pool, family room, dining room. $375,000.

3-bedroom, 2-bath, living room, fireplace, 1,440 sq. ft. $237,000.

Napa

3-bedroom, 2.5-bath, new Victorian, hardwood floor, custom tile, breakfast nook, formal dining, marble fireplace. $257,500.

Napa

3-bedroom, 2-bath, family room, fireplace, central air, hot tub, pool. $187,900.

St. Helena

2-bedroom, 2-bath, fireplace, hardwood floors, large corner lot, fenced, central heat, air conditioned. $220,000.

3-bedroom, 2.5-bath, dining, breakfast room, fireplace, 2-car garage, patio, $249,500.

Yountville

3-bedroom, 2-bath, farmhouse, luxury finish, new, 2,427 square feet. $340,000.

3-bedroom, 2-bath, den, 2-car garage, pool, tennis close by. $289,500.

Source: Survey of classified ads, summer and fall, 1991.

---

elementary schools in town: Donaldson Way and Napa Junction. Then kids head off to Silverado Junior High and Vintage High School.

Academic rankings bounce around but many are well above the 50th percentile, and the high school is hitting the top 30th percentile in state.

Crime not tracked by FBI. Patrolled by sheriff's deputies. Small airport.

Cityhood should be a plus. It will give American Canyon control over its planning and intensify efforts to build a commercial base along Highway 29.

Angwin

Hamlet in the hills, off Howell Mountain Road. Population 3,503, many of them students at Pacific Union College, the great influence in the town.

A place for the young at heart and just plain young. About 61 percent of Angwin is under age 30. Parks, tennis courts. A few shops and offices in plaza. Homes hidden in trees and shrubs, the college buildings. Landing strip nearby.

One elementary school. Rankings bounce all over but some in the 70th and 80th percentile.

Angwin sits on a mesa. Drive a bit and down you go. Place has air of mountain village.

Calistoga

Resort city, pretty, increased its population by 15 percent in the 1980s but in real numbers this came out to only 589 people. Total population 4,468.

Some new housing on the north side of town but most of Calistoga has been around for a while, pre-World War II, the 1950s and 1960s. Well-kept. A few Victorians. Away from the main drag, Lincoln Avenue, Calistoga has a retiring

Number & Value of Owner-Occupied Dwellings

City or Area	< $100K -199K	$200K -299K	$300K -399K	$400K -499K	$500K -plus
American Canyon	1,306	241	5	1	3
Angwin	197	73	31	12	10
Calistoga	327	145	51	21	18
Deer Park	98	74	36	15	54
Napa, City of	7,917	3,058	771	180	159
St. Helena	358	327	157	61	76
Yountville	163	100	24	2	3
Countywide	11,897	5,001	1,846	686	905

Source: 1990 Census. The chart shows the number of owner-occupied dwellings within a set price range.

Median & Average Price of Owner-Occupied Homes

City or Area	Units	Median	Average
American Canyon	1,556	$135,700	$147,039
Angwin	323	175,300	211,362
Calistoga	562	187,900	215,774
Deer Park	277	267,200	306,101
Napa, City of	12,085	175,000	194,825
St. Helena	979	234,200	266,386
Yountville	292	189,900	200,925
Countywide	20,335	183,000	217,930

Source: 1990 Census. Median means half way. In 100 homes the 50th home will be the median home.

air and, in fact, folks age 55 and older make up about 36 percent of population (1990 census).

Legend has it town got its name when founding father Sam Brannan stood up at a grand party to introduce Calistoga as the "Saratoga of California." Calistoga has hot springs and mud baths, much like the resort town of Saratoga in New York. Sam, having hoisted a few, instead popped out with "Calistoga of Sarafornia." Name stuck. Sounds like it was a great party.

Crime not tracked by FBI but towns of this size and nature generally come in peaceful. Calistoga has own police department.

School rankings bounce all over, low and high, and suggest a mix of suburban and rural. Rural scores are often low.

Calistoga is the northernmost town in the county, a long way from the East Bay and San Fran. But back roads run over to Highway 12 and Highway 101, and from there Santa Rosa is but a short drive. Being a resort town, Calistoga has its own employment base: restaurants, inns, hotels, spas, stores, country club nearby.

Library, community center. Petrified forest, Mt. St. Helena, state park nearby.

Deer Park

Located east of St. Helena, off Deer Park Road. Site of St. Helena Hospital. Homes hidden among trees. Hilly. Population 1,825.

Short drive to valley floor.

Napa City

Largest city in county and seat of county government. Rises from valley floor into hills. Picturesque downtown. Victorians, government buildings, shopping plaza. Napa River. A lot of thinking went into making the downtown an attractive place to shop and dine.

Like many older towns, Napa started with a core that slowly grew over 100 years then rapidly expanded after World War II and the suburban revolution. The city started 1950 with 13,579 residents and added 10,000 to 14,000 people in each of the following four decades. The population is now 61,482.

In and about the downtown are the older neighborhoods: grid streets lined with trees; garages separate from houses, a leftover from the horse and buggy days; large Victorians, some of them subdivided into apartments; bungalows; large rambling homes, circa 1920s and 1930s; homes built after the war, two-car garages. Some of the stuff is rundown; a lot of it is neat, well-kept or restored, and charming.

Napa High School is just north of downtown. When school lets out, the kids can be seen walking and chatting in groups some eight or 10 blocks away. There's a certain intimacy to the older sections, a feeling that the institutions and residents have grown up together.

Moving north and west and east, the homes become more modern and streets start ending in cul-de-sacs, the suburban design. Behind Queen of the Valley Hospital, off Trancas Street, the homes say 1960s and 1970s, two-car garages, mix of blue- and white-collar middle class.

Stores and small shopping plazas along Trancas serve the north end.

Traveling east along Redwood and Brown's Valley roads, you'll find the upper-middle and well-to-do neighborhoods of the city. The homes are larger and newer, custom jobs mixed among upscale tracts.

In the southern section, River Park fronts its homes on the Napa River, an upscale neighborhood that glides north into a commercial-residential section.

That's the broad pattern; exceptions abound. Brown's Valley has older homes, some run down; the quality of the downtown neighborhoods vary from section to section.

Rental Units & Rates in Napa County

City or Area	< $100 -249	$250 -499	$500 -749	$750 -999	$1,000 -plus
American Canyon	19	62	161	69	8
Angwin	22	216	93	22	7
Calistoga	39	358	299	67	6
Deer Park	21	117	104	21	9
Napa, City of	567	2,361	4,622	1,285	419
St. Helena	71	237	280	142	60
Yountville	14	87	95	44	15
Countywide	856	3,877	6,191	1,817	584

Source: 1990 Census. The chart shows the number of rental units counted within a set range of rates.

Median & Average Rents of Renter-Occupied Dwellings

City or Area	Units	Median	Average
American Canyon	330	$607	$617
Angwin	370	438	470
Calistoga	796	492	517
Deer Park	285	496	525
Napa, City of	9,436	572	595
St. Helena	816	564	594
Yountville	258	547	598
Countywide	13,775	561	583

Source: 1990 Census. Median means half way. In 100 homes the 50th home will be the median home.

Homes and buildings near the river flooded in 1986 rains.

Crime about low suburban average, more petty thefts than major stuff (but lock the doors). One homicide in 1990, zero in 1989, three in 1988, zero in 1987.

Commute is not that bad considering the distance. Coming north, Highway 29 splits off Highway 221 (the Silverado Trail) and both run though Napa City.

Down toward Vallejo, traffic lights have been installed, which slows all, and the Highway 37 cutover near Marine World is still being overhauled (a mess during peak hours).

But if you have a local job or something in Contra Costa County ... it's do-able. Tourist traffic in summer and on weekends irritates a few.

Napa City's amusements include two movie houses (11 screens), bowling alleys, racquetball, four golf courses (36-18-18-9 holes), horse center, art galleries, museums, three regional parks and 33 other parks in assorted sizes (mini, neighborhood and community). River fishing and boating, and in the city or nearby, wineries and first-class restaurants. Also Napa Community College, many classes and activities.

Government is the biggest employer: schools, 2,300; Napa State Hospital, 2,100; plus the hundreds in city and county governments and the college.

School rankings up there, generally the 60th and 70th percentiles, some schools hitting the 90s.

Overall: a pleasing town, Middle America, but moving up the scale.

St. Helena

Heart of the wine country. Many of the major wineries are located in town or nearby and St. Helena does a lively trade in tourists and tasters. A stable town. Started 1980 with 4,898 residents, finished with 4,990, an increase of 92 people. About a third of the residents are 55 or older, the retiring age.

Trailer park on the east side of town. Regular housing on the west. St. Helena has some fairly new homes but much of the housing was built decades ago, many before World War II. Generally, the homes are well-kept. Lots of trees and greenery. Vineyards start at city borders and on some streets within.

Away from Main Street, St. Helena comes across as a country town that in a small way has been "discovered" by people who appreciate the good life: the wineries, the restaurants, a morning cappuccino. Main Street is also Highway 29, frequently congested, especially in tourist season. Movie house, restaurants, delis, small shops, some Victorians — a quaint main drag.

Two elementary schools, one intermediate, one high. Academic rankings generally up there, 70s, 80s, 90s. Town also has a Catholic school.

Crime not tracked by FBI but towns like St. Helena almost invariably land on the peaceful side. People know one another. Parking meters on Main Street.

Commute ... if you have a local job or one in Napa City ... excellent. If you labor in the City, our sympathies.

Yountville

After George Yount, first white settler in Napa Valley. Increased its population by 366 in the last decade and is still building but slowly. Now has 3,259 residents, reports census.

Location of veterans home and one of few towns in state where men outnumber women — 2,040 to 1,219. The vets, census figures suggest, make up about 41 percent of Yountville. Families number just over 500, census says.

Tourist-wine country burg. Hotels. Old winery converted into shops and restaurants. Place to make connections for hot-air balloon rides.

Crime not tracked by FBI but low.

Children attend schools in Napa Valley Unified School District.

Nice place to visit, to linger, but the small size restricts choice of housing.

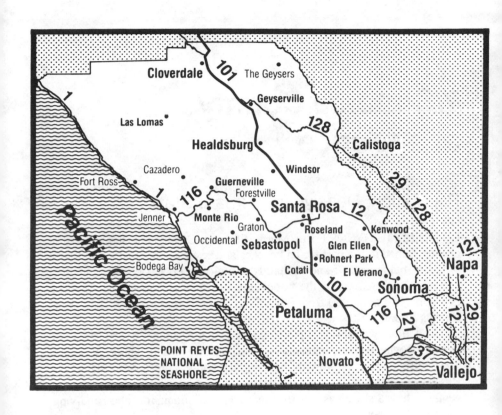

Sonoma County

7/Sonoma County at a Glance

Population, Dewey vs. Truman, Stats

LOCATED JUST NORTH of Marin, Sonoma County is a suburban-rural county, famed in the past for its beaches and resorts and its wines and farm products, but nowadays known mainly as a pleasant place to live.

In the last 20 years, the population has almost doubled itself, rising between 1970 and 1980 from 204,885 to 299,681 and to 388,421 by 1990 (census figures).

The allure was always there. Zephyrs ease the summer heat. The Pacific warms the winters. Snow rarely falls. Rain confines itself to winter and spring. The Pacific rolls up the western shore — miles of beaches, soaring vistas. The Russian and Petaluma Rivers meander through the interior. Flatlands give way gently to hills and valleys. But the means to tap Sonoma for suburban living, foremost transportation, were not.

The Coming of Highway 101

Following World War II, San Francisco, as a metropolis, spread to the East and South Bay and to Marin County, which gradually built Highway 101 to carry traffic to the City. The farther north 101 was extended, the more accessible Sonoma became and in the 1970s and 1980s the suburban swing become more pronounced.

Also pushing suburbia north was a sharp rise in the general population of California and housing costs that priced other sections, especially Marin, beyond the pocketbook of many home buyers. Marin in the 1980s increased its population by 7,504 residents. Petaluma alone in that decade added 9,350 inhabitants.

Indeed, so favorable were home prices that many Marin residents and

Sonoma County Population

City or Area	Male	Female	Total	*Total
Bodega Bay	585	542	1,127	NA
Boyes Hot Springs	2,999	2,974	5,973	NA
Cloverdale	2,432	2,492	4,924	5,000
Cotati	2,765	2,949	5,714	5,825
El Verano	1,733	1,765	3,498	NA
Fetters Ht Sprgs-Ag. Cal.	991	1,033	2,024	NA
Forestville	1,178	1,265	2,443	NA
Glen Ellen	580	611	1,191	NA
Guerneville	1,039	927	1,966	NA
Healdsburg	4,545	4,924	9,469	9,625
Monte Rio	561	497	1,058	NA
Occidental	662	638	1,300	NA
Petaluma	20,993	22,191	43,184	43,500
Rohnert Park	17,721	18,605	36,326	37,000
Roseland	4,346	4,422	8,779	NA
Santa Rosa	54,142	59,171	113,313	115,900
Sebastopol	3,189	3,815	7,004	7,200
Sonoma	3,555	4,566	8,121	8,225
South Santa Rosa	2,055	2,073	4,128	NA
Windsor	6,626	6,745	13,371	NA
Remainder	57,575	55,734	113,309	NA
Countywide	190,272	197,950	388,222	396,800

Source: 1990 Census. *Population estimates by the California Department of Finance, Jan. 1, 1991.

established residents from other counties sold their homes and with the equity bought bigger and better homes in Sonoma County.

Enticing for Home and Hearth

About 1990, the equity market began to dry up and with it went the roaring housing market of the 1980s. Still, Sonoma is considered a good buy for people interested in stretching the housing dollar.

Beside the blessings of nature, the county offers many other enticements: vineyards, wineries, classy restaurants, a state university, a community college, swimming, boating, fishing, golf, skating, softball — a wealth of activities.

Crime is generally low, school rankings generally high. Services, in most cases, have kept pace with development: hospitals, police and fire protection.

But in one area, the whole North Bay has fallen down: traffic. Highway 101, which feeds to the Golden Gate, remains practically the only major road

Coming & Going
(Driver License Address Changes)

County	Moved to Sonoma from	Moved from Sonoma to	Net
Alameda	968	596	372
Alpine	2	2	0
Amador	15	33	-18
Butte	202	302	-100
Calaveras	25	31	-6
Colusa	9	9	0
Contra Costa	718	488	230
Del Norte	34	68	-34
El Dorado	121	157	-36
Fresno	189	172	17
Glenn	15	21	-6
Humboldt	257	232	25
Imperial	13	6	7
Inyo	16	12	4
Kern	104	98	6
Kings	15	13	2
Lake	357	840	-483
Lassen	22	23	-1
Los Angeles	1,630	715	915
Madera	16	37	-21
Marin	2,938	1,365	1,573
Mariposa	7	14	-7
Mendocino	607	661	-54
Merced	59	44	15
Modoc	11	13	-2
Mono	8	1	7
Monterey	148	108	40
Napa	533	469	64
Nevada	88	97	-9
Orange	610	293	317
Placer	118	155	-37
Plumas	26	40	-14
Riverside	206	206	0
Sacramento	553	801	-248
San Benito	19	13	6
San Bernardino	214	143	71
San Diego	541	407	134
San Francisco	1,600	866	734

Coming & Going
(Driver License Address Changes)

County	Moved to Sonoma from	Moved from Sonoma to	Net
San Joaquin	192	201	-9
San Luis Obispo	146	138	8
San Mateo	1,143	388	755
Santa Barbara	169	150	19
Santa Clara	989	513	476
Santa Cruz	189	145	44
Shasta	116	230	-114
Sierra	10	5	5
Siskiyou	68	68	0
Solano	323	484	-161
Stanislaus	131	144	-13
Sutter	39	36	3
Tehama	29	64	-35
Trinity	22	30	-8
Tulare	73	78	-5
Tuolumne	49	48	1
Ventura	156	92	64
Yolo	135	200	-65
Yuba	33	33	0
All Counties	17,026	12,598	4,428
Out of State	3,878	3,720	158
Total	20,904	16,318	4,586

Source: California Department of Finance, 1991. Data covers fiscal year July 1, 1990-June 30, 1991. Out-of-state counts have been adjusted for non-compliers.

to San Francisco. Residents would love to widen it or duplicate it and add a second deck on the bridge but cannot bring themselves to accept the population splurge the improvements would bring.

History

Before the Europeans, there were the Indians, Pomos, Miwoks and others. They hunted, they fished, they ate acorns and berries and simple foods derived from the wild fields. They were utterly unprepared for what was to befall them.

In 1492, Columbus, working for Spain, discovered America. The Spanish moved quickly into Mexico and other parts of Central and South America but they didn't get around to California, which they claimed, until the eve of the American Revolutionary War.

Sonoma County Ethnic Makeup

City or Area	White	Black	Hisp.	Asn./PI	N. Am.
Bodega Bay	1,030	0	74	21	1
Boyes Hot Springs	4,666	22	1,131	107	39
Cloverdale	4,023	8	791	28	69
Cotati	4,804	147	487	206	63
El Verano	2,910	11	426	100	47
Fetters Hot Spr.-Ag. Cal.	1,714	20	226	42	22
Forestville	2,113	7	266	35	22
Glen Ellen	1,119	8	43	9	9
Guerneville	1,636	23	261	23	22
Healdsburg	7,281	12	2,026	59	83
Monte Rio	977	8	50	15	8
Occidental	1,225	6	51	14	4
Petaluma	37,084	513	3,985	1,354	208
Rohnert Park	30,160	933	3,247	1,646	293
Roseland	5,515	324	2,267	434	209
Santa Rosa	95,768	1,910	10,727	3,626	1,152
Sebastopol	6,250	21	560	97	68
Sonoma	7,510	28	418	140	23
South Santa Rosa	2,971	184	760	113	95
Windsor	10,209	119	2,597	272	159
Remainder	98,464	964	10,830	1,893	1,067
Countywide	327,429	5,268	41,223	10,234	3,663

Source: 1990 Census. Key: Hisp. (Hispanic); Asn./PI (Asian/Pacific Islander); N. Am. (Native American including American Indian, Eskimo and Aleut). Not included, a small number identified by census as "other race."

In 1769 Gaspar de Portola discovered the Bay. Once established in Northern California, the Spanish and their heirs (Mexico won independence in 1821 and took over the Spanish claim) moved energetically but the Southwest Indians again closed overland migration. On the eve of the Mexican-American War in 1846, fewer than 7,000 Spanish-Mexicans inhabited the entire state.

The Mission

Gradually the first settlers moved north from the Presidio in San Francisco and in 1823 Father Jose Altimira opened the Mission of San Francisco de Solano at what is now the city of Sonoma. From noble intentions — to care for and convert the Indians — came tragic results. Having no immunity to European diseases, the Indians died in large numbers from measles and smallpox.

In 1834, Mariano Vallejo, Commandant-General and a man of great energy, took over mission lands and built a small town and fort. The county,

Average Household Income

City or Area	1990	1991
Cloverdale	$33,600	$35,000
Coastal-Gualala	38,000	39,600
Cotati	32,500	33,900
Healdsburg	37,100	38,700
Healdsburg, Rural Areas	37,900	39,500
Petaluma	40,100	41,800
Petaluma, Rural Areas	42,500	44,300
Rohnert Park	37,000	38,600
Rohnert Park, Rural Areas	36,500	38,000
Rural Northeast	37,700	39,300
Russian River	31,200	32,500
Santa Rosa	38,600	40,300
Santa Rosa, Rural Areas	42,100	43,900
Sebastopol	34,200	35,700
Sebastopol, Rural Areas	39,100	40,800
Sonoma	35,200	36,700
Sonoma Valley, Rural	24,600	25,700
Windsor	39,600	41,300
Countywide	38,000	39,600

Source: *Projects '90,* Association of Bay Area Governments, January, 1990; U.S. Bureau of Labor Statistics. Income is stated in constant 1988 dollars, rounded off to the nearest $100. Income for 1991 is an estimate based on 1990 income adjusted by the Bay Area consumer price Index for the September, 1990-September, 1991, period. A full-year adjustment may vary.

which is named after an Indian chief, was divided into great rancheros (Vallejo's covered 175,000 acres), soldiers were sent out to subdue the Indians and the great days of the Californios began.

Vast herds of cattle roamed the countryside. After vaqueros branded the cattle in the spring, fiestas were thrown that lasted for days. Music, dancing, barbecues, rodeos, unfettered hospitality — the Days of the Dons are still celebrated in California folklore. But their time in the sun would quickly pass.

The Russians

As the Spanish were moving into Northern California, the Russians were crossing the Bering Strait and claiming Alaska. Not surprisingly, Russian explorers soon ventured down into California and in 1812, to the distress of the Spanish, built a settlement and fort on the Sonoma coast.

The Spanish hinted it would be nice if the Russians returned from whence

Voter Registration

City	Demo.	Repub.	All
Cloverdale	1,293	808	2,406
Cotati	1,657	778	2,818
Healdsburg	2,690	1,902	5,156
Petaluma	12,977	7,144	23,109
Rohnert Park	9,129	5,800	17,346
Santa Rosa	33,367	23,810	64,050
Sebastopol	2,343	1,143	3,943
Sonoma	2,712	1,943	5,158
Windsor	3,758	2,587	7,199
Unincorporated	49,698	28,534	89,366
Countywide	115,866	71,862	213,252

Source: Sonoma County Registrar of Voters, November, 1991.

they came. But, behind their cannons, the Russians chose not to hear.

They muddled along, trading with Indians and Californios, exploring the countryside, and taking care not to rile authorities. Spanish-Mexican distrust of the Russians soon receded before fears of the Yankees.

The Yankee Invasion

Although nominally Spanish or Mexican, California in the early 1800s was claimed by several nations. A sparsity of settlers created a situation where the country that could field the largest numbers would probably carry the day.

In 1803, Thomas Jefferson purchased the Midwest and as it was settled, mountain men and pioneers began pushing west toward California. The Monroe Doctrine — no more European colonies in the Americas — apparently impressed the czar and nothing was done to expand the settlement at Fort Ross. The Russians hunted the local otter to extinction and in 1841, after selling the fort to John Sutter, of golden fame, sailed off. As more Americans arrived, disputes arose. The Californios claimed all; the Yankees saw land poorly defended, scarcely inhabited, ideal for trade and farming. They began plotting.

On June 11, 1846, buckskinned Americans, many shoeless, seized Vallejo at Sonoma and took him to Sutter's Fort in Sacramento — the Bear Flag Revolt, which preceded but soon became part of the war between Mexico and the United States. Skirmishes were fought up and down the state, but most of the blood was shed in the invasion of Mexico. Two years after the shooting stopped, California, in 1850, was admitted into the Union.

Squatters and settlers moved onto the great rancheros. Vallejo, who died poor, is remembered in local histories as a great man and a tragic figure.

Taking the long view, the true victims of the era were the Indians. They

Presidential Voting in Sonoma County

Year	Democrat	Votes	Republican	Votes
1948	Truman*	16,026	Dewey	22,077
1952	Stevenson	17,046	Eisenhower*	34,088
1956	Stevenson	20,616	Eisenhower*	33,659
1960	Kennedy*	29,147	Nixon	34,641
1964	Johnson*	44,354	Goldwater	27,677
1968	Humphrey	33,587	Nixon*	38,088
1972	McGovern	43,746	Nixon*	57,697
1976	Carter*	50,353	Ford	50,555
1980	Carter	45,596	Reagan*	60,722
1984	Mondale	71,295	Reagan*	76,447
1988	Dukakis	91,262	Bush*	67,625

Source: California Secretary of State's office. * Election winner.

preceded the Californios (and the Americans, who also were cruel) by a thousand years. Few escaped with their lives. The Californio interlude in Sonoma County lasted 25 years, in Northern California less than 100 years.

The New Californians

First almost all headed for the gold fields after the strike of 1848, then, having struck out, they came to Sonoma in the Fifties and took up farming.

Hay and wheat, beef and potatoes, cheese, eggs and milk — from the fields and farms of Sonoma to the bellies and ships of San Francisco. Redwoods grew in great abundance in west Sonoma. With the exceptions of a few groves, all were felled to help build the West.

Second-growth redwoods, however, have restored the forested look.

The Railroad

In 1870, the San Francisco and Northern Pacific Railroad laid a line between Petaluma (accessible to ship) and Santa Rosa, and within a few years the line was extended to Cloverdale.

What the freeway is to Sonoma late 20th century, the railroad was to

---

SUGGESTED READING

San Francisco Bay Area Neighborhood Handbook, *by Brad Inman, who writes a real estate column for local newspapers. The book covers 80 neighborhoods. Foghorn Press. $12.95 at bookstores.*

Inman and the S.F. Examiner also sponsor a popular home-buyers fair every Spring.

Sonoma late 19th century. Within five years, Santa Rosa shot from 1,000 to 6,000 residents. Perhaps more important, rails gave Sonoma County much better access to the commerce of the world.

Wine

The mission padres dabbled in grapes and produced simple, sweet wines, better than nothing but incapable of exciting the palate.

In the early 1800s in Hungary, a showdown pitted Liberals against Conservatives. Agoston Haraszthy, a nobleman, threw in with the Libs, and when they lost, packed his bags and headed for the New World.

After an adventuresome and prosperous sojourn in Wisconsin, he made for California, was elected sheriff of San Diego County and in 1856 wound up in Sonoma County. The colonel, the title which he claimed, knew his wines and what he didn't know about viticulture he remedied during an 1861 tour of European wine countries. Returning with 300 varieties of vines, Haraszthy planted, literally, the foundation of the California wine industry.

Chickens and Eggs

Thousands of chicken farms flourished in and about Petaluma, which even had a pharmacy for chickens. In some years, the town shipped out over 600 million eggs, all over the world.

Rising labor and feed costs in the 1930s started the industry on a slow decline. Many farms were consolidated into few. Cattle, sheep and homes replaced hens and roosters but it's still possible to get fresh eggs and every May the town celebrates with the Butter and Eggs Parade. Kids one to eight, if costumed, get a chance to win the title of "Cutest Little Chick in Town."

Golden Gate Bridge and World War II

Completed in 1937, the Golden Gate Bridge began what Highway 101 finished, the development, in part, of Sonoma County as a suburb.

World War II, following four years later, brought millions to the West Coast — soldiers, sailors and marines in transit to the Pacific, workers for the war industries. Many of former came back, many of the latter stayed. The population boomed. The countryside beckoned, but not until the 1950s was the key built to open the door — Highway 101.

The Future

Right now Sonoma County is catching its breath on growth, but more is coming, along with more arguments on how to handle it. The next hot spot might be in the south county, near the Sears Point race track.

Highway 101 is close by and Highway 37 (to Vallejo) might siphon off East Bay traffic. When traffic becomes truly as opposed to merely intolerable, some solution might be found, perhaps a BART line from San Francisco.

8/Sonoma County School Rankings

Elementary, Middle and High, by Districts

THESE RANKINGS ARE drawn from state tests given over three years, 1988, 1989, 1990. For the most part, they will follow a pattern. High one year will be high the next, low will be low.

When the numbers fluctuate wildly, the number of children who took the tests will often be low. In a small class, one or two kids having a bad or good day will cause wide swings. Sometimes the children fail to understand instructions and this lowers their grade. Sometimes they just have an off day.

A Cautionary Note

Ranking systems don't recognize overall gains or losses. If every school in California raised raw scores 20 percent, some schools would still be ranked at the bottom, a few at the top. The same if every raw score dropped. A ranking system shows how one school did against all other schools. There is no one perfect method of testing. Family background, particularly education of parents, greatly influences how children will score in schools. See introduction to Marin scores (Chapter 2) and chapter on How Public Schools Work.

ALEXANDER UNIFIED
District-Wide

Third Grade	1988	1989	1990
Reading	96	52	42
Writing	95	60	59
Math	86	43	15
No. Tested	13	20	17
Sixth Grade	1988	1989	1990
Reading	95	86	98
Writing	59	62	72

Sixth Grade	1988	1989	1990
Math	97	94	97
No. Tested	10	17	14

Alexander Valley Elem., Healdsburg

Third Grade	1988	1989	1990
Reading	93	52	43
Writing	90	59	58
Math	78	45	19
No. Tested	13	20	17

ALEXANDER UNIFIED (Continued)
Alexander Valley Elem., Healdsburg

Sixth Grade	1988	1989	1990
Reading	90	82	96
Writing	56	61	68
Math	94	90	95
No. Tested	10	17	14

ANALY UNION HIGH SCHOOL DISTRICT
District-Wide

Twelfth Grade	1988	1989	1990
Reading	87	86	90
Writing	—	73	76
Math	84	82	91
No. Tested	387	410	349

Analy High, Sebastopol

Twelfth Grade	1988	1989	1990
Reading	94	82	87
Writing	—	84	71
Math	88	83	88
No. Tested	245	222	187

El Molino High, Forestville

Twelfth Grade	1988	1989	1990
Reading	56	81	88
Writing	—	60	77
Math	61	76	87
No. Tested	138	179	157

BELLEVUE UNION ELEM. DISTRICT
District-Wide

Third Grade	1988	1989	1990
Reading	59	58	35
Writing	56	50	35
Math	39	29	33
No. Tested	138	142	172

Sixth Grade	1988	1989	1990
Reading	49	66	57
Writing	45	75	52
Math	39	54	51
No. Tested	135	124	129

Bellevue Elem., Santa Rosa

Third Grade	1988	1989	1990
Reading	49	61	45
Writing	52	66	49
Math	35	42	38
No. Tested	79	77	91

Sixth Grade	1988	1989	1990
Reading	45	75	52
Writing	37	78	57
Math	31	58	36
No. Tested	75	61	65

Kawana Elem., Santa Rosa

Third Grade	1988	1989	1990
Reading	67	52	27
Writing	64	33	20
Math	47	24	32
No. Tested	59	65	81

Sixth Grade	1988	1989	1990
Reading	51	50	57
Writing	56	59	51
Math	55	50	69
No. Tested	60	63	64

BENNETT VALLEY UNION DISTRICT
District-Wide

Third Grade	1988	1989	1990
Reading	91	96	93
Writing	85	93	97
Math	88	87	88
No. Tested	135	150	125

Sixth Grade	1988	1989	1990
Reading	98	97	93
Writing	94	96	98
Math	97	97	96
No. Tested	119	143	163

Bennett Valley Elem., Santa Rosa

Sixth Grade	1988	1989	1990
Reading	89	93	88
Writing	89	91	94
Math	94	90	86
No. Tested	71	86	99

Strawberry Elem., Santa Rosa

Third Grade	1988	1989	1990
Reading	86	89	88
Writing	90	85	91
Math	94	80	76
No. Tested	51	54	47

Sixth Grade	1988	1989	1990
Reading	98	96	88
Writing	89	95	92
Math	96	96	96
No. Tested	48	57	64

Yulupa Elem., Santa Rosa

Third Grade	1988	1989	1990
Reading	84	96	89
Writing	69	89	94
Math	64	78	82
No. Tested	84	96	78

CINNABAR ELEM. DISTRICT
District-Wide

Third Grade	1988	1989	1990
Reading	92	98	55
Writing	90	96	66
Math	98	91	52
No. Tested	41	35	36
Sixth Grade	1988	1989	1990
Reading	99	96	78
Writing	98	98	88
Math	98	98	61
No. Tested	29	34	25

Cinnabar Elem., Petaluma

Third Grade	1988	1989	1990
Reading	86	97	56
Writing	83	93	63
Math	95	85	52
No. Tested	41	35	36
Sixth Grade	1988	1989	1990
Reading	98	91	70
Writing	95	95	84
Math	97	96	60
No. Tested	29	34	25

CLOVERDALE UNIFIED DISTRICT
District-Wide

Third Grade	1988	1989	1990
Reading	45	50	68
Writing	50	34	50
Math	47	35	59
No. Tested	101	121	130
Sixth Grade	1988	1989	1990
Reading	31	59	63
Writing	35	58	47
Math	30	42	65
No. Tested	82	83	94
Eighth Grade	1988	1989	1990
Reading	59	74	61
Writing	62	—	—
Math	76	80	57
History	74	48	66
Science	88	87	69
No. Tested	72	79	71
Twelfth Grade	1988	1989	1990
Reading	22	26	74
Writing	—	42	93
Math	33	17	78
No. Tested	74	68	58

Cloverdale High, Cloverdale

Twelfth Grade	1988	1989	1990
Reading	29	35	72
Writing	—	46	89
Math	35	18	77
No. Tested	69	66	58

Washington Elem., Cloverdale

Third Grade	1988	1989	1990
Reading	46	49	65
Writing	50	36	50
Math	46	38	59
No. Tested	101	121	130
Sixth Grade	1988	1989	1990
Reading	31	56	59
Writing	35	57	45
Math	32	43	62
No. Tested	82	83	94
Eighth Grade	1988	1989	1990
Reading	55	71	59
Writing	60	—	—
Math	73	78	62
History	73	49	66
Science	86	85	71
No. Tested	72	79	71

COTATI-ROHNERT PARK DISTRICT
District-Wide

Third Grade	1988	1989	1990
Reading	78	63	68
Writing	75	60	61
Math	79	60	56
No. Tested	504	572	571
Sixth Grade	1988	1989	1990
Reading	67	52	82
Writing	80	77	79
Math	82	67	80
No. Tested	461	455	496
Eighth Grade	1988	1989	1990
Reading	64	56	62
Writing	62	—	—
Math	63	51	67
History	67	52	75
Science	68	59	75
No. Tested	427	434	458
Twelfth Grade	1988	1989	1990
Reading	50	73	66
Writing	—	75	63
Math	48	72	48
No. Tested	314	323	279

COTATI-ROHNERT PARK (Continued)
Rancho Cotate High, Rohnert Park

Twelfth Grade	1988	1989	1990
Reading	49	74	69
Writing	—	76	71
Math	47	71	51
No. Tested	307	311	258

Cotati Middle, Cotati

Sixth Grade	1988	1989	1990
Reading	51	26	74
Writing	53	61	87
Math	72	35	78
No. Tested	81	90	85

Eighth Grade	1988	1989	1990
Reading	40	39	57
Writing	50	—	—
Math	59	33	63
History	57	55	73
Science	63	55	86
No. Tested	96	75	83

Crane (Richard) Elem., Rohnert Park

Third Grade	1988	1989	1990
Reading	59	49	38
Writing	46	49	35
Math	50	49	42
No. Tested	57	86	74

Sixth Grade	1988	1989	1990
Reading	58	44	28
Writing	54	64	39
Math	72	42	44
No. Tested	47	43	55

Evergreen Elem., Rohnert Park

Third Grade	1988	1989	1990
Reading	75	83	63
Writing	76	88	63
Math	77	79	62
No. Tested	79	108	95

Sixth Grade	1988	1989	1990
Reading	35	41	85
Writing	64	71	78
Math	52	48	74
No. Tested	71	71	80

Gold Ridge Elem. Rohnert Park

Third Grade	1988	1989	1990
Reading	69	76	90
Writing	74	62	80
Math	75	75	79
No. Tested	73	62	72

Sixth Grade	1988	1989	1990
Reading	84	72	61
Writing	85	77	60
Math	90	85	72
No. Tested	25	31	42

Hahn (Marguerite) Elem., Rohnert Park

Third Grade	1988	1989	1990
Reading	83	85	79
Writing	94	72	77
Math	93	76	70
No. Tested	67	79	70

Sixth Grade	1988	1989	1990
Reading	71	86	86
Writing	85	97	74
Math	84	94	88
No. Tested	55	45	51

La Fiesta Elem., Rohnert Park

Third Grade	1988	1989	1990
Reading	63	29	62
Writing	46	35	53
Math	59	44	54
No. Tested	63	70	74

Sixth Grade	1988	1989	1990
Reading	73	57	98
Writing	69	83	94
Math	78	76	95
No. Tested	70	73	75

Page (Thomas) Elem., Cotati

Third Grade	1988	1989	1990
Reading	73	38	78
Writing	75	30	86
Math	51	32	72
No. Tested	48	38	44

Sixth Grade	1988	1989	1990
Reading	73	80	15
Writing	55	22	51
Math	59	45	27
No. Tested	18	14	26

Reed (John) Elem., Rohnert Park

Third Grade	1988	1989	1990
Reading	547	37	31
Writing	35	35	30
Math	48	38	25
No. Tested	55	78	82

Sixth Grade	1988	1989	1990
Reading	27	39	54
Writing	47	37	46
Math	34	57	33
No. Tested	44	44	28

Rohnert (Waldo) Elem., Rohnert Park

Third Grade	1988	1989	1990
Reading	92	66	76
Writing	82	57	47
Math	87	47	49
No. Tested	62	51	60
Sixth Grade	1988	1989	1990
Reading	—	69	76
Writing	—	66	51
Math	—	72	60
No. Tested	—	44	54

Rohnert Park Jr. High, Rohnert Park

Eighth Grade	1988	1989	1990
Reading	66	55	61
Writing	62	—	—
Math	65	57	66
History	69	51	75
Science	67	58	72
No. Tested	331	359	375

DUNHAM ELEM. DISTRICT
District-Wide

Third Grade	1988	1989	1990
Reading	99	94	56
Writing	90	86	85
Math	88	65	70
No. Tested	5	16	13
Sixth Grade	1988	1989	1990
Reading	78	96	91
Writing	84	97	80
Math	97	90	96
No. Tested	12	22	17

Dunham Elem., Petaluma

Third Grade	1988	1989	1990
Reading	98	89	57
Writing	83	78	79
Math	80	60	65
No. Tested	5	16	13
Sixth Grade	1988	1989	1990
Reading	74	92	85
Writing	76	94	76
Math	95	84	92
No. Tested	12	22	17

FORESTVILLE UNION ELEM. DISTRICT
District-Wide

Third Grade	1988	1989	1990
Reading	61	75	68
Writing	73	82	71
Math	59	72	59
No. Tested	87	71	74

Sixth Grade	1988	1989	1990
Reading	99	77	96
Writing	98	86	79
Math	98	90	89
No. Tested	76	89	96
Eighth Grade	1988	1989	1990
Reading	84	93	91
Writing	93	—	—
Math	91	91	89
History	97	95	93
Science	98	94	89
No. Tested	69	71	77

Forestville Elem., Forestville

Third Grade	1988	1989	1990
Reading	59	70	65
Writing	68	76	67
Math	58	66	59
No. Tested	87	71	74
Sixth Grade	1988	1989	1990
Reading	98	73	92
Writing	95	82	73
Math	97	85	85
No. Tested	76	89	96
Eighth Grade	1988	1989	1990
Reading	81	91	89
Writing	89	—	—
Math	89	89	86
History	96	93	91
Science	97	93	87
No. Tested	69	71	77

FORT ROSS ELEM. DISTRICT
District-Wide

Third Grade	1988	1989	1990
Reading	94	99	83
Writing	66	86	83
Math	50	68	73
No. Tested	6	8	8
Sixth Grade	1988	1989	1990
Reading	84	99	97
Writing	93	73	92
Math	98	99	99
No. Tested	6	9	8
Eighth Grade	1988	1989	1990
Reading	97	99	99
Writing	91	—	—
Math	93	95	99
History	92	99	99
Science	96	94	92
No. Tested	8	7	7

FORT ROSS ELEM. (Continued)
Fort Ross Elem., Cazadero

Third Grade	1988	1989	1990
Reading	88	97	77
Writing	64	79	77
Math	49	62	69
No. Tested	6	8	8

Sixth Grade	1988	1989	1990
Reading	79	98	95
Writing	87	67	87
Math	96	98	98
No. Tested	6	9	8

Eighth Grade	1988	1989	1990
Reading	96	99	98
Writing	88	—	—
Math	91	93	99
History	90	98	99
Science	96	93	90
No. Tested	8	7	7

GEYSERVILLE UNIFIED
District-Wide

Third Grade	1988	1989	1990
Reading	61	17	94
Writing	81	23	99
Math	91	32	99
No. Tested	36	29	19

Sixth Grade	1988	1989	1990
Reading	36	93	89
Writing	95	93	81
Math	95	96	88
No. Tested	19	26	17

Eighth Grade	1988	1989	1990
Reading	43	88	44
Writing	45	—	—
Math	83	57	71
History	64	72	18
Science	66	60	68
No. Tested	14	20	13

Twelfth Grade	1988	1989	1990
Reading	53	24	17
Writing	—	17	96
Math	26	2	71
No. Tested	12	24	17

Geyserville Education High, Geyserville

Twelfth Grade	1988	1989	1990
Reading	42	81	31
Writing	—	95	94
Math	27	24	70
No. Tested	11	13	16

Geyserville Elem., Geyserville

Third Grade	1988	1989	1990
Reading	59	20	90
Writing	75	25	98
Math	85	34	98
No. Tested	36	29	19

Geyserville Middle, Geyserville

Sixth Grade	1988	1989	1990
Reading	39	88	84
Writing	91	88	76
Math	91	91	83
No. Tested	19	26	17

Eighth Grade	1988	1989	1990
Reading	46	85	45
Writing	44	—	—
Math	78	57	70
History	65	68	20
Science	63	60	69
No. Tested	14	20	13

GRAVENSTEIN UNION
ELEM. DISTRICT
District-wide

Third Grade	1988	1989	1990
Reading	56	95	97
Writing	53	94	95
Math	38	78	89
No. Tested	80	69	78

Sixth Grade	1988	1989	1990
Reading	85	89	88
Writing	95	97	95
Math	89	97	91
No. Tested	95	52	90

Eighth Grade	1988	1989	1990
Reading	90	97	94
Writing	75	—	—
Math	83	88	79
History	78	95	89
Science	88	92	87
No. Tested	54	71	78

Gravenstein Elem., Sebastopol

Eighth Grade	1988	1989	1990
Reading	85	95	93
Writing	69	—	—
Math	79	84	78
History	76	93	86
Science	85	90	84
No. Tested	54	71	78

Hillcrest Elem., Sebastopol

Third Grade	1988	1989	1990
Reading	54	90	95
Writing	54	89	90
Math	40	70	81
No. Tested	80	69	78
Sixth Grade	1988	1989	1990
Reading	79	84	81
Writing	90	94	91
Math	81	93	86
No. Tested	95	52	90

GUERNEVILLE ELEM. DISTRICT
District-Wide

Third Grade	1988	1989	1990
Reading	72	50	37
Writing	45	31	27
Math	48	23	50
No. Tested	67	48	74
Sixth Grade	1988	1989	1990
Reading	60	49	91
Writing	68	49	91
Math	45	33	82
No. Tested	63	68	59
Eighth Grade	1988	1989	1990
Reading	88	58	80
Writing	82	—	—
Math	74	53	73
History	71	52	50
Science	87	92	68
No. Tested	53	53	54

Guerneville Elem., Guerneville

Third Grade	1988	1989	1990
Reading	67	50	39
Writing	43	33	29
Math	47	25	51
No.Tested	67	48	74
Sixth Grade	1988	1989	1990
Reading	57	49	85
Writing	66	49	86
Math	48	32	75
No. Tested	63	68	59
Eighth Grade	1988	1989	1990
Reading	84	55	77
Writing	78	—	—
Math	71	54	72
History	70	51	50
Science	83	91	69
No. Tested	53	53	54

HARMONY UNION ELEM. DISTRICT
District-Wide

Third Grade	1988	1989	1990
Reading	22	31	74
Writing	15	16	56
Math	14	16	75
No. Tested	74	48	60
Sixth Grade	1988	1989	1990
Reading	96	70	89
Writing	94	84	58
Math	97	67	87
No. Tested	45	52	74
Eighth Grade	1988	1989	1990
Reading	90	93	89
Writing	92	—	—
Math	91	97	90
History	78	86	90
Science	94	94	91
No. Tested	50	49	49

Harmony Elem., Occidental

Third Grade	1988	1989	1990
Reading	25	36	71
Writing	19	20	56
Math	16	19	72
No. Tested	74	48	60
Sixth Grade	1988	1989	1990
Reading	93	66	83
Writing	89	78	58
Math	92	62	82
No. Tested	45	52	74
Eighth Grade	1988	1989	1990
Reading	85	92	86
Writing	89	—	—
Math	87	96	86
History	77	82	87
Science	92	92	90
No. Tested	50	49	49

HEALDSBURG UNION ELEM. DISTRICT
District-Wide

Third Grade	1988	1989	1990
Reading	61	65	61
Writing	51	64	59
Math	66	50	74
No. Tested	139	159	170
Sixth Grade	1988	1989	1990
Reading	55	48	78
Writing	46	43	43
Math	49	49	80
No. Tested	129	176	47

HEALDSBURG UNION (Continued)

Fitch Mountain Elem., Healdsburg

Third Grade	1988	1989	1990
Reading	47	73	57
Writing	32	58	54
Math	47	49	75
No. Tested	70	72	54

Healdsburg Elem., Healdsburg

Third Grade	1988	1989	1990
Reading	73	54	62
Writing	72	67	60
Math	77	51	69
No. Tested	69	87	116
Sixth Grade	1988	1989	1990
Reading	54	48	70
Writing	47	44	43
Math	50	48	74
No. Tested	129	176	47

HEALDSBURG UNION HIGH DISTRICT
District-Wide

Eighth Grade	1988	1989	1990
Reading	35	83	74
Writing	41	—	—
Math	60	66	75
History	61	88	72
Science	69	83	78
No. Tested	180	204	166
Twelfth Grade	1988	1989	1990
Reading	22	56	49
Writing	—	52	60
Math	36	71	46
No. Tested	197	222	209

Healdsburg High, Healdsburg

Twelfth Grade	1988	1989	1990
Reading	31	56	50
Writing	—	54	57
Math	43	72	45
No. Tested	186	216	202

Healdsburg Jr. High, Healdsburg

Eighth Grade	1988	1989	1990
Reading	35	80	74
Writing	41	—	—
Math	62	67	74
History	60	78	71
Science	67	81	78
No. Tested	180	204	166

HORICON ELEM. DISTRICT
District-Wide

Third Grade	1988	1989	1990
Reading	4	31	19
Writing	31	36	17
Math	67	68	1
No. Tested	10	13	6
Sixth Grade	1988	1989	1990
Reading	53	63	43
Writing	4	49	21
Math	38	48	45
No. Tested	11	7	9
Eighth Grade	1988	1989	1990
Reading	96	91	71
Writing	61	—	—
Math	74	62	50
History	94	49	63
Science	92	59	61
No. Tested	7	12	9

Horicon Elem., Annapolis

Third Grade	1988	1989	1990
Reading	18	34	24
Writing	33	37	20
Math	64	62	4
No. Tested	10	13	6
Sixth Grade	1988	1989	1990
Reading	52	60	43
Writing	17	48	23
Math	41	46	44
No. Tested	11	7	9
Eighth Grade	1988	1989	1990
Reading	94	88	71
Writing	59	—	—
Math	72	63	50
History	93	50	63
Science	90	57	62
No. Tested	7	12	9

KENWOOD ELEM. DISTRICT
District-Wide

Third Grade	1988	1989	1990
Reading	94	91	88
Writing	67	94	71
Math	98	96	91
No. Tested	18	23	34
Sixth Grade	1988	1989	1990
Reading	97	87	89
Writing	97	52	60
Math	99	71	89
No. Tested	25	24	27

Kenwood Elem., Kenwood

Third Grade	1988	1989	1990
Reading	89	85	83
Writing	65	90	67
Math	96	91	85
No. Tested	18	23	34
Sixth Grade	1988	1989	1990
Reading	94	82	83
Writing	94	52	60
Math	98	66	85
No. Tested	25	24	27

LIBERTY ELEM. DISTRICT
District-Wide

Third Grade	1988	1989	1990
Reading	93	92	84
Writing	93	53	64
Math	96	85	39
No. Tested	13	19	23
Sixth Grade	1988	1989	1990
Reading	82	96	78
Writing	82	58	73
Math	76	60	75
No. Tested	16	20	24

Liberty Elem., Petaluma

Third Grade	1988	1989	1990
Reading	87	86	79
Writing	88	55	62
Math	92	77	39
No. Tested	13	19	23
Sixth Grade	1988	1989	1990
Reading	76	82	70
Writing	75	57	69
Math	68	59	69
No. Tested	16	20	24

MARK WEST UNION ELEM. DISTRICT
District-Wide

Third Grade	1988	1989	1990
Reading	77	82	74
Writing	61	78	89
Math	67	87	91
No. Tested	115	144	149
Sixth Grade	1988	1989	1990
Reading	84	96	93
Writing	68	89	93
Math	52	88	92
No. Tested	73	108	121

Mark West Elem., Santa Rosa

Sixth Grade	1988	1989	1990
Reading	78	91	88
Writing	65	84	88
Math	51	80	86
No. Tested	73	108	121

San Miguel Elem., Santa Rosa

Third Grade	1988	1989	1990
Reading	72	75	71
Writing	61	74	82
Math	64	79	85
No. Tested	115	144	149

MONTE RIO UNION ELEM. DISTRICT
District-Wide

Third Grade	1988	1989	1990
Reading	83	50	61
Writing	77	34	49
Math	80	68	81
No. Tested	15	23	20
Sixth Grade	1988	1989	1990
Reading	96	64	68
Writing	43	61	73
Math	85	27	61
No. Tested	23	17	27
Eighth Grade	1988	1989	1990
Reading	45	58	85
Writing	28	—	—
Math	35	80	92
History	66	91	95
Science	60	90	78
No. Tested	15	21	26

Monte Rio Elem., Monte Rio

Third Grade	1988	1989	1990
Reading	76	49	60
Writing	71	36	49
Math	74	62	76
No. Tested	15	23	20
Sixth Grade	1988	1989	1990
Reading	91	62	61
Writing	44	60	69
Math	77	26	60
No. Tested	23	17	27
Eighth Grade	1988	1989	1990
Reading	47	55	82
Writing	28	—	—
Math	37	78	89
History	65	88	94
Science	60	87	77
No. Tested	15	21	26

MONTGOMERY ELEM. DISTRICT
District-Wide

Third Grade	1988	1989	1990
Reading	69	28	68
Writing	79	32	69
Math	29	49	77
No. Tested	12	8	7
Sixth Grade	1988	1989	1990
Reading	65	63	83
Writing	57	82	80
Math	49	76	66
No. Tested	7	11	7
Eighth Grade	1988	1989	1990
Reading	68	64	63
Writing	61	—	—
Math	37	26	71
History	58	75	79
Science	52	99	51
No. Tested	13	6	8

Montgomery Elem., Cazadero

Third Grade	1988	1989	1990
Reading	64	31	65
Writing	74	34	64
Math	30	50	73
No. Tested	12	8	7
Sixth Grade	1988	1989	1990
Reading	61	60	77
Writing	54	76	75
Math	50	70	63
No. Tested	7	11	7
Eighth Grade	1988	1989	1990
Reading	65	61	61
Writing	58	—	—
Math	41	28	69
History	56	73	77
Science	54	98	51
No. Tested	13	6	8

OAK GROVE UNION ELEM. DISTRICT
District-Wide

Third Grade	1988	1989	1990
Reading	44	40	68
Writing	59	25	59
Math	85	50	72
No. Tested	34	39	59
Sixth Grade	1988	1989	1990
Reading	89	64	90
Writing	66	56	86
Math	83	79	84
No. Tested	40	41	46

Eighth Grade	1988	1989	1990
Reading	27	93	92
Writing	21	—	—
Math	22	45	92
History	42	73	86
Science	39	67	92
No. Tested	32	47	39

Oak Grove Elem., Sebastopol

Third Grade	1988	1989	1990
Reading	45	40	65
Writing	60	27	58
Math	78	50	68
No. Tested	34	39	59

Willowside Elem., Santa Rosa

Sixth Grade	1988	1989	1990
Reading	83	62	84
Writing	64	54	81
Math	76	74	78
No. Tested	40	41	46
Eighth Grade	1988	1989	1990
Reading	29	92	90
Writing	23	—	—
Math	26	46	89
History	41	70	83
Science	38	67	90
No. Tested	32	47	39

OLD ADOBE UNION ELEM. DISTRICT
District-Wide

Third Grade	1988	1989	1990
Reading	87	87	84
Writing	85	86	77
Math	80	75	77
No. Tested	226	272	289
Sixth Grade	1988	1989	1990
Reading	75	91	89
Writing	60	78	85
Math	59	82	85
No. Tested	215	234	222

Bernard Eldredge Elem., Petaluma

Third Grade	1988	1989	1990
Reading	86	77	75
Writing	83	82	73
Math	74	63	72
No. Tested	57	83	82
Sixth Grade	1988	1989	1990
Reading	86	94	94
Writing	60	81	76
Math	63	78	82
No. Tested	55	60	62

La Tercera Elem., Petaluma

Third Grade	1988	1989	1990
Reading	88	83	87
Writing	80	75	77
Math	87	68	82
No. Tested	74	80	80
Sixth Grade	1988	1989	1990
Reading	47	78	75
Writing	57	65	93
Math	47	72	84
No. Tested	91	73	69

Miwok Valley Elem., Petaluma

Third Grade	1988	1989	1990
Reading	59	71	71
Writing	74	73	66
Math	57	66	71
No. Tested	69	85	98
Sixth Grade	1988	1989	1990
Reading	71	80	78
Writing	58	67	60
Math	64	69	71
No. Tested	52	71	67

Old Adobe Elem., Petaluma

Third Grade	1988	1989	1990
Reading	69	95	84
Writing	79	90	60
Math	65	84	54
No. Tested	22	24	29
Sixth Grade	1988	1989	1990
Reading	89	93	78
Writing	47	82	72
Math	87	92	78
No. Tested	17	30	24

PETALUMA CITY ELEM. DISTRICT
District-Wide

Third Grade	1988	1989	1990
Reading	71	79	61
Writing	51	62	50
Math	74	72	65
No. Tested	292	303	347
Sixth Grade	1988	1989	1990
Reading	82	83	54
Writing	89	82	72
Math	86	79	70
No. Tested	261	284	284

Cherry Valley Elem., Petaluma

Third Grade	1988	1989	1990
Reading	86	84	52
Writing	56	70	24

Third Grade	1988	1989	1990
Math	97	84	51
No. Tested	37	40	47
Sixth Grade	1988	1989	1990
Reading	45	87	44
Writing	44	78	58
Math	52	72	71
No. Tested	37	40	38

Grant Elem., Petaluma

Third Grade	1988	1989	1990
Reading	54	79	86
Writing	50	67	83
Math	63	89	75
No. Tested	49	41	56
Sixth Grade	1988	1989	1990
Reading	95	91	61
Writing	93	97	87
Math	91	81	66
No. Tested	19	36	38

McDowell Elem., Petaluma

Third Grade	1988	1989	1990
Reading	52	63	57
Writing	48	43	59
Math	46	31	87
No. Tested	32	51	47
Sixth Grade	1988	1989	1990
Reading	66	89	77
Writing	93	89	80
Math	92	94	96
No. Tested	48	52	54

McKinley Elem., Petaluma

Third Grade	1988	1989	1990
Reading	43	42	35
Writing	15	34	28
Math	16	25	20
No. Tested	44	46	39
Sixth Grade	1988	1989	1990
Reading	84	39	14
Writing	65	46	48
Math	61	29	10
No. Tested	27	42	43

McNear Elem., Petaluma

Third Grade	1988	1989	1990
Reading	64	74	66
Writing	68	70	56
Math	78	86	58
No. Tested	46	47	65
Sixth Grade	1988	1989	1990
Reading	95	90	52

PETALUMA CITY ELEM. (Continued)
McNear Elem., Petaluma

Sixth Grade	1988	1989	1990
Writing	89	78	58
Math	88	72	44
No. Tested	50	54	50

Penngrove Elem., Penngrove

Third Grade	1988	1989	1990
Reading	52	69	38
Writing	46	43	25
Math	64	43	52
No. Tested	39	42	45
Sixth Grade	1988	1989	1990
Reading	40	35	40
Writing	79	38	45
Math	63	53	56
No. Tested	39	43	33

Valley Vista Elem., Petaluma

Third Grade	1988	1989	1990
Reading	90	96	64
Writing	82	94	64
Math	84	89	77
No.Tested	45	36	48
Sixth Grade	1988	1989	1990
Reading	77	80	70
Writing	89	90	84
Math	70	93	92
No. Tested	41	17	28

PETALUMA JOINT UNION DISTRICT
District-Wide

Eighth Grade	1988	1989	1990
Reading	68	71	69
Writing	58	—	—
Math	64	73	64
History	64	75	70
Science	68	67	76
No. Tested	574	565	596
Twelfth Grade	1988	1989	1990
Reading	59	56	58
Writing	—	51	57
Math	68	59	61
No. Tested	564	591	556

Casa Grande High, Petaluma

Twelfth Grade	1988	1989	1990
Reading	81	47	50
Writing	—	57	56
Math	77	54	57
No. Tested	258	274	257

Petaluma High, Petaluma

Twelfth Grade	1988	1989	1990
Reading	44	67	68
Writing	—	54	62
Math	63	67	73
No. Tested	281	295	273

Kenilworth Jr. High, Petaluma

Eighth Grade	1988	1989	1990
Reading	73	58	69
Writing	65	—	—
Math	69	58	57
History	72	60	76
Science	69	65	74
No. Tested	295	285	297

Petaluma Jr. High, Petaluma

Eighth Grade	1988	1989	1990
Reading	54	79	70
Writing	44	—	—
Math	62	77	72
History	57	83	63
Science	63	71	79
No. Tested	279	280	299

PINER-OLIVET UNION ELEM. DISTRICT
District-Wide

Third Grade	1988	1989	1990
Reading	57	54	74
Writing	66	48	64
Math	41	27	80
No. Tested	142	161	167
Sixth Grade	1988	1989	1990
Reading	91	91	86
Writing	75	95	93
Math	87	78	86
No. Tested	107	148	126

Olivet Elem., Santa Rosa

Third Grade	1988	1989	1990
Reading	55	54	71
Writing	64	46	63
Math	42	30	75
No. Tested	142	161	167

Piner Elem., Santa Rosa

Sixth Grade	1988	1989	1990
Reading	84	86	80
Writing	69	91	88
Math	79	72	81
No. Tested	107	148	126

RINCON VALLEY UNION DISTRICT
District-Wide

Third Grade	1988	1989	1990
Reading	96	96	97
Writing	95	96	97
Math	94	95	96
No. Tested	361	361	364
Sixth Grade	1988	1989	1990
Reading	98	93	91
Writing	98	93	92
Math	93	90	89
No. Tested	362	410	386

Binkley Elem., Santa Rosa

Sixth Grade	1988	1989	1990
Reading	94	82	81
Writing	91	84	80
Math	83	86	67
No. Tested	113	132	116

Madrone Elem., Santa Rosa

Third Grade	1988	1989	1990
Reading	84	92	83
Writing	86	91	86
Math	89	88	85
No. Tested	108	103	133

Matanzas Elem., Santa Rosa

Sixth Grade	1988	1989	1990
Reading	84	88	84
Writing	97	84	82
Math	76	65	85
No. Tested	87	87	83

Whited (Douglas) Elem., Santa Rosa

Third Grade	1988	1989	1990
Reading	89	89	88
Writing	92	93	92
Math	68	79	90
No. Tested	58	58	49
Sixth Grade	1988	1989	1990
Reading	92	79	79
Writing	85	89	88
Math	79	83	83
No. Tested	44	54	70

Sequoia Elem., Santa Rosa

Third Grade	1988	1989	1990
Reading	95	98	98
Writing	95	96	98
Math	96	94	89
No. Tested	55	57	55
Sixth Grade	1988	1989	1990
Reading	98	95	89
Writing	98	95	95

Sixth Grade	1988	1989	1990
Math	98	96	89
No. Tested	63	77	65

Spring Creek Elem., Santa Rosa

Third Grade	1988	1989	1990
Reading	97	93	98
Writing	92	95	92
Math	96	95	98
No. Tested	85	87	79

Village Elem., Santa Rosa

Third Grade	1988	1989	1990
Reading	82	88	91
Writing	78	83	97
Math	81	88	95
No. Tested	55	56	48
Sixth Grade	1988	1989	1990
Reading	94	90	94
Writing	95	93	94
Math	85	87	98
No. Tested	55	60	52

ROSELAND ELEM. DISTRICT
District-Wide

Third Grade	1988	1989	1990
Reading	29	45	4
Writing	34	41	18
Math	29	56	21
No. Tested	113	112	105
Sixth Grade	1988	1989	1990
Reading	64	76	40
Writing	41	67	74
Math	42	67	45
No. Tested	99	96	74

Roseland Elem., Santa Rosa

Third Grade	1988	1989	1990
Reading	37	37	19
Writing	33	31	18
Math	29	58	20
No. Tested	47	56	52
Sixth Grade	1988	1989	1990
Reading	55	71	35
Writing	26	47	59
Math	43	62	38
No. Tested	53	49	50

Sheppard Elem., Santa Rosa

Third Grade	1988	1989	1990
Reading	27	51	14
Writing	41	50	25
Math	29	52	29
No. Tested	66	56	53

ROSELAND ELEM.(Continued)
Sheppard Elem., Santa Rosa

Sixth Grade	1988	1989	1990
Reading	66	71	50
Writing	57	82	87
Math	49	62	60
No. Tested	46	47	24

SANTA ROSA ELEM. DISTRICT
District-Wide

Third Grade	1988	1989	1990
Reading	47	50	50
Writing	48	48	46
Math	46	45	42
No. Tested	574	571	635
Sixth Grade	1988	1989	1990
Reading	67	57	69
Writing	66	58	72
Math	76	69	82
No. Tested	491	562	531

Biella (Al) Elem., Santa Rosa

Third Grade	1988	1989	1990
Reading	—	—	59
Writing	—	—	67
Math	—	—	75
No. Tested	—	—	71
Sixth Grade	1988	1989	1990
Reading	—	—	49
Writing	—	—	69
Math	—	—	85
No. Tested	—	—	45

Brook Hill Elem., Santa Rosa

Third Grade	1988	1989	1990
Reading	29	33	8
Writing	17	15	9
Math	20	30	16
No. Tested	50	42	60
Sixth Grade	1988	1989	1990
Reading	33	23	64
Writing	41	26	57
Math	52	35	67
No. Tested	49	58	45

Burbank (Luther) Elem., Santa Rosa

Third Grade	1988	1989	1990
Reading	27	3	10
Writing	18	11	13
Math	30	15	8
No. Tested	39	41	43

Sixth Grade	1988	1989	1990
Reading	29	66	12
Writing	35	32	31
Math	49	66	32
No. Tested	40	29	30

Doyle Park Elem., Santa Rosa

Third Grade	1988	1989	1990
Reading	45	49	49
Writing	51	50	63
Math	53	52	66
No. Tested	41	51	43
Sixth Grade	1988	1989	1990
Reading	42	59	70
Writing	44	44	78
Math	59	55	80
No. Tested	39	40	41

Fremont (John C.) Elem., Santa Rosa

Third Grade	1988	1989	1990
Reading	39	37	29
Writing	27	56	33
Math	35	68	29
No. Tested	43	39	42
Sixth Grade	1988	1989	1990
Reading	50	56	49
Writing	40	71	31
Math	48	39	57
No. Tested	39	43	34

Lincoln (Abraham) Elem., Santa Rosa

Third Grade	1988	1989	1990
Reading	34	20	26
Writing	27	20	17
Math	24	26	22
No. Tested	63	65	68
Sixth Grade	1988	1989	1990
Reading	41	4	48
Writing	47	10	39
Math	50	18	52
No. Tested	51	56	50

Monroe (James) Elem., Santa Rosa

Third Grade	1988	1989	1990
Reading	44	58	54
Writing	41	60	33
Math	48	49	42
No. Tested	85	85	74
Sixth Grade	1988	1989	1990
Reading	38	44	60
Writing	45	43	66
Math	62	59	70
No. Tested	66	85	57

Proctor Terrace Elem., Santa Rosa

Third Grade	1988	1989	1990
Reading	71	82	97
Writing	91	53	96
Math	72	55	74
No. Tested	49	42	42
Sixth Grade	1988	1989	1990
Reading	95	85	91
Writing	94	72	93
Math	92	91	93
No. Tested	32	44	42

Steele Lane Elem., Santa Rosa

Third Grade	1988	1989	1990
Reading	62	53	83
Writing	62	72	69
Math	49	62	68
No. Tested	74	56	66
Sixth Grade	1988	1989	1990
Reading	50	76	57
Writing	45	82	76
Math	50	84	75
No. Tested	59	68	66

Lehman (Helen M.) Elem., Santa Rosa

Third Grade	1988	1989	1990
Reading	41	53	46
Writing	65	41	38
Math	40	36	28
No. Tested	73	99	69
Sixth Grade	1988	1989	1990
Reading	66	68	38
Writing	70	81	54
Math	53	69	50
No. Tested	59	83	64

Hidden Valley Elem., Santa Rosa

Third Grade	1988	1989	1990
Reading	71	96	87
Writing	64	86	85
Math	82	74	57
No. Tested	57	51	57
Sixth Grade	1988	1989	1990
Reading	99	80	98
Writing	99	91	94
Math	98	93	98
No. Tested	57	56	57

SANTA ROSA HIGH DISTRICT
District-Wide

Eighth Grade	1988	1989	1990
Reading	75	80	83
Writing	72	—	—

Eighth Grade	1988	1989	1990
Math	74	81	82
History	79	82	86
Science	79	87	85
No. Tested	1,404	1,449	1,524
Twelfth Grade	1988	1989	1990
Reading	63	78	82
Writing	—	70	73
Math	66	73	77
No. Tested	1,210	1,315	1,209

Montgomery High, Santa Rosa

Twelfth Grade	1988	1989	1990
Reading	49	90	84
Writing	—	72	75
Math	65	80	83
No. Tested	386	441	380

Piner High, Santa Rosa

Twelfth Grade	1988	1989	1990
Reading	40	53	71
Writing	—	67	71
Math	48	61	52
No. Tested	351	386	344

Santa Rosa High, Santa Rosa

Twelfth Grade	1988	1989	1990
Reading	87	78	82
Writing	—	73	72
Math	72	74	84
No. Tested	460	463	462

Cook (Lawrence) Jr. High, Santa Rosa

Eighth Grade	1988	1989	1990
Reading	43	64	46
Writing	36	—	—
Math	43	68	46
History	45	58	48
Science	49	72	67
No. Tested	287	294	313

Slater (Herbert) Jr. High, Santa Rosa

Eighth Grade	1988	1989	1990
Reading	93	88	93
Writing	93	—	—
Math	92	92	93
History	91	87	94
Science	92	94	93
No. Tested	311	308	337

Rincon Valley Jr. High, Santa Rosa

Eighth Grade	1988	1989	1990
Reading	90	91	90
Writing	86	—	—

SANTA ROSA HIGH (Continued)

Rincon Valley Jr. High, Santa Rosa

Eighth Grade	1988	1989	1990
Math	88	90	90
History	94	94	92
Science	92	95	94
No. Tested	288	256	238

Santa Rosa Jr. High, Santa Rosa

Eighth Grade	1988	1989	1990
Reading	40	54	75
Writing	36	—	—
Math	37	50	74
History	58	63	84
Science	50	62	71
No. Tested	227	227	246

Hilliard Comstock Jr. High, Santa Rosa

Eighth Grade	1988	1989	1990
Reading	60	74	80
Writing	55	—	—
Math	61	73	78
History	68	72	76
Science	72	78	78
No. Tested	291	364	390

SEBASTOPOL UNION ELEM. DISTRICT
District-Wide

Third Grade	1988	1989	1990
Reading	70	61	74
Writing	62	51	62
Math	58	50	68
No. Tested	120	121	148
Sixth Grade	1988	1989	1990
Reading	89	82	75
Writing	94	57	73
Math	89	69	79
No. Tested	134	133	133
Eighth Grade	1988	1989	1990
Reading	63	67	82
Writing	45	—	—
Math	71	76	71
History	60	73	96
Science	72	66	70
No. Tested	136	117	132

Brook Haven Elem., Sebastopol

Sixth Grade	1988	1989	1990
Reading	82	59	66
Writing	89	56	69
Math	81	65	73
No. Tested	134	133	133

Eighth Grade	1988	1989	1990
Reading	59	64	80
Writing	44	—	—
Math	69	74	70
History	57	71	95
Science	72	66	72
No. Tested	136	117	132

Pine Crest Elem., Sebastopol

Third Grade	1988	1989	1990
Reading	64	61	71
Writing	62	53	60
Math	57	50	64
No. Tested	120	121	148

SONOMA VALLEY UNIFIED
District-Wide

Third Grade	1988	1989	1990
Reading	94	93	91
Writing	95	92	89
Math	92	92	85
No. Tested	297	281	353
Sixth Grade	1988	1989	1990
Reading	92	83	83
Writing	90	85	72
Math	90	77	85
No. Tested	272	278	284
Eighth Grade	1988	1989	1990
Reading	83	80	83
Writing	76	—	—
Math	84	88	82
History	75	75	88
Science	83	89	90
No. Tested	245	292	304
Twelfth Grade	1988	1989	1990
Reading	77	84	68
Writing	—	54	60
Math	66	59	69
No. Tested	275	238	265

Sonoma Valley High, Sonoma

Twelfth Grade	1988	1989	1990
Reading	75	80	67
Writing	—	56	57
Math	63	57	69
No. Tested	268	236	256

Altimira Inter., Sonoma

Eighth Grade	1988	1989	1990
Reading	80	78	80
Writing	72	—	—
Math	80	84	79
History	74	74	85

Eighth Grade	1988	1989	1990
Science	80	87	88
No. Tested	245	292	304

Dunbar Elem., Glen Ellen

Third Grade	1988	1989	1990
Reading	86	85	86
Writing	87	90	80
Math	82	80	81
No. Tested	50	43	67
Sixth Grade	1988	1989	1990
Reading	87	91	92
Writing	88	96	76
Math	71	92	85
No. Tested	41	37	37

El Verano Elem., El Verano

Third Grade	1988	1989	1990
Reading	83	91	75
Writing	79	85	68
Math	72	74	61
No. Tested	66	68	87
Sixth Grade	1988	1989	1990
Reading	97	74	72
Writing	91	90	61
Math	94	66	85
No. Tested	60	72	67

Flowery Elem., Boyes Springs

Third Grade	1988	1989	1990
Reading	78	86	92
Writing	77	80	95
Math	69	85	73
No. Tested	69	51	59
Sixth Grade	1988	1989	1990
Reading	71	82	61
Writing	68	67	60
Math	76	78	85
No. Tested	44	56	45

Prestwood Elem., Sonoma

Third Grade	1988	1989	1990
Reading	98	89	92
Writing	99	93	88
Math	96	98	97
No. Tested	55	61	75
Sixth Grade	1988	1989	1990
Reading	79	69	84
Writing	78	58	72
Math	76	56	66
No. Tested	71	60	76

Sassarini Elem., Sonoma

Third Grade	1988	1989	1990
Reading	88	83	83
Writing	95	88	73
Math	93	64	62
No. Tested	57	58	65
Sixth Grade	1988	1989	1990
Reading	86	75	69
Writing	84	67	69
Math	87	64	78
No. Tested	56	53	59

TWIN HILLS UNION ELEM. DISTRICT
District-Wide

Third Grade	1988	1989	1990
Reading	98	95	91
Writing	96	91	86
Math	96	96	94
No. Tested	98	78	84
Sixth Grade	1988	1989	1990
Reading	77	77	96
Writing	76	73	85
Math	87	84	96
No. Tested	88	95	97
Eighth Grade	1988	1989	1990
Reading	90	94	70
Writing	80	—	—
Math	75	79	83
History	80	79	86
Science	92	97	92
No. Tested	95	67	97

Apple Blossom Elem., Sebastopol

Third Grade	1988	1989	1990
Reading	95	91	86
Writing	92	86	79
Math	92	92	89
No. Tested	98	78	84

Twin Hills School, Sebastopol

Sixth Grade	1988	1989	1990
Reading	72	73	91
Writing	70	67	79
Math	79	78	93
No. Tested	88	95	97
Eighth Grade	1988	1989	1990
Reading	85	93	70
Writing	76	—	—
Math	72	77	80
History	78	77	83
Science	90	96	91
No. Tested	95	67	97

TWO ROCK UNION ELEM. DISTRICT
District-Wide

Third Grade	1988	1989	1990
Reading	94	95	81
Writing	81	91	69
Math	98	99	75
No. Tested	15	24	26
Sixth Grade	1988	1989	1990
Reading	89	89	91
Writing	95	62	66
Math	63	29	85
No. Tested	13	19	19

Two Rock Elem., Petaluma

Third Grade	1988	1989	1990
Reading	89	91	75
Writing	75	84	66
Math	96	97	72
No. Tested	15	24	26
Sixth Grade	1988	1989	1990
Reading	83	84	85
Writing	91	61	65
Math	59	29	79
No. Tested	13	19	19

WAUGH ELEM. DISTRICT
District-Wide

Third Grade	1988	1989	1990
Reading	55	86	70
Writing	90	70	32
Math	97	91	58
No. Tested	7	12	12
Sixth Grade	1988	1989	1990
Reading	78	63	89
Writing	96	94	80
Math	50	84	91
No. Tested	3	11	7

Waugh Elem., Petaluma

Third Grade	1988	1989	1990
Reading	52	79	66
Writing	84	67	32
Math	94	85	58
No. Tested	7	12	12
Sixth Grade	1988	1989	1990
Reading	73	61	84
Writing	92	90	76
Math	50	77	86
No. Tested	3	11	7

WEST SIDE UNION ELEM. DISTRICT
District-Wide

Third Grade	1988	1989	1990
Reading	72	93	39
Writing	50	62	35
Math	71	94	48
No. Tested	22	22	11
Sixth Grade	1988	1989	1990
Reading	38	87	62
Writing	55	75	82
Math	42	37	56
No. Tested	8	12	9

West Side Elem., Healdsburg

Third Grade	1988	1989	1990
Reading	67	88	39
Writing	50	60	35
Math	67	88	49
No. Tested	22	22	11
Sixth Grade	1988	1989	1990
Reading	41	83	57
Writing	53	70	78
Math	46	37	55
No. Tested	8	12	9

WILLMAR UNION ELEM. SCHOOL DISTRICT
District-Wide

Third Grade	1988	1989	1990
Reading	52	58	88
Writing	77	72	75
Math	94	52	88
No. Tested	19	21	30
Sixth Grade	1988	1989	1990
Reading	62	83	82
Writing	76	85	49
Math	76	84	42
No. Tested	27	25	31

Wilson Elem., Petaluma

Third Grade	1988	1989	1990
Reading	50	58	83
Writing	71	69	69
Math	89	51	80
No. Tested	19	21	30
Sixth Grade	1988	1989	1990
Reading	58	78	76
Writing	70	79	48
Math	68	78	43
No. Tested	27	25	31

WINDSOR UNION SCHOOL DISTRICT
District-Wide

Third Grade	1988	1989	1990
Reading	61	42	33
Writing	61	47	37
Math	54	27	28
No. Tested	106	108	182
Sixth Grade	1988	1989	1990
Reading	31	2	31
Writing	41	17	28
Math	25	17	34
No. Tested	96	99	109
Eighth Grade	1988	1989	1990
Reading	25	33	43
Writing	26	—	—
Math	36	64	41
History	43	29	50
Science	50	42	55
No. Tested	84	86	99

Windsor Middle, Windsor

Sixth Grade	1988	1989	1990
Reading	30	11	31
Writing	41	19	29
Math	26	18	37
No. Tested	96	99	109
Eighth Grade	1988	1989	1990
Reading	28	34	44
Writing	28	—	—
Math	39	66	44
History	42	29	50
Science	50	41	54
No. Tested	84	86	99

Windsor Elem., Windsor

Third Grade	1988	1989	1990
Reading	58	42	33
Writing	61	45	35

Third Grade	1988	1989	1990
Math	54	31	32
No. Tested	106	108	182

WRIGHT ELEM. DISTRICT
District-Wide

Third Grade	1988	1989	1990
Reading	77	68	55
Writing	75	60	46
Math	88	66	49
No. Tested	122	152	165
Sixth Grade	1988	1989	1990
Reading	67	71	79
Writing	94	79	92
Math	76	54	61
No. Tested	120	125	101

Wilson (J. X.) Elem., Santa Rosa

Third Grade	1988	1989	1990
Reading	71	68	78
Writing	62	60	73
Math	70	63	74
No. Tested	66	86	88
Sixth Grade	1988	1989	1990
Reading	72	83	83
Writing	87	89	79
Math	71	64	65
No. Tested	69	66	52

Wright Elem., Santa Rosa

Third Grade	1988	1989	1990
Reading	71	61	30
Writing	76	56	19
Math	88	58	24
No. Tested	56	66	77
Sixth Grade	1988	1989	1990
Reading	48	45	61
Writing	91	49	93
Math	63	41	54
No. Tested	51	59	49

9/Sonoma City Profiles

Home Values, Rents, Home Price Sampler, Towns and Cities on Parade

FOR A BRIEF DISCUSSION of the roles of local governments, see the beginning of Marin City Profiles, Chapter 3.

Agua Caliente, Boyes Hot Springs, El Verano, Fetters Hot Springs

Hamlets to north of city of Sonoma. Quiet neighborhoods, generally well kept, noted for their spas, restaurants and resorts. Golf course. Several parks.

Although they claim separate identities, these neighborhoods should be considered part of greater Sonoma. Contiguous to the city, they follow the same pursuits (tourism, government work, commuting, retirement) and shop in Sonoma.

Census populations, 1990, Boyes Hot Springs, 5,973; El Verano, 3,498; Fetter's Hot Springs-Agua Caliente, 2,024.

Some new construction, townhouses and single homes. Unincorporated, governed from Santa Rosa by the board of supervisors. New hotel, designed upon the lines of what was popular in 19th century Russia, recently got OK for construction.

All, including Sonoma, are part of the Sonoma Unified School District. Academic rankings up there, generally top 30th percentile in state.

Bodega Bay

Fishing, tourist, vacation town on the south Sonoma coast. Named after a Spanish captain who sailed into the bay in 1775. Good place for a salmon or crab dinner. Bodega has one of the largest "small" harbors on the West Coast. Many fishing boats put out from the town. Also boats for whale watching.

Population 1,127 (census). About 35 percent of residents over age 55.

For many, a second-home town, a place for weekend retreats, close enough to San Francisco for a Friday afternoon cutout, but a little too distant for a commute, although no doubt some manage it. Many people rent their homes by the weekend or month.

Windy in summer, often clear in winter, the coastal pattern. Mix of homes, many on bluff overlooking Bay. Coast Guard station. Marine lab.

Sand dune park, salt marshes, tidal flats, sea birds, abalone for divers, a lot of outdoorsy stuff, beaches. Spring Fishermen's Festival. Sheep graze in hills. A nice town to relax in. Hitchcock shot scenes for "The Birds" in Bodega Bay.

Cloverdale

Last town in Sonoma Country traveling north on 101, about 19 miles from Santa Rosa. Wine country to east and west. Increased population by 23 percent in last decade. Now has about 5,000 residents. Another old-time burg moving into suburbia.

Highway 101 fades to a country road just south of Cloverdale, dumping all the traffic into town and leaving an impression of trucks and noise. A freeway bypass is now under construction.

The Russian River snakes up the east side of Cloverdale. Away from the main drag, Cloverdale exudes the calm of the small town. Kids on bikes, a well tended baseball field, shady streets, a Boys and Girls Club, hometown paper.

Mix of housing, '50s tract types, bungalows, Victorians, trailers, some new one- and two-story stuccos north of town, fairly new housing to south. According to 1990 state count, housing units totaled 2,109, of which 1,470 were single family, 18 single attached, 429 apartment units, 192 mobile homes.

For much of its history, Cloverdale was a lumber town. But in 1991, the last mill was closed, a loss of 57 jobs.

School rankings bounce around too much for a confident assessment but many are well above the 50th percentile.

FBI doesn't track crime in cities under population 10,000 but Cloverdale is not the Wild West.

The future: the housing market is going to catch its breath and then discover Cloverdale, never mind the distance from San Francisco.

Cotati

A small town that has been growing — increased its population by 64 percent in the 1980s — but is overshadowed by its bigger and more dynamic neighbor, Rohnert Park.

Cotati, about 5,800 residents, straddles Highway 101 just south of Rohnert Park and calls itself the "Hub of Sonoma County," a harmless pretension. The town is named after an Indian chief.

When a region grows, it's important for cities to get businesses to locate within their borders. Otherwise the cities will not be able to capture tax

Number & Value of Owner-Occupied Dwellings

City or Area	< $100K -199K	$200K -299K	$300K -399K	$400K -499K	$500K -plus
Bodega Bay	43	58	88	65	45
Boyes Hot Spring	675	379	55	12	8
Cloverdale	765	129	21	6	5
El Verano	319	219	56	7	10
Fettrs Hot Sp.-Ag. Cal.	236	85	14	2	2
Forestville	339	149	43	13	10
Glen Ellen	117	69	33	9	10
Guerneville	259	63	6	2	1
Healdsburg	1,297	436	178	45	24
Monte Rio	206	28	4	2	0
Occidental	172	61	31	11	14
Petaluma	4,440	4,018	600	143	73
Rohnert Park	3,650	1,818	212	10	5
Roseland	983	52	1	4	7
Santa Rosa	12,086	6,946	1,767	677	583
Sebastopol	664	452	142	24	12
Sonoma, City of	570	660	252	102	58
South Santa Rosa	534	117	16	13	10
Windsor	1,224	992	301	66	30
Countywide	36,506	24,181	7,883	2,912	2,318

Source: 1990 Census. The chart shows the number of owner-occupied dwellings within a set price range.

revenues to pay for roads, utilities and services.

Despite its growth, Cotati has few businesses. It comes across as a sleepy hamlet, many open spaces, a few new housing tracts, many homes fairly old.

In neighboring Rohnert Park, businesses are plentiful and more are setting up or have recently set up: Price Club, Home Club, Walmart, etc.

From Cotati's perspective, Rohnert Park is capturing the growth money and dumping the problems (traffic) into Cotati. The two cities have been bickering for years and lately they seem to have staggered into some kind of arrangement where Rohnert Park gives Cotati some offsetting funds.

If you buy in Cotati, you, in effect, buy the Rohnert Park package. That city is loaded with activities open to Cotati residents. There is a strong argument for merging both cities into one, and in fact the two share the same school district. California State University is located just down the road. See Rohnert Park.

In the early 1980s, Cotati almost went bankrupt and the city council has a history of firing managers, an indication of instability. Cotati in 1991 hired its

Median & Average Price of Owner-Occupied Homes

City or Area	Units	Median	Average
Bodega Bay	299	$355,100	$362,701
Boyes Hot Spring	1,129	184,300	195,723
Cloverdale	926	153,000	161,789
Cotati	1,107	167,000	185,917
El Verano	611	196,300	208,677
Fettrs Hot Sp.-Ag. Cal.	339	175,600	183,178
Forestville	554	172,400	195,440
Glen Ellen	238	202,800	233,929
Guerneville	331	145,700	157,364
Healdsburg	1,980	181,500	202,074
Monte Rio	240	120,700	136,573
Occidental	289	157,200	200,381
Petaluma	9,274	204,000	215,868
Rohnert Park	5,695	184,000	192,185
Roseland	1,047	146,500	149,607
Santa Rosa	22,059	193,800	219,246
Sebastopol	1,294	197,900	213,727
Sonoma, City of	1,642	235,700	255,597
South Santa Rosa	690	147,700	169,007
Windsor	2,613	205,900	222,986
Countywide	73,800	201,400	228,273

Source: 1990 Census.

first woman city manager. Good luck to her.

The state in 1990 tallied 2,403 housing units:1,226 single homes, 274 single attached, 796 apartments, 107 mobile homes.

Crime not tracked by FBI. Academic rankings middling to high in the district. Bond passed in 1990 to build schools, improve high school. Rancho-Cotate High recently opened math and science building, cost $2.4 million.

The Cotati downtown is designed around a hexagon and efforts have been made to build on the town's history. If Cotati decides to pursue growth, it has the land, especially west of the freeway.

Forestville

Rural burg along Highway 116, trees and brush on outskirts but no forests. Named after a guy named Forest. Population 2,443 in 1990.

Town lightens life with Poison Oak Festival. Awards are presented for the best rash, best patch, even the best floral arrangement, which sometimes leads to winning the best rash.

Downtown covers a few blocks: dentists, lawyers, restaurants, hardware, real estate, bank, post office, shops. Bus service to other towns. Churches, baseball diamond, volunteer fire dept. Ordinary town with sense of community.

One school, Forestville Elementary. Academic rankings in the 80s and 90s, among tops in state.

About 1.5 hours from San Fran. Residents a mix of homeowners, renters, retirees, vacationers. Modest homes, mobile homes downtown, further out, larger, newer homes.

Geyserville

Located north of Healdsburg, just off Highway 10. A wine country village. Russian River ambles by just east of town. Restaurants. Quality wineries.

Glen Ellen

Winery hamlet, homes tucked out of sight. Population 1,191 in 1990. A few shops. Set in the middle of miles of orchards and vineyards. Jack London Park. Museum.

Jack London, entranced with the nearby Valley of the Moon, built Wolf House here, 26 rooms, nine fireplaces, volcanic rock and redwood. Shortly before he was to move in, the place burned down. Its ruins still stand.

An exciting writer ("The Call of the Wild") and a native son, London is remembered with great fondness in California, and indeed many parts of the world. For London fans, Wolf House has become a sort of pilgrimage.

Off Highway 12, about seven miles north of City of Sonoma.

Guerneville

Russian River village. Population about 2,000. Pronounced Gurn-ville. After a founding father who cut down most of the giant redwoods in the vicinity.

A resort town, fetching in a quiet way. In the summer a dam is thrown across the river, backing it up so swimmers and canoeists won't scrape bottom.

Vacation homes line the river. Some condos, some hotels, cabins for rent. Housing mixed. Many older homes. Water system getting overhauled, a project that may take a few years. Restaurants, saloons, shops, a bakery, video rentals, a Safeway with a deli. Mini water slide, go-carts, video games, miniature golf.

A popular town with gays. Generally low key, don't-flaunt-it style but no apologies. Annual Women's Weekend, lesbian event. When someone writes Santa Rosa paper complaining of homosexual love, you can count on a rebuttal letter from Guerneville. Many straights also. Live-and-let-live kind of burg.

School district also serves nearby Rio Nido and Vacation Beach. Academic rankings bounce below and way above the 50th percentile.

Armstrong redwoods a short hike up, a pleasing remnant of the ancient giants. Many second-growth redwoods. If buying a home near the river, ask about flooding. River has jumped banks in past. New bridge going in.

Healdsburg

A town of about 9,500 that has that elusive and rare quality, charm.

Located north of Santa Rosa, just east of 101, part of the wine-tourist circuit. Fitch Mountain, a tall hill, rises about 1,000 feet to the east. The Russian River takes pleasantly wide loop around the east side of the town.

Healdsburg has preserved its history and was designed along lines that 30 or 40 years ago would have brought snorts of derision from any city planner but now strike us moderns as quaint and reassuring. The downtown has a square and, in the middle, a gazebo. Antique shops, art galleries, book stores, boutiques, restaurants travel around the square and into adjoining streets.

The streets are laid out on a grid pattern — logical, few suburban curlicues. Around the old town are scattered homes from around the turn of the century and the early 1900s: Queen Annes, bungalows, cottages, homes built in the styles of Italianate, Greek, Mediterranean. Lived in, well cared for, cherished. Some apartments faded — can't do it all — but overall Healdsburg impresses.

As you travel east on Fitch Mountain Road, the homes get newer and near the river custom homes and middle-class tracts can be found, the latter well kept. Further out, vacation cottages line the river.

State in 1990 counted 3,781 housing units: 2,885 single homes, 54 single attached, 752 apartments, 90 mobile homes.

In the 1980s, Healdsburg added about 2,200 residents, not runaway growth but nonetheless a sharp increase, about 31 percent. If working in Santa Rosa, a great commute. If working in San Francisco, a long drive.

School rankings come in generally above 50th percentile. Town is moving toward upper middle class, which usually means very high rankings.

Healdsburg Union High School District also serves fast-growing Windsor and the high school is crowded. If money can be found, new high schools will be built in both towns.

Baseball, soccer, swimming (river and city pool), fishing, canoeing, nine-hole golf course, many wineries nearby. Two ball fields for kids opened in 1991. Five parks, a museum. Summer film festival. River is dammed in the spring to raise the water level for swimming and boating. Healdsburg encourages tourists. Over a dozen bed-and-breakfast places.

Fairly new library. Summer jazz in the gazebo park. Small airport on the other side of the freeway.

Jenner

Small town built on the side of a wind-protected hill overlooking the mouth of Russian River. Couple of restaurants, shops. About 60 homes. Goat Rock, just south of the mouth, dominates the landscape. Seals loll on a sandbar where the river meets the ocean. Picturesque town. Chilly summers, mild winters.

Ranch couple, well-known and liked, murdered in 1991, shot. Young stranger arrested. Police said he did it to steal credit cards.

Kenwood

Winery hamlet in the Sonoma Valley. Plaza. Small park. Shops, stores, restaurants. Noted for wine and restaurants. Volunteer firefighters every year sponsor Fourth of July Pillow Fight.

Has own school district, one elementary school. Academic rankings in 80s and 90s.

Monte Rio

Small resort town that straddles the Russian River west of Guerneville. Population 1,058. One of few towns where men outnumber women, 561 to 497.

Monte Rio helps with the annual hi-jinks at the nearby Bohemian Grove, playground for world movers and shakers.

Parts flooded in 1986, including school, which needed to be replaced anyhow. This prompted state to put up funds. New school opened 1991. Residents call it the prettiest in the county.

Occidental

Tourist village on Route 116 between Sebastopol and Russian River. Population 1,300. Surrounded by redwood forest and ridges that, locals say, hold back the fog and define neighborhoods, upper ridge and lower ridge.

Shops, restaurants along three blocks. Tiny library. Victorians peek out of hillsides, horses and sheep graze the upper ridges. Picturesque town, a favorite of people who want to drive the redwoods and take in an Italian dinner.

One-school town, Harmony Elementary. Rankings generally high.

A nice place to drive to — California B.B. (before bulldozers): vineyards, lots of pine, redwood, poppies, wild fern and laurel.

Petaluma

Second largest city in Sonoma County. Located near the southern border and straddled by Highway 101. Best commute in the county to San Francisco.

Old Petaluma to the west of the freeway, new Petaluma to the east. Old artsy, new suburban.

Petaluma made headlines in the 1970s when it limited residential growth, with some exceptions, to 500 units a year. This gave the town a reputation for no-growth but in truth, like the rest of Sonoma County, it has been adding people at a steady clip. Between 1980 and 1990, city added about 9,000 residents, an increase of 28 percent. Present population is about 43,000.

Housing units in 1990 totaled 16,760, of which 11,819 were single homes, 1,248 single-family attached, 2,815 apartments, 878 mobile homes.

Mariano Vallejo, commandante of Mexican excursion, built a hacienda-fort at Petaluma. It has been restored and is now a park.

In the latter half of the 19th century, Petaluma became a great farming center. Mansions, many of them still standing, were built in the old town.

Home Price Sampler from Classified Ads

Cloverdale
3-bedroom, 2-bath. $169,500.
4-bedroom, 3-bath. $279,000.

Cotati
2-bedroom, 1-bath, sunny patio, spacious rooms, storage, new blinds. $110,000.
2-bedroom, 1.5-bath, /$126,000.

Guerneville
2-bedroom secluded retreat in the redwoods, living room whitewashed knotty pine, fireplace, 2-car garage, large work area, parking. $148,950.

Healdsburg
2-bedroom cozy home & small cottage on quiet street, close to town. $182,500.
3-bedroom, 3-bath, $355,000.

Petaluma
3-bedroom, 2-bath, open floor plan, mature landscaping with low maintenance backyard. $192,000.
1-bedroom, 1-bath, big lot, new windows, walls, tile, skylights, detached garage, boat shed, room for expansion. $167,500.

Rohnert Park
3-bedroom, 2-bath, formal living and dining, family rooms, professional landscape, $220,000.
4-bedroom, 3-bath, giant bonus room, family room, vaulted ceiling, tiled kitchen and bath. $279,000.

Santa Rosa
3-bedroom, 2.5-bath, Cape Cod, cathedral ceilings, family room, many upgrades, flagstone patio, RV parking, prime neighborhood. $209,950.
3-bedroom, 2.5-bath, 2,500 square feet, large family room, formal dining, custom tile-oak throughout, decks, landscaped. $365,000.

Sebastopol
4-bedroom, 2.5-bath, 2,800 square feet, 1 year old, all upgrades, professionally decorated, rural, apple country. $449,000.
3-bedroom, 2-bath, den, one acre, separate guest studio, custom. $439,000.

Sonoma
4-bedroom, 3-bath, oak floors, 2 fireplaces, pool, spa, landscaping. $360,000.
3-bedroom, 2-bath, covered patio, gazebo, hot tub, landscaping. $262,000.

Windsor
4-bedroom, 2.5-bath, large lot, lake-mountain views, gourmet kitchen, work center, solarium, vaulted ceiling, RV parking. $319,000.
4-bedroom, 3-bath, formal dining, mature oaks and more, new, in Victoria Estates. $289,000.

Source: Local newspaper classified ad listings, fall, 1991.

The 20th century saw Petaluma become probably the egg capital of the world. Rising feed and labor costs drastically reduced the trade but a million hens still lay 204 million eggs annually and in the countryside many dairy farms can be found. Each May Petaluma celebrates its past with a Butter and Eggs Parade.

The town and its environs are served by seven elementary school districts, most consisting of just one school. Pressure is building to consolidate some of the smaller districts. Two largest are Old Adobe and Petaluma.

After elementary, kids attend either Kenilworth or Petaluma junior highs, then either Casa Grande or Petaluma Union high schools. New junior high on way if school board can find the money and an affordable site.

Academic rankings bounce all over, some in the 80s and 90s.

In 1991, Petaluma High students attempted to stage "Heathers," a play based on a movie that starred Winona Ryder. Miss Ryder, then Noni Horiwitz, spent her sophomore year at the school. Well into rehearsals, the principal reviewed the play and citing sensitive themes — murder and suicide — and foul words, said no-go.

Parents and volunteers rallied behind kids but did not tackle school. Instead, the play was staged one night at a local theater — a response that suggests a certain sophistication about Petaluma.

Santa Rosa City College has a satellite campus in Petaluma. Sonoma State University is just up the freeway.

Crime rate about suburban average, on the low side. Zero homicides in 1990 and 1989, one in 1988.

Homeless shelter opened in 1991 on Petaluma Boulevard South.

For recreation: 22 tennis courts, two baseball fields, two softball, plus fields for kids (soccer, baseball etc.), nine parks, swim center, three gyms, bowling alley, 18-hole golf course. City runs recreation programs.

Petaluma fronts on Petaluma River, which runs down to San Pablo Bay. Fishing, boating. City recently opened a marina, and is trying to build the water side of the tourist trade.

County fair, summer music festival, farmers' market, library, museum, movies, two playhouses (opera, drama, ballet), sprint and stock car races at the fairgrounds, river festival, World Wristwrestling Championship, heritage tours, Boys and Girls Club, two dozen delis, Chinese, Japanese, Mexican, French, Italian, seafood, American restaurants, plus the old standbys, McDonald's, etc.

The downtown, backdrop for several movies, is stuffed with restaurants, art galleries, antique stores, offices and small shops, but it also has supermarkets. Tourists and Petalumans from other side of freeway do a lot to sustain downtown but its bread and butter resides in the homes, many of them on hillsides, surrounding the downtown.

If shopping for a home and wanting to avoid tract look, drive these neighborhoods. You'll find the old, the ornate and the quaint, but mostly an assortment of ordinary homes, many built before World War II, that have been remodeled and given a lot of care.

Small shopping plaza (Meryvn's and Penney's) near freeway.

City has approved construction of an outlet mall near freeway, river and Corona Road. Supposed to yield $500,000 annually in tax revenues, a nice shot for city coffers. But Sierra Club and some residents have sued to stop project, saying it would degrade river, snarl traffic and weaken downtown businesses.

Petaluma, east of the freeway, has been building tracts for decades. The farther east you travel, the newer and larger the homes, but almost all fall within the description of middle class. Near freeway the first tracts are starting to fade.

Hoo-hah of 1991. Petaluma Auto plaza, using $260,000 in redevelopment (public) funds, built near the freeway a sign that rose 60 feet and had an electronic reader board. Can't miss it and no one did. Not a few exclaimed, What the blickety-blank hell is that damned thing, or something similar.

City council is discovering why some of our ancestral apes evolved into lawyers.

Rohnert Park

The third largest city in Sonoma County, Rohnert Park was built from nothing beginning in the late 1950s, pure suburbia, no history, no traditions, just tract after tract plunked down over the flat land south of Santa Rosa.

But if bland, Rohnert Park is also dynamic, a city that started with a plan and a vision of how it wanted to grow. The presence of a state university has also helped.

With no city council to deal with, the developer, Paul Golis, had a free hand to impose a master design. He favored neighborhood units, 200-250 homes per unit, each with 10 acres for a school and five acres for park and pool.

Special attention was given to recreation. Rohnert Park has two 18-hole golf courses. It has baseball fields, basketball and tennis courts, a skating rink, four public swimming pools, a bowling alley, a chess club, softball league (100 teams), a Fuchsia Society, cribbage, 11 parks, a community center, a senior center. Summer camp for kids.

A performing arts center opened in 1990, dance, ballet for kids, theater and music, 500-seat theater. City symphony. First food festival, honoring the melon, was held in 1991.

Rohnert Park has Sonoma State University, a big plus, books, libraries, theater, plays, off-beat movies, educated people, culture. Also college basketball and football.

When your town lands a university, a lot percolates beneath the surface that comes up positive. Rohnert Park schools, with some exceptions, generally score above the 50th percentile. (Cotati and Rohnert Park are in the school district.)

School bond passed in 1990, the $85 million to buy land for and build two elementary, one middle school over next 15 years, and for improvements to Rancho Cotate High, which recently added a math and science building.

Crime suburban average, on low side. Zero homicides in 1990, 1989, 1988. Cops are trying to discourage kids from joining a county gang that favors Raiders jackets, burglaries and drugs.

Good mix of homes and apartments. The state in its 1990 report counted 14,274 housing units: 6,936 single family, 1,040 single attached, 5,162 apartments, 1,136 mobile homes. Many of the apartments are located along Snyder Lane, an approach to the university.

Seniors complex, 230 units, opened in 1991. Independent living. Located on Enterprise Drive.

Some neighborhoods are showing their age, flaky paint, lawns needing care. But a mix. Five older homes will be spiffed up; the sixth faded.

Innovative city government. Cops and firefighters are cross trained; combat both fire and crime. One big chief, not two. Ground broken in 1991 for a $7 million public safety building.

On the way or recently constructed near the freeway: a Price Club, a Home

Rental Units & Rates in Sonoma County

City or Area	< $100 -249	$250 -499	$500 -749	$750 -999	$1,000 -plus
Bodega Bay	6	43	36	10	18
Boyes Hot Spring	48	419	433	116	20
Cloverdale	113	321	215	51	5
El Verano	7	71	115	19	1
Fettrs Hot Sp.-Ag. Cal.	7	132	112	43	6
Forestville	13	72	98	23	8
Glen Ellen	3	51	86	17	7
Guerneville	18	173	141	30	4
Healdsburg	88	400	649	183	17
Monte Rio	14	130	66	5	1
Occidental	8	47	44	11	2
Petaluma	220	1,124	2,228	1,240	319
Rohnert Park	175	773	3,369	1,208	293
Roseland	185	399	831	159	11
Santa Rosa	941	4,780	8,989	3,180	831
Sebastopol	90	418	564	179	17
Sonoma, City of	51	326	625	238	180
South Santa Rosa	27	190	194	53	6
Windsor	149	234	328	175	66
Countywide	3,010	13,767	23,250	8,361	2,284

Source: 1990 Census. The chart shows the number of rental units counted within a set range of rates.

Depot, a Walmart and many other stores, and a business park.

Major employers include Hewlett-Packard, 1,400 employees, university, 1,000, State Farm, 1,000.

The problems, the criticisms: road and sewer and utility improvements will be needed to serve the new stores and buildings. Some concern about the traffic these stores will generate.

Neighboring Cotati is worried it will get a lot of the traffic from these projects and none or little of the tax revenues necessary for improvements.

A middle school, 1,000 students, is to be built on 30 acres at Keiser Avenue and Snyder Lane. Neighbors don't like the idea.

Having shelled out for services and buildings, city hall struggled in 1991 to balance its books without wiping out its reserve.

School district also had money woes, and had to cut $2 million in personnel and programs. On the other hand, the new superintendent is trying to work closely with the university for the good of the local kids.

Median & Average Rents of Renter-Occupied Dwellings

City or Area	Units	Median	Average
Bodega Bay	121	$538	$626
Boyes Hot Spring	1,055	517	542
Cloverdale	730	424	451
Cotati	857	526	543
El Verano	621	616	634
Fettrs Hot Sp.-Ag. Cal.	312	521	551
Forestville	236	544	565
Glen Ellen	169	596	597
Guerneville	392	488	504
Healdsburg	1,378	539	558
Monte Rio	220	430	444
Occidental	139	506	520
Petaluma	5,234	641	655
Rohnert Park	5,881	634	665
Roseland	1,606	545	531
Santa Rosa	19,020	579	611
Sebastopol	1,298	542	551
Sonoma, City of	1,458	623	672
South Santa Rosa	497	518	533
Windsor	1,008	544	577
Countywide	52,479	576	600

Source: 1990 Census. Median means half way. In 100 homes the 50th home is median home.

Too much, too fast, say some environmentalists, a common complaint throughout Sonoma County.

If you wonder about that flower on the town signs, it's a sweet pea. Used to be grown locally. History, folks, is where you find it.

Santa Rosa

Largest city, county seat of Sonoma County. Flat lands, hills and valleys. Split by Highway 101. Named by a padre who had a narrow escape from Indians on feast day of St. Rose of Lima.

A changing city that added about 30,000 people in the 1980s, became more sophisticated, but still retains much of its small-town flavor. The county fair is the Big Event.

Used by Alfred Hitchcock in "Shadow of a Doubt" to symbolize the virtues of small-town America (Evil uncle flees big city, comes to Santa Rosa where he is undone by niece and cops.)

When Hollywood shot a television version in 1991, the location was switched to Petaluma. How fleeting fame!

Santa Rosa home prices, as compared to Marin County's, give a good idea of why Sonoma County's population boomed in the 1980s.

The 1990 census correlated dollar values to housing. For owner-occupied homes, 15 percent of Santa Rosa homes were worth $100,000 to $125,000. Up a notch, 36 percent were worth $150,000 to $200,000, and 21 percent came in at $200,000 to $250,000.

Put another way, if the census can be believed, 7 out of every 10 owned homes in Santa Rosa can be bought for between $100,000 and $250,000.

For Marin County, homes worth $100,000 to $200,000 made up 8 percent of the total, and those from $200,000 to $250,000, about 11 percent. The total between these brackets, about 1 in 5 homes.

Taking Marin, population 230,096, in its entirety, it has for potential sale 4,015 owner homes worth $100,000 to $200,000.

Santa Rosa, with half the population, carried 11,252 homes in this bracket. And Sonoma County in this range offers for potential sale 32,412 homes.

So when you say Santa Rosa and Sonoma County, you're saying, choice, selection, variety. And middle-class "affordable" (by California's standard. Iowans and Texans would cringe at these prices.)

You're also saying, more house for the buck. You can buy 4-bedrooms, new, in Sonoma County for under $250,000. In Marin ... forget it.

The tradeoff: If you work in San Fran, you'll spend maybe an hour or more a day on the freeway. Some people hate this.

And a different, though hard to pin down, style of life. Take a look at the Marin school rankings. A lot of 90s. A lot of sons and daughters of college grads, of bosses.

In Santa Rosa, a lot of 90s, but also scores that bounce across the spectrum, especially in the elementary grades. Scores that suggest sons and daughters of lawyers and laborers, managers and mechanics.

The why: money, of course, but also background, parental education, values. The average Marinite may value education more than the average Santa Rosa resident and these values may rub off on the young.

The hidden message to the ambitious Santa Rosa mom or dad: you may have to work harder with your child.

When you buy a home, you buy into the values of a neighborhood or town, and although they may not be professed in obvious ways, every place has values.

Why are so many people moving to Santa Rosa? The home prices, yes; very important. But also because they like it as a town, they sense it is a friendly place, with a lot to offer.

Close to wine country. Two centers for the arts. Two libraries, 38 parks, two public lakes, ice arena, roller skating arena, movie theaters, bowling, softball, basketball, tennis, volleyball. Rose Festival Parade in May. Symphony orchestra.

Besides county fair, many events at fairgrounds, including annual Scottish Games. Draws 45,000. Supposed to be largest Scottish gathering in North America. County fair attracts 400,000. Community college in the downtown. State university in nearby Rohnert Park.

Neighborhood shopping plazas and two regional plazas: the downtown (Macy's, Sears, Mervyn's) and Coddington Center (Macy's, Emporium, Penney's), located west of 101 and about a mile north of the downtown.

The best choice of housing in the county: 48,019 housing units: 28,942 single homes, 4,136 single attached, 12,831 apartments, 2,110 mobile homes (1990 state count).

In many towns, the higher the elevation, the better the view, the higher the price. To some extent, Santa Rosa follows this rule. Fountaingrove, probably the ultimate in Santa Rosa housing, looks down from the north hills.

But a fair amount of first-class stuff was plopped on the valley floor west of Highway 101. And on some eastern hills, the housing runs suburban tract.

Market forces greatly influenced Santa Rosa housing. When plain sold, it built plain. When fancy sold, it built fancy. If your budget says 1950 flat top, two bedrooms, drive some of the downtown neighborhoods. East of Highway 101, the town sends fingers down into valleys. Drive Bennett Valley Road, Yulapa Avenue, Summerfield Road. Lot of fairly new stuff.

Oakmont, a retirement community, stole a march down Highway 12 into the Sonoma Valley, wine country.

City in the next 20 years will be pushing development east of Highway 101 in the southern section. Number of residents is expected to increase by 20,000.

Highway 12 splits the town west to east and ends abruptly a few miles east of Highway 101, then picks up three or four miles to east. Not a few residents would like a straight connector that would pass through Spring Lake Park — and presumably over the bodies of the seemingly thousands who plan to throw themselves in front of bulldozers. But, still, an idea that refuses to die. If buying in the area, consult a map.

Crime about suburban average, pushed a little high by thefts (shopping plazas attract thieves). One homicide in 1990, five in 1989, five in 1988, two in 1987. New jail opened in 1991 in downtown.

SMOKE GETS IN YOUR EYES

A crackling fire, a glass of wine and thou. How, haff-kaff, delightful. How polluting.

Air quality people say that old-fashioned fireplaces and inefficient stoves are polluting Healdsburg, Guerneville and North Sonoma. Law is in the works to require non-polluting stoves and fireplace inserts in new homes.

Much anguish about homeless sleeping under bridges. In 1991, police rousted about 60 bridge sleepers, 20 of them teenagers. In winter, the armory is used as a shelter.

Airport southwest of city. Prop jets to L.A. Noise doesn't seem to be a big problem but if buying in the area check with neighbors.

Novel idea coming in 1992: School (kindergarten and first grade) to open near Hewlett Packard. Instead of neighborhood oriented, workplace oriented. The better for working parents to visit and pick up kids.

If voters pass bond, school construction will get a boost.

Finally, in an age where freeways bypassed and killed a lot of downtowns, Santa Rosa's is breathing well (thanks in part to heavy infusions of public money but why quibble). Mixed shops, department stores, restaurants, government buildings and some history. A pleasant place to stroll and shop.

Two big unincorporated neighborhoods to south of city. Roseland, west of Highway 101, and South Santa Rosa.

Older homes, many vintage 1950s. Many kids. In Roseland 31 percent of residents are under age 18, South Santa Rosa, 28 percent. Good place to look if you lack bucks and want to break into the housing market.

Patroled by sheriff's deputies. Some complaints about crime in Roseland. Sheriff's office has stepped up patrols.

Sebastopol

Small city, famed for Gravenstein apples, that in the 1980s added about 1,400 residents and quietly went upscale.

Grateful Bagel on Main Street, Nuclear Free Zone, activist politics for the good life. When the city council got hung up about cutting down two sick redwoods, the local paper accused the council of trying to be "politically correct."

In and about the downtown, a good many ordinary homes, nice but not

---

SEWER LINES WERE NOT FLUSH

In August 1990, shortly after the opening of 188 apartments, business people near Sonoma Highway and Mission Boulevard could not help but smell a powerful stench. Inspectors from the Regional Water Quality Control Board sniffed and searched but no cause was found. Still the stench persisted.

About six months and many complaints later, someone looked at a map and speculated that maybe the sewage line from the apartments had not been properly connected to the trunk line. A manhole was popped open — Eureka and peeugh.

Seems the lines were built years apart by different developers. Two hours of work made the connection. No harm done. Blackberries and poison oak flourished thanks to the bubbled-up effluent, a million plus gallons.

distinctive, but away from Main Street custom homes pop up here and there, and the town has many well-kept older homes.

What's the allure? Try: quiet, intimate, friendly, big enough to provide the basics (Safeway, shops on Main Street), small enough to be comprehended. Just outside city limits the country starts.

School rankings generally up there, some in top 10th percentile.

Crime not tracked by FBI but small towns with high academic rankings are usually peaceful. New police station opened in 1991.

The 1990 state count showed 2,971 housing units, of which 1,874 were single homes, 181 single attached, 851 apartments, 65 mobile homes.

Three parks, five playgrounds, public swimming pool, golf course, Center for the Arts, community center with many activities for kids and adults.

Russian River nearby. Lots of outdoors stuff. Apple Blossom Parade in May, Apple Fair in August. Plenty of apple trees but more outside city limits than in. Farmers Market in the summer.

Sebastopol commute is as good as most from Sonoma County. Highway 12 and 116 shoot over to Highway 101, a distance of about seven miles along Highway 12. Sebastopol is a quick hop to the regional malls.

Sea Ranch

Second-home community on the north coast. About 2,400 lots on 1,200 acres with another 4,000 acres or so set aside for buffer. Sea Ranch runs 10.5 miles along the coast.

So far, a little over 1,000 homes built, with new homes going up 85 to 100 a year. Active resale market.

Diverse group of residents, many educators, doctors, professionals, some artists. One fellow described them as a "community of overachievers."

About 600 people, half of them retired, live year-round. The two dozen kids attend Horicon Elementary in Annapolis, high school in Pt. Arena.

Small landing strip but most come by car, up Route 1. When the roads are clear, 2 hours and 10 minutes from Golden Gate.

Community is run by homeowners group, which employs about two dozen, assesses fee on property owners for common maintenance. Design committee reviews plans for new homes.

Summer fog but realtors say that winds allow more sunshine than other locations on coast. Trails. Great views. Beach strolls. Golf course. Recreation centers, restaurant. Tennis. Fishing. Swimming pool.

Many homes are rented out by two-day or week.

Sonoma

Historic town, popular with tourists but also attracting upscale residents, nestled at the base of hills in the Sonoma Valley wine country.

Entering the town traveling north on Highway 12, you smack into the

Sonoma Plaza, anchored by imposing city hall. On the opposite side stand the barracks built in 1835 by Mariano Vallejo, commandant-general of the northern frontier during the days when Mexico owned California.

Just east of the barracks stands the Sonoma Mission, the end of Camino Real, the old King's Highway that runs up California from San Diego.

Both buildings have been carefully restored. A block east of the mission you'll find the Sebastiani winery. And around the plaza, homes have been restored, and restaurants, antique stores, art galleries and shops built.

History, the real stuff, rare in California. Throughout the year thousands drive up to Sonoma and do the history-wine country tour. Or lay up at a spa and get their bodies massaged and caressed into working order.

Parks, baseball, football, small theater, public pool (at high school), 18-hole golf course, soccer, equestrian activities, farmers market, miniature steam trains (can be ridden).

The state in 1990 counted 4,137 housing units: 2,047 single homes, 602 single attached, 1,065 apartments, 423 mobile homes. Population 8,121, an increase of 34 percent over last decade. Census showed that about 40 percent of residents are over age 55. Many retirees like to hang their hats in the town.

School rankings, for the most part, way up there, in the 80th and 90th percentiles. School district is thinking about building a new high school.

FBI doesn't track crime for cities under 10,000 population but if it did Sonoma would come in pretty safe.

Traffic is a bit of a pain: tourists, whom the city actively encourages to visit. A good map will reveal the detours.

For general employment, several government and private institutions are located in the Sonoma area, the largest being the Sonoma Development Center for the mentally ill and retarded.

Housing generally built in the 1950s and 1960s, some much earlier. Sonoma on many of its side streets has a suburban look.

On a few streets, the homes blast off into opulence, mansions of stone and brass and massive chimneys. This is the new Sonoma — discovered to be within driving distance of the urban centers. More upscale stuff is on the way.

Sonoma's about 23 miles from Vallejo and the East Bay. Petaluma and Highway 101 are about 10 miles to the east. Santa Rosa 20 miles to the north.

As for the commute, it just depends on where you're going, and if to San Fran, how much pain you're willing to endure to live here. The reward: you will live in a nice town with some class and history.

Windsor

Fast-growing town that in November 1991 voted to incorporate itself as a city. Loaded with new homes. Located about six miles north of Santa Rosa and growing toward that city.

To meet the housing demand for the 1980s and yet protect agricultural lands, the county government shunted development to Windsor. The town is right off Highway 101 and served by the Redwood Highway, and probably would have gone suburban sooner or later.

The result: a series of developments, one-two stories, two-three car garages, nice in the way of middle-class tracts, some upscale. Shopping mall, offices. Raley's market.

A planned community with sites designated for parks and schools. Between 1986 and the 1990 census, the population about doubled and is now about 14,000. Pending developments may add another 6,000 people in this decade.

Although building has slowed, many new units are still available and a resale market has developed. Several mobile home parks in the region.

Kids attend local schools and Healdsburg Junior and Senior High. Plans are to build a new high school in Windsor, if money can be raised.

Many school rankings below the 50th percentile, a cause for concern but district is moving from rural to suburban and with influx of middle class, scores should be coming up.

Short commute to Santa Rosa; to San Fran, still a long haul.

Three parks, four neighborhood parks on the way. Annual Hot Air Balloon Festival. Still a lot of open country around the town. Russian River, Santa Rosa City College, Cal State University in Rohnert Park — all within a short drive of Windsor.

The problems, which some might call challenges: Windsor has developed so fast that municipal services have not kept pace. Construction was slowed when sewage capacity was exceeded. Traffic snarls at peak hours because arterials and freeway accesses have yet to be overhauled.

School construction has lagged, in part because of shortcomings throughout the state but also because of the rapid growth. Many kids attend class in portables.

But there is movement. An elementary school, now under construction, will open in fall 1992. Road improvements are being made.

Cityhood, which will give Windsor control over its planning, should help.

County governments, basically regional bodies, often stumble when they get into municipal services and in Windsor's case, the county was clearly indicating it would like to see a city formed and a council take over.

10/How Public Schools Work

Marin, Napa & Sonoma SAT Scores, Ethnic Enrollments, Vacation Dates, Colleges

SCORES. WHAT DO they mean? If the scores in your children's school are low, should you place them in a private school or another public school? If you can't afford a private school, what can you do to assure your children a good education in the local school? What's in store for your children when you buy a home in a neighborhood with a marginal school?

The answers start with what is called socioeconomics — a theory loved and hated by educators but widely believed by the California educational establishment.

Socioeconomics — The Bottom Line

In its crudest form, socioeconomics means rich kids score high, middle-class kids score about the middle and poor kids score low. Not all the time, not predictably by individual. Many children from poor and middle-class homes succeed in school and attend the best colleges. But as a general rule socioeconomics enjoys much statistical support.

Compare the rankings in the preceding chapters with income by towns. In the higher income Marin cities — Kentfield, Mill Valley and Ross, percentile rankings among the tops in the state. In middle to upper middle, San Rafael and Novato, rankings in the 70s, 80s and 90s. If you took, say, the San Rafael district and tracked the schools according to neighborhood income, chances are very good that the higher-scoring schools would be in the affluent neighborhoods, the middle scoring in the less affluent.

Sausalito, a rich town, is married in its educational system to Marin City, a poor neighborhood. Rankings middling. Sonoma County makes a tougher case because it's more evenly middle class and less likely to show wide swings and because many of its school districts enroll few children, which makes statistics suspect.

But the difference in rankings between Rincon Valley Union District as opposed to those in Roseland Elementary District probably owes more to social influences than teacher quality or educational factors.

Scores in the Napa Valley Unified School District are generally up there but the highest scores — the 90s — are usually to be found in the high-income neighborhoods. The pattern shows up around the state, the country and in other countries. The federal study, "Japanese Education Today," notes a "solid correlation between poverty and poor school performance ...."

Family and Culture

In its refined form, socioeconomics moves away from the buck and toward culture and family influence.

Historically, millions of poor American children have succeeded in public schools because their parents badgered, bullied and encouraged them every step of the way and made sacrifices so they would succeed. The Vietnamese provide the modern example. They arrived in this country penniless; many seem to be doing quite well in school, excepting the language difficulty. And this should fade with the generation born in America.

So thoroughly does the California Department of Education believe in socioeconomics that it worked the theory into a mathematical model. Teachers collected data on almost all students: are they on welfare, do they have language problems (immigrants), how educated are their parents? The information was fed to a computer and used to predict how students would score on tests.

Ability Grouping

California and American schools dealt with socioeconomics by organizing "comprehensive" schools or school districts. If students have varying talents and interests, the reasoning went, schools should provide programs that reflect this diversity. The ideal was to educate all students in the fundamentals of English, reading and math then, as they grew older, to divide them by ability and interest and teach accordingly — vocational, general, prep.

Although there have been many changes in recent years, most California school districts operate basically this way.

In the first six years in an average school, the children receive some special help according to ability, but for the most part they share the same class experiences and get the same instruction.

About the seventh grade the students are divided into classes for low achievers, middling students and high achievers, or low-middle and advanced. Texts are sometimes different for each group, the homework is different, the expectations are different. Some students straddle the groupings, taking "easy" and "tough" classes.

Parents can always request a transfer from one group to another (whether they can get it is another matter). But the reality often is that remedial children can't keep pace with the middle children and the middling can't keep up with the high achievers.

In the last 30 years or so, recognizing the importance of educating children while they are very young, schools introduced special programs into the early grades. These programs are aimed at low achievers, immigrant children who speak English poorly, children with learning disabilities and high achievers.

Although they vary greatly, the programs typically pull the children out of class for instruction in small groups then return them to the regular class.

College Influence

The junior high divisions sharpen at high school. Colleges exercise great influence over what students are taught in high school. So many local students attend the University of California and California State University schools that public and private high schools must of necessity teach the classes demanded by these institutions.

So the typical high school will have a prep program that meets University of California requirements. The school will also offer general education classes in math and English but these will not be as tough as the prep courses and will not be recognized by the state universities. And usually the school will teach some trades so those inclined can secure jobs upon graduation.

Can a school with mediocre or even low basic scores field a successful college prep program? With comprehensive programs, the answer is yes.

How "Mediocre" Schools Succeed — College Admissions

The state traces public college freshman, age 19 and under, to their high schools. The data can mislead but it shows the strengths of the middling schools (See Chart on Page 121).

If a student attends a California State University, a community college or a University of California (Berkeley, Los Angeles, San Diego, Davis, etc.), the state generally will know where he or she attended high school in California. The chart, using data from fall 1990, tracks freshmen in California public colleges back to their high schools. The UCs generally restrict themselves to the top 13 percent in the state. The Cal States take the top third.

Notice Piner High School in Santa Rosa, a school that straddles the middle academic rankings. It sent 10 kids to the University of California and 23 to Cal State Universities. The 1990 information on community colleges was not available but in 1989 Piner graduated 201 students to community colleges.

Or Casa Grande High in Petaluma. On the basic rankings, it comes in about the 50th percentile. It graduated 21 students to the University of California, 26 to Cal States, and in 1989 sent 131 to community colleges.

Sonoma, Napa and Marin do not have high schools ranking at the bottom

Scholastic Aptitude Test (SAT) Scores

Marin County

High School	No. Tested	Verbal	Math
Novato High	134	448	515
Redwood	267	474	554
San Marin	134	454	524
San Rafael	101	454	509
Sir Francis Drake	84	446	481
Tamalpais	175	454	507
Terra Linda	110	437	495
Tomales	16	432	487
County Avg.	—	456	519

Napa County

High School	No. Tested	Verbal	Math
Calistoga	11	373	390
Napa	93	413	489
Vintage	124	435	494
St. Helena	61	437	505
County Avg.	—	426	490

Sonoma County

High School	No. Tested	Verbal	Math
Analy	81	475	511
Casa Grande	115	423	471
Cloverdale	23	471	508
El Molino	68	472	495
Healdsburg	77	402	463
Montgomery	149	463	524
Petaluma	106	446	495
Piner	73	457	520
Rancho Cotate	76	429	501
Santa Rosa	176	460	533
Sonoma Valley	120	450	489
County Avg.	—	449	503

Source: California Department of Education, 1990 tests. **Note**: SAT scores are greatly influenced by who and how many take the test. The California Department of Education, under Bill Honig, has been pushing schools to have more students take the SAT. A school that has more marginal students taking the test will, by one line of reasoning, be doing a good job, but the scores are likely to be lower.

but throughout the state there are high schools in the bottom 10th percentile sending a few kids on to top colleges. What these figures indicate is that almost all high schools have a prep program in place, although the quality of course offerings probably varies widely.

So if your local rankings are mediocre, even low, there's hope. Get the kids into the college-track classes.

Where does this information mislead? The Cal States and UCs run on academics, the community colleges run on academics and vocational classes. Just because a student attends a community college does not mean he or she is pursuing a bachelor's degree.

Secondly, students who qualify for a Cal State or even a UC often take their freshman and sophomore years at a community college. It's cheaper — $60 maximum per semester — and closer to home. They then transfer as juniors into the four-year colleges.

The chart does not track private colleges. It doesn't tell us how many local students went to Stanford or Harvard or the Dominican College of San Rafael. Or public colleges out of the state.

The chart does confirm the influence of socioeconomics: the rich towns send more kids to the UCs than the poorer ones. But socioeconomics does not sweep the field. Not every student from a high-scoring school goes on to college. Many students from low- and middle-income towns come through.

Dissatisfaction at Home

If this is true, why are so many people dissatisfied with public schools? Why do parents pay thousands to educate their children in private schools?

Before diving into that maelstrom, let's note that as logical as this system sounds, it is not universally practiced. Japan does not divide students by ability, even for reading difficulties, until the 10th grade. The Einsteins and the low achievers are all educated in the same class, use the same books and are taught a common curriculum (But many students attend private afternoon schools and many of these group by ability.)

Many people are dissatisfied with California education because it works fitfully. Although the dropout rate has fallen, dropouts are still numerous, scores are low in many urban districts, employers report that high school grads are unable to read or write. Colleges complain honor high school students often need remedial math and English.

Average SAT scores nationally have rebounded 13 points since 1980 but in the preceding decades they dropped 90 points, The New York Times reported in 1990. In 1991, the newspapers reported that SAT scores dipped again (but some said this was because a higher number of students took the test).

The Major Disputes

It is not the intention of this book to reform American education or dwell

California College Admissions of Public School Graduates
Marin County

High School	UC	CSU	Com	Total
Novato	31	24	NA	NA
Redwood	77	42	NA	NA
San Marin	22	40	NA	NA
San Rafael	27	12	NA	NA
Sir Francis Drake	15	15	NA	NA
Tamalpais	44	25	NA	NA
Terra Linda	23	28	NA	NA
Tomales	2	7	NA	NA
All Public Schools	241	193	NA	NA

Napa County

High School	UC	CSU	Com	Total
Calistoga	0	4	1	5
Napa	17	23	71	111
St. Helena	16	17	NA	NA
Vintage	19	27	70	116
All Public Schools	52	71	NA	NA

Sonoma County

High School	UC	CSU	Com	Total
Analy	16	14	NA	NA
Casa Grande	21	26	NA	NA
Cloverdale	3	2	NA	NA
El Molino	12	7	NA	NA
Healdsburg	7	15	NA	NA
Montgomery	29	17	NA	NA
Petaluma	23	31	NA	NA
Piner	10	23	NA	NA
Rancho Cotate	15	27	NA	NA
Santa Rosa	26	40	NA	NA
Sonoma Valley	26	21	NA	NA
All Public Schools	189	231	NA	NA

Source: California Postsecondary Education Commission. **Key:** UC (University of California system); CSU (Cal State system); Com (Community Colleges); NA (Not Available). Chart tracks high school graduates entering California public colleges as freshmen in fall, 1990. NA (not available), data for community colleges in Marin and Sonoma were not available at press time.

on its shortcomings. But to explain how local schools work, it is necessary to touch on some of the major disputes. These are:

• Clustering children by abilities or problems. Although widespread, this

UCs Chosen by Public School Graduates
Marin County

High School	Berk.	Davis	Irvine	UCLA	River.	SD	SB	SC	Total
Novato	1	16	—	2	3	3	5	1	31
Redwood	14	13	1	14	2	2	13	18	77
San Marin	4	8	—	2	—	2	4	2	22
San Rafael	4	10	—	2	1	2	4	4	27
Sir Fr. Drake	3	4	—	—	—	—	1	7	15
Tamalpais	5	5	1	4	—	6	8	15	44
Terra Linda	3	10	2	—	—	2	2	4	23
Tomales	1	1	—	—	—	—	—	—	2

Napa County

High School	Berk.	Davis	Irvine	UCLA	River.	SD	SB	SC	Total
Napa	1	10	1	1	—	1	2	1	17
St. Helena	2	8	1	—	—	1	1	3	16
Vintage	2	9	—	—	—	3	2	3	19

Sonoma County

High School	Berk.	Davis	Irvine	UCLA	River.	SD	SB	SC	Total
Analy	3	7	—	—	—	1	1	4	16
Casa Grande	—	12	1	—	—	2	4	2	21
Cloverdale	1	—	—	—	—	2	—	5	12
El Molino	4	1	—	—	—	2	—	5	12
Healdsburg	4	2	—	—	—	—	—	1	7
Montgomery	2	8	2	3	—	2	6	6	29
Petaluma	2	9	1	—	—	1	2	8	23
Piner	2	5	—	—	—	1	1	1	10
Rancho Cotate	2	3	—	5	1	1	3	—	15
Santa Rosa	2	5	1	1	—	6	9	2	26
Sonoma Valley	2	7	—	3	—	2	4	8	26

Source: Callifornia Department of Education, fall, 1990. **Key**: Berk. (Berkeley); River. (Riverside); SD (San Diego); SB (Santa Barbara); SC (Santa Cruz).

practice has many opponents and often its supporters are uneasy in its defense.

Opponents argue that children labeled "low achievers" will fulfill that prophecy. The sad fact is that many programs aimed at low achievers have not worked or work poorly. This provokes bitter arguments: supporters saying that more money and programs are needed, opponents pushing for an end or curtailment of the programs.

Meanwhile, supporters of gifted (high achiever) and bilingual programs argue that more money needs to be spent on these children.

• Different expectations. Low-achieving students are often assigned little or no homework and, in higher grades, given books with simple words and sentences. High achievers get more homwork and books that require dictionaries.

Men, Women and College

Marin County

Sex	UC	CSU	Com	Totals
Men	148	111	NA	NA
Women	164	130	NA	NA
Total	312	241	NA	NA

Napa County

Sex	UC	CSU	Com	Totals
Men	32	42	97	171
Women	43	51	79	173
Total	75	93	176	344

Sonoma County

Sex	UC	CSU	Com	Totals
Men	101	132	NA	NA
Women	119	149	NA	NA
Total	220	281	NA	NA

Source: California Postsecondary Education Commission. Chart tracks all high school graduates, private and public, entering California public colleges as freshmen in fall, 1990. Key: NA, not available. Data was not avaible from the state at press time.

• Money and how it is spent. Many educators argue that the California system is underfunded. Others contend the money is adequate but wasted.

Special programs are expensive. They require more training for teachers, additional classrooms, an expanded bureaucracy, much paper work.

In recent years sentiment has been growing to spend much more on pre-school programs, for children while they are three, four and five years old.

• Class size and teaching days. Many teachers argue that class sizes, which often run beyond 30 in California, are too big. The California Teachers Association, a union, wants 20 students per teacher.

The typical California school runs 175-180 teaching days. Too few, say many. The Japanese school year is over 230 days.

Oregon is moving to gradually extend its school year to 220 days.

• Teacher competency. Once tenured, teachers are almost impossible to fire, which leaves schools open to accusations of coddling incompetents.

Lately, however, some schools have been taking a harder line on teacher competency, especially in screening teachers before they win tenure. Because of a local glut of teachers, many school districts can be selective.

• Educational methods. Furious arguments rage over what will work and what needs fixing. One example: dropouts.

Policies favor keeping kids in school, no matter how low they score and

Marin County Enrollments & Key 1992 Dates

School District	Enroll	Spr. Break	Last Day
Bolinas-Stinson	219	4/13-4/17	June 10
Dixie	1,486	4/13-4/17	June 10
Kentfield	903	4/13-4/17	June 12
Laguna Joint	21	4/20-4/24	June 11
Lagunitas	394	4/13-4/17	June 10
Larkspur	819	4/13-4/17	June 10
Mill Valley	1,850	4/13-4/17	June 16
Nicasio	NA	4/13-4/17	June 11
Novato Unified	8,032	4/17-4/24	June 11
Reed Union	864	4/13-4/17	June 17
Ross	331	4/13-4/17	June 11
Ross Valley	1,618	4/13-4/17	June 11
San Rafael Elem.	2,863	4/13-4/17	June 11
San Rafael High	1,706	4/13-4/17	June 11
Sausalito	341	4/13-4/17	June 16
Shoreline Unified	843	4/13-4/17	June 11
Tamalpais Union High	2,638	4/13-4/17	June 11
Union Joint	24	4/20-4/24	June 11

Source: Marin County Office of Education and phone survey of individual school districts. Some districts take a ski week off.

how little interest they show. Expulsions are rare even when teenagers misbehave (schools often isolate the more troublesome in separate classes.)

On the other hand, schools believe that unless they keep the kids in school, they will have no opportunity to educate them.

Almost anyone over age 18 can enroll in a California community college. There are no academic admission requirements. Dropouts are many and, to bring students up to college level, the colleges have been forced to offer many remedial classes.

• Minorities and integration. One of the touchiest topics in the state. California minorities are growing rapidly and will soon be a majority in the state. Some groups, notably Blacks and Hispanics, are doing poorly in schools. Asians score high.

Some educators argue that what is taught in public schools fails to instill pride in the accomplishments of various cultures and ethnic groups, that too much attention is paid to European civilization, too little to Asian and African.

From this, it is deduced that if texts and curriculum were revised, minority children would do better in school. The state is now introducing textbooks that emphasize the accomplishments of minorities and women and approach

Napa County Enrollments & Key 1992 Dates

School District	Enroll	Spr. Break	Last Day
Calistoga Joint Unified	719	4/13-4/20	June 12
Howell Mountain	170	4/13-4/24	June 11
Napa Valley Unified	14,000	4/13-4/17	June 11
Pope Valley Union	66	4/11-4/19	June 11
St. Helena Unified	1,508	4/13-4/17	June 11

Source: Napa County Office of Education and phone survey of individual school districts. Some districts take a ski week off.

history from diverse perspectives. Criticism has also been leveled against ability clustering, which tends to place many minorities in the low-scoring classes.

• Vouchers or unrestricted transfers. Many public educators are against them, arguing that they would make a shambles out of planning and segregate poor minorities in inner-city schools. Supporters say that public schools will never reform, never meet the needs of inner-city kids until they (the schools) are jolted by competition.

Vouchers, in one form or another, may appear on a 1992 ballot.

• Parental influence. Almost everyone agrees that schools would work better, students would score higher, if parents did a better job at home. This is a major but often muted complaint among teachers: society (family, television, social influences) is failing the schools, not the schools failing the society.

The problem: how to get parents to do a better job, how to influence home life.

Back to Socioeconomics

Suffice it to say that socioeconomics, being a popular theory, has its critics. Some educators argue that, never mind parents, the schools should be able to do it all. Carried to its logical extreme — parents are the be all and end all — socioeconomics becomes absurd. Clearly schools, teaching methods, teachers, greatly influence the children.

Although applied usually to students, the theory can be applied to parental influence on schools. Achieving students score high because they are pushed by parents and, possibly, because the parents push or manipulate the schools.

At high-achieving schools, parents often wear out their welcome by butting into school affairs. They complain, they meddle and they forever ask why this, why that.

But they also raise money for programs, praise the praiseworthy, slander through gossip the undeserving and generally keep the heat on school personnel to do well.

Several years ago a Marin principal, summing up social influences, said, "I think ... that our parents and our teachers and our kids deserve credit for the (high) scores through the high expectations that they set. I think we ask a lot of our kids, and I'm convinced the more you ask, the more you get."

Myth or Fact?

On one important aspect the debate becomes hopelessly muddled. Since the rich suburbs have the highest-scoring schools, parents often assume that they have the best teachers, administrators and programs. Or that these schools have some hard-to-define quality that sets them apart, a special esprit de corps.

Housing guides use teacher salaries and per-pupil expenditures as indicators of quality. Teacher salaries, however, and per-pupil expenditures vary widely throughout the state and in many instances the low- and middle-scoring districts pay more than the high-scoring districts.

When parents see that a school scores high on basic tests, they think, this must be an excellent school. Everyone is doing so well.

When a school administrator sees a high-scoring school, he thinks: this school has excellent students (high income, educated parents) but I wonder if it is managed well, if it has the right programs.

The Parent's Role

What's a parent to do? You would be foolish to ignore the socioeconomic message: To succeed in school, children need strong support from the home. Bookstores and libraries are full of books with advice on how you can work with your child. You as a parent, with a little work and discipline, can make a real difference in the quality of your child's education.

You should probably look for outside help even if your child is doing well.

This is a hard call. Since 1978, when the California tax system was drastically revised (Proposition 13), educators every year have had to beg and threaten to get minimal funding. At the same time, through collective bargaining, the power of the teachers has risen, with the effect that while overall funding has tightened, salaries have risen competitively. California teachers, on the average, are the sixth highest paid in the country.

Proposition 13 greatly eroded the taxing power of local schools and made Sacramento the money bags of education. The hand that dispenses the bucks also, to a large extent, decides how the bucks will be spent. A great deal of policy is now set in Sacramento, far beyond the reach of parents and school boards.

There are pros and cons to all this. Teachers should be adequately paid. In a state as diverse as California, a central authority should be setting some policy, and so on.

But the overall effect has been to grow a system that has become increasingly complex and strapped for money. Up and down the state, school

Sonoma County Enrollments & Key 1992 Dates

School District	Enroll	Spr. Break	Last Day
Alexander Valley Union	124	4/17-4/24	June 12
Analy Union High	2,011	4/17-4/24	June 11
Bellevue Union	1,317	4/17-4/24	June 12
Bennett Valley Union	970	4/17-4/24	June 11
Cinnabar	270	4/17-4/24	June 11
Cloverdale Unified	1,321	4/20-4/24	June 11
Cotati-Rohnert Park	7,227	4/17-4/24	June 12
Dunham	87	4/17-4/24	June 12
Forestville Union	794	4/17-4/24	June 11
Fort Ross	85	4/17-4/24	June 10
Geyserville Unified	347	4/20-4/24	June 11
Gravenstein Union	716	4/17-4/24	June 11
Guerneville	615	4/17-4/24	June 11
Harmony Union	611	4/17-4/24	June 11
Healdsburg Union Elem.	1,428	4/20-4/24	June 11
Healdsburg Union High	1,573	4/20-4/24	June 11
Horicon	106	4/13-4/24	June 12
Kenwood	182	4/17-4/24	June 11
Liberty	156	4/17-4/24	June 12
Mark West Union	1,208	4/17-4/24	June 12
Monte Rio Union	193	4/17-4/24	June 12
Montgomery	80	4/17-4/24	June 11
Oak Grove Union	505	4/17-4/24	June 11
Old Adobe Union	2,170	4/17-4/24	June 11
Petaluma City	2,376	4/17-4/24	June 12
Petaluma Jt. Union High	3,832	4/17-4/24	June 12
Piner-Olivet Union	1,282	4/17-4/24	June 11
Rincon Valley Union	2,733	4/17-4/24	June 12
Roseland	924	4/17-4/24	June 11
Santa Rosa City Elem.	4,764	4/17-4/24	June 11
Santa Rosa City High	9,631	4/17-4/24	June 11
Sebastopol Union	1,327	4/17-4/24	June 11
Sonoma Valley Unified	4,572	4/16-4/24	June 12
Twin Hills Union	829	4/17-4/24	June 11
Two Rock Union	197	4/17-4/24	June 12
Waugh	124	4/17-4/24	June 11
West Side Union	120	4/20-4/24	June 11
Wilmar Union	220	4/17-4/24	June 12
Windsor Union	1,691	4/17-4/24	June 12
Wright	1,183	4/17-4/24	June 12

Source: Sonoma County Office of Education. Some districts take a ski week off.

Marin County Ethnic Enrollments by School District

District	White	Black	Asn/PI	Filipino	Hisp	Nat.
Bolinas-Stinson	99	1	0	0	1	1
Dixie	89	2	6	1	4	0
Kentfield	97	1	2	*0	1	0
Laguna Joint	71	0	0	0	29	0
Lagunitas	93	2	1	*0	3	0
Larkspur	85	2	8	*0	5	*0
Lincoln Elem.	87	0	0	0	13	0
Mill Valley	86	4	7	0	3	*0
Nicasio	78	0	0	0	22	0
Novato Unified	87	3	5	*0	5	*0
Reed Union	94	3	2	1	1	0
Ross	98	1	*0	0	1	0
Ross Valley	91	2	2	1	3	*0
San Rafael Elem.	62	7	9	*0	22	*0
San Rafael High	71	5	9	*0	14	*0
Sausalito	50	43	3	0	4	*0
Shoreline Unified	79	1	*0	0	20	*0
Tamalpais Union High	88	4	4	*0	4	*0
Union Joint Elem.	50	0	0	0	50	0

Source: California Dept. of Education, 1990. Figures are percentages, rounded to the nearest whole number. Total may exceed or be less than 100 percent. **Key**: Asn/PI (Asian and Pacific Islander); Hisp. (Hispanics); Nat. (Alaskan & American Indian). Asterisk (*) zeros are for figures less than 0.5 percent.

districts are cutting periods here and there, scrimping on supplies, pushing as many children as possible into classrooms.

For the foreseeable future, improvements will probably not be made. The California economy is limping. Despite large tax increases in 1991, the state is still short of money and will probably have to cut more programs in 1992.

In well-to-do neighborhoods and rich towns, parents are informally taxing themselves to raise money for schools. These are clever, well-educated people. They have studied the state laws and figured out ways to get around restrictions designed to level out spending among school districts.

Little clubs are formed and when a child enters kindergarten or a family moves to the district, the parents are quietly informed by other parents that the right thing to do is donate $100 or $200 or more to a fund that pays for teachers' aides or computers or other educational items.

Parents clubs these days are putting a lot more energy into fund raisers to get the schools extra classes, and in some instances they are running classes

Napa County Ethnic Enrollments by School District

District	White	Black	Asn/PI	Filipino	Hisp.	Nat.
Calistoga Unified	62	1	*0	*0	37	*0
Howell Mtn. Elem.	56	6	6	0	32	0
Napa Valley Unified	80	1	2	2	15	1
St. Helena Unified	73	1	1	0	25	*0

Source: California Dept. of Education, 1990. Figures are percentages, rounded to the nearest whole number. Total may exceed or be less than 100 percent. Key: Asn/PI (Asian and Pacific Islander); Hisp. (Hispanics); Nat. (Alaskan & American Indian). Asterisk (*) zeros are for figures less than 0.5 percent.

outside the school district. Poor and middle-class parents find it hard, if not impossible, to duplicate the efforts of the richer towns.

Shop for Bargains

This dumps the burden on financially struggling families who have high educational ambitions for their children. Shop for bargains: reading classes in the summer, local tutors who might work with small groups, day schools that have afternoon programs. Perhaps a private school.

The editors, as a matter of policy, do not endorse private schools over public or vice versa, but private schools, having more flexibility than public institutions, clearly have a place in the educational picture.

Choosing the Right School

Almost all public schools have attendance zones, usually the immediate neighborhood. The school comes with the neighborhood; often you have no choice. If you don't know your school, call the school district office.

Many parents mix private day care with public education. The day care center takes the kid to the public school in the morning and picks him up in the afternoon. Many public schools, in recent years, have installed day care.

If you don't like your neighborhood school, you can request a transfer to another school in the district or to a school outside the district. But the school won't provide transportation.

Transfers to schools inside the district are easier to get than transfers outside the district. For every student enrolled, the state allots a district a certain amount of money. When a student transfers out, the allotment goes with him or her.

A recent law supposedly makes it easier for parents to get a transfer to towns where they work. If your child has a special problem that may demand your attention — say a medical condition — speak to the school administrators about a transfer to a school close to your job.

The Low-Scoring School

Should you place your child in a low-scoring school? The argument against the very low-scoring schools is not that they have incompetent teachers or rundown facilities. Often the teachers are quite dedicated and the buildings funded as well as any public school. Rather, the teacher may be forced to move at a pace well below your child's capability.

In a class of 30 where 22 score low, 5 in the middle and 3 high, the teacher would be derelict if she didn't pace the class to the low end. Educators often scorn the idea that students influence one another academically but when trying to get pupils to shun sex and drugs schools sing the praises of peer influence. To state the obvious, a child at a low-scoring school meets children who are not bothered by low grades. What effect this has? Who knows?

Does Ability Grouping Work?

This is a minefield of conflicting studies. Nothing would seem more logical than to give a child special attention when he or she falters in class. And some children clearly do benefit. But, critics argue, singling a child out for this attention often implants the idea that he is inferior, that he can't do the work without special help. Also, the teacher may lower her expectations for the pullout group, may move them at a pace slower than they are capable of.

This argument frequently emerges in language programs. Special instruction proponents contend kids learn faster when they are taught both in their native languages and in English. Immersion proponents argue kids would learn English faster and do better all around if they dived into a pool of English only.

If your child is pulled out for remedial education, don't assume that the problem is solved. The kid may need extra help at home.

Gifted Programs

The labeling accusation, in different form, surfaces when schools implement gifted programs for very young children. By labeling one group extra smart, the rest of the children may conclude they are dumb, the argument runs. Where the gifted are clustered in their own classes (magnet programs), the fault is supposedly accentuated. On the other side, parents of these children argue that they should be allowed to learn as fast as they can.

Speaking of gifted kids, here's how the Gifted and Talented Education (GATE) program usually works. About the third grade, usually at the teacher's

---

MORE FALLOUT FROM CHERNOBYL

The Russian city of Vetka was up for consideration as a sister city to Petaluma. It turned out, however, that Vetka is located near Chernobyl and was on the list for evacuation. Thumbs down.

One councilmember favored a city "more our size and not irradiated."

Sonoma County Ethnic Enrollments by School District

District	White	Black	Asn/PI	Filipino	Hisp.	Nat.
Alexander Valley Elem.	69	0	3	0	26	2
Analy Union High	88	1	2	*0	8	1
Bellevue Union Elem.	63	6	3	1	27	2
Bennett Valley Elem.	94	1	3	*0	2	*0
Cinnabar Elem.	96	1	2	0	2	0
Cloverdale Unified	83	1	1	0	16	*0
Cotati-Rohnert Park	82	3	4	1	8	1
Dunham Elem.	87	2	1	0	10	0
Forestville Union Elem.	90	1	2	*0	6	1
Fort Ross Elem.	97	0	2	0	1	0
Geyserville Unified	60	0	1	0	35	5
Gravenstein Elem.	87	2	2	0	9	*0
Guerneville Elem.	89	2	0	0	9	0
Harmony Union Elem.	93	1	1	0	6	0
Healdsburg Elem.	76	*0	1	0	23	*0
Healdsburg Union High	69	1	1	0	27	2
Horicon Elem.	78	0	2	0	18	2
Kenwood Elem.	93	0	2	2	3	1
Liberty Elem.	87	0	1	0	12	0
Mark West Union Elem.	90	*0	2	0	6	2
Monte Rio Elem.	99	1	0	0	0	0
Montgomery Elem.	100	0	0	0	0	0
Oak Grove Elem.	80	1	1	0	18	*0
Old Adobe Union Elem.	87	2	3	*0	8	*0
Petaluma City Elem.	89	1	2	*0	8	*0
Petaluma Joint High	86	2	3	*0	9	1
Piner-Olivet Elem.	91	1	2	1	5	*0
Rincon Valley Elem.	91	2	3	*0	4	*0
Roseland Elem.	57	6	8	*0	22	7
Santa Rosa Elem.	69	4	8	*0	16	3
Santa Rosa High	80	3	5	*0	10	2
Sebastopol Elem.	93	*0	1	0	5	3
Sonoma Valley Unified	87	1	2	*0	10	*0
Twin Hills Elem.	89	1	2	0	8	1
Two Rock Elem.	74	3	2	3	18	0
Waugh Elem.	73	0	2	2	23	0
West Side Elem.	79	0	1	0	20	0
Wilmar Elem.	81	1	1	0	18	0
Windsor Elem.	64	1	1	*0	32	3
Wright Elem.	74	5	5	1	13	2

Source: California Dept. of Education, 1990. Figures are percentages, rounded to the nearest whole number. Total may exceed or be less than 100 percent. **Key**: Asn/PI (Asian and Pacific Islander); Hisp. (Hispanics); Nat. (Alaskan & American Indian). Asterisk (*) zeros are for figures less than 0.5 percent.

recommendation, the advanced children are given an I.Q. or achievement test. Those who score about I.Q. 132 or in the top 2 percent will be admitted to the program. This generally means they spend about three hours a week on special projects or in activities with other gifted children.

The schools are also supposed to pull out kids with artistic talents but many schools lack art programs. If you think your child is gifted and the teacher hasn't given him the nod, ask to have him tested.

Tips for Parents: Tap Into the School's Gossip

Schools never release evaluations of teachers, but parents informally work out their own rankings. Join the PTA. Get to know other parents.

Although teachers are rarely dismissed, it doesn't follow that many deserve to be fired. Don't approach the schools with a chip on your shoulder. They will resent you. Schools, like private businesses, have their lackluster people but most teachers are diligent and greater efforts are being made to improve teacher quality.

If your kid gets an incompetent, request a transfer to another class. For that matter, ask for a particular teacher before the teaching assignments are made. In Sonoma County, often, there are no alternate choices. Many small districts run one class per grade level.

Don't Trust the Official Rhetoric

School officials cannot say anything public against individual teachers. To do so would violate the union contract and expose the district to a lawsuit for slander. Even when teachers are dismissed or dropped before they reach tenure, the school district will not say anything. When asked, most administrators will say teachers are "wonderful," "underpaid" and "the salt of the earth." If the teacher is screwing up, get the principal behind a closed door and tell her.

"My school — my district — is the best." All administrators say this in one form or another. Rules of the game. More attendance means more money, less chance of layoffs, cutbacks. Everything is "great."

Take a school with low scores that has just cut its teaching day and reduced

---

WHY EVIL EMPIRE COLLAPSED

Forget Gorby. Forget an economic system conceived by idiots. The Soviet Union collapsed because for 25 years Carmelite nuns at a monastery in Marinwood prayed for its demise.

To be precise, when they made a brief appearance in public in 1991 they gave the credit to Himself, and indirectly to Mother Miriam. She founded the community in 1969 and died in December 1990.

"She went off to God and since then things in the Soviet Union have been falling apart," said one nun.

its electives. You walk in the door with your kid and ask, how good is this school? You're going to get a positive answer. That principal is going to find something nice to say, is not going to knock the school.

When you go to buy something at Macy's, the clerk doesn't say, "Stop. Emporium is having a sale today." He sells his products. The same with principals; they sell their schools.

Schools frequently proclaim they and teachers welcome parental comments and help. Up to a point, this is true. If you make sure your kids do their homework, teachers will love you.

But in the experience of the editor, many teachers dislike dealing with parents. Teachers are not trained for it. They generally don't have the time or background to deal with problems outside the class. They don't see themselves as social workers, except in rare cases, say child abuse.

Know When to Back Off

Half a loaf. You've been a perfect parent, read to the kid every night since he was in the cradle and attended every school function. But the ingrate has always hated school, will read only at gunpoint and you're crying into your pillow and kissing off Stanford.

What next? Here is some advice from a school administrator who had a difficult son. The guy said he backed off, determined the requirements for a California State University and worked to convince his kid to take the right classes and keep his grades reasonably good — B's with some A's — with the goal of getting the boy into a Cal State campus.

California State University takes the top third of high school seniors. The University of California takes the top 13 percent, although some UC campuses are tougher than others. UC Berkeley is probably the toughest.

If your son or daughter balks at taking prep classes or is not smart enough to handle the load, mix prep with general education and aim at preparing him for community college. At the end of two years, many community college students transfer to California State University or a UC campus.

Know When to Get Outside Help

If your child falls behind and is put in a remedial class, it often doesn't mean the school will bring him up to grade level. It may mean that the teacher will try to keep him from falling further behind.

A Little Effort Helps

Make the open houses and conferences. Teachers are human beings: if you take an interest in what they are doing, they are more likely to take an interest in your child. One study indicated that when parents attend open houses, their children are much more likely to take an interest in school. If you can't visit the school during the day, have the teacher phone you that evening.

When Not to Shut Up

Complain. Your son's teacher has been sick for three weeks and the school keeps changing substitutes. Schools have their priorities. You have yours. Sometimes they may clash. If you can't get satisfaction from the teacher or the principal, try the superintendent or the school board.

Kindergarten

To get into kindergarten a child must be 4 years, 9 months by September.

11/Private Schools & Colleges

Pros, Cons, Advice, Directory of Schools

PRIVATE SCHOOLS make a tacit promise for which they should always be held to account. They promise to deliver the goods on academics.

There are other considerations, foremost religious instruction, in deciding whether to enroll your child in a private school. But a quality education should always be expected. By their nature, private schools enjoy certain advantages over many public schools.

The Advantages

Public schools must accept all students, have little power to dismiss incompetent teachers and are at the mercy of their neighborhoods for the quality of students — the socioeconomic correlation. Disruptive students are frequently suspended from public schools but rarely expelled, a problem in some districts.

Much has been said about the ability of private schools to rid themselves of problem children and screen them out in the first place. But tuition probably does more than anything else to assure private schools quality students.

Parents who pay extra for their child's education and often agree to work closely with the school are, usually, demanding parents. The result: fewer discipline problems, fewer distractions in class, more of a willingness to learn.

When you place your child in a good private school, you are, to an extent, buying him or her scholastic classmates. They may not be the smartest — many private schools accept children of varying ability — but generally they will have someone at home breathing down their necks to succeed in academics.

The same attitude, a reflection of family values, is found in the high-achieving public schools. When a child in one of these schools or a private school turns to his left and right, he will see and later talk to children who read books and newspapers. A child in a low-achieving school, public or private, will talk to classmates who watch a lot of television and rarely read.

(These are, necessarily, broad generalizations. Much depends on whom the children pick for friends. High-achieving students certainly watch television but, studies show, much less than low-achieving students. Many critics contend that even high-scoring schools are graduating students that need bonehead English when they reach college.)

The Quality of Teaching

Do private schools have better teachers than public schools? Impossible to tell. Both sectors sing the praises of their teachers.

Private schools have much more freedom to dismiss teachers but this can be abused. The private schools themselves advise parents to avoid schools with excessive teacher turnover. Public schools generally pay teachers more than private schools. In recent years public schools, by tighter hiring procedures, supposedly have weeded out more incompetents.

Private schools claim to attract people fed up with the limitations of public schools, particularly restrictions on disciplining and ejecting the unruly. Some proponents argue private schools attract teachers "who really want to teach."

Religion and Private Schools

Private schools talk about religion and many teach a specific creed. Because of controversy, religion as an influence or a topic of discussion has just about disappeared from public schools. Moses, Joseph, David and Goliath, Samson and Delilah, Peter and Paul, Jesus, Muhammad — these names are rarely heard in public schools (although new texts are paying more attention to religion).

Many religious schools, Catholic and Protestant, accept students of different religions or no religion. Some schools offer these students broad courses in religion — less dogma. Ask about the program.

Money

Private school parents pay taxes for public schools and they pay tuition. Public school parents pay taxes but not tuition. Big difference.

Ethnic Diversity

Many private schools are integrated and the great majority of private school principals — the editor knows no exceptions — welcome minorities. Some principals fret over tuition, believing that it keeps many poor students out of private schools. Money, the lack of it, weighs heavily on private schools. Scholarships, however, are awarded, adjustments made, family rates offered. Never hurts to ask.

UCs Chosen by Private School Graduates
Marin County

High School	Berk.	Davis	Irvine	UCLA	River.	SD	SB	SC	Total
Bransn-Mt. Tam.	2	3	1	2	0	2	2	4	16
Marin Acad.	1	1	2	1	0	3	1	8	17
North Bay	0	1	0	0	0	0	0	0	1
Marin Catholic	5	13	1	2	0	2	5	2	30
San Dominico	2	1	0	3	0	1	0	0	7

Napa County

High School	Berk.	Davis	Irvine	UCLA	River.	SD	SB	SC	Total
Justin-Siena	1	11	0	1	0	1	8	1	23

Sonoma County

High School	Berk.	Davis	Irvine	UCLA	River.	SD	SB	SC	Total
Card. Newman	2	1	0	1	0	1	3	1	9
Rio Lindo Adv.	0	1	0	0	0	0	0	0	1
Ursuline	0	5	0	1	0	2	4	2	15

Source: Callifornia Department of Education, fall, 1990. The chart shows which UC a 1990 graduate selected for freshman enrollment. **Key**: Berk. (Berkeley); River. (Riverside); SD (San Diego); SB (Santa Barbara); SC (Santa Cruz).

Class Size

Public schools often run 25 to 30 per teacher. Many private schools run the same or higher. Catholic elementary schools in many parts of the Bay Area put more than 30 students in a class. Catholic schools, nonetheless, are the most popular, a reflection in part of the high number of Catholics in the Bay Area.

Many private "schools" are one-family affairs, mom and pop — one usually a teacher and damned if she'll put her kids through public schools — at home. A support network that supplies books and materials has grown up for these people.

Some regular private schools have low teacher-pupil ratios, fewer than 15 students per teacher.

Variety

Private schools come in great variety, Christian, Jewish, Montessori, Carden, Waldorf, prep schools, schools that emphasize language or music, boarding and day schools, schools that allow informal dress, schools with dress codes, boys' schools, girls' schools.

Choosing a Private School

1. Inspect the grounds, the school's buildings, ask plenty of questions. "I would make myself a real pest," advised one private school official. If possible,

sit in on a class. Good schools welcome this kind of attention.

2. Choose a school with a philosophy congenial to your own, and your child's. Carden schools emphasize structure. Montessori schools, while somewhat structured, encourage individual initiative and independence.

Ask whether the school is accredited. Private schools are free to run almost any program they like, to set any standards they like, which sounds nice but in some aspects hurts the schools. A few bad ones spoil the reputation of the good ones. To remedy this an increasing number of private schools are submitting to inspections by independent agencies such as the Western Association of Schools and Colleges and the California Association of Independent Schools. These agencies try to make sure that schools meet their own goals.

To save money some good schools do not seek accreditation.

3. Have all details about tuition carefully explained. How is it to be paid? Are there extra fees? Book costs? Is there a refund if the student is withdrawn or dropped from the school?

4. Progress reports. Parent conferences. How often are they scheduled?

5. What are the entrance requirements? When must they be met? Although many schools use entrance tests, often they are employed to place the child in an academic program, not exclude him from the school.

6. For prep schools, what percentage of the students go on to college and to what colleges?

7. How are discipline problems handled?

8. What are the teacher qualifications? What is the teacher turnover rate?

9. How sound financially is the school? How long has it been in existence? There is nothing wrong per se with new schools. But you want a school that has the wherewithal to do the job.

10. Don't choose in haste but don't wait until the last minute. Some schools fill quickly, some fill certain classes quickly.

Lastly, don't assume that because your child attends a private school you can expect everything will go all right, that neither school nor student needs attention. The quality of private schools in California varies. The prudent parent will keep a watchful eye, and good schools will welcome your interest.

Adult Schools

Although rarely in the headlines, adult schools serve thousands of Marin, Napa and Sonoma residents. Upholstery, microwave cooking, ballroom dancing, computers, cardiopulmonary resuscitation, aerobics, how to invest in stocks, art, music, how to raise children — all these and much more are offered.

These schools and programs are run by school districts and by cities. Many schools also run adult sports programs. Call for a catalog.

Getting the Older Students

As the public's needs have changed, so have the colleges. The traditional college audience — high school seniors — is still thriving but increasingly colleges are attracting older students and working people. Many colleges offer evening and weekend programs, especially in business degrees and business-related subjects. Some programs — an MBA — can take years, some classes only a day. Here is a partial list of local colleges and specialty schools. As with any venture, the student should investigate before enrolling or paying a fee.

Community Colleges

Cheap. $60 a semester, the maximum. Many students attend these two-year public colleges then transfer as juniors to state universities or University of California schools, or other colleges.

Day and evening sessions. Many classes, academic and vocational. No entrance requirement for degree programs but many students drop out along the way. Special classes to ease women and minorities into college life. Many students take one or two classes a year, usually vocational, as needed.

Associate degrees, certificates, training for licenses (reg. nurse, medical technician, real estate, many others.) Sports, activities. Pretty campuses but many students take the classes and run. Commuter colleges. Phone for more info and catalogs or visit campuses.

• College of Marin, College Avenue, Kentfield. (415) 457-8811.

• Indian Valley College, 1800 Ignacio Blvd., Novato. (415) 883-2211.

• Napa Valley College, Napa-Vallejo Highway, Napa. (800) 826-1077. Also has a small campus at north end of valley.

• Santa Rosa City College, 1501 Mendocino Ave. Santa Rosa. (707) 527-4431. Also run by Santa Rosa City College: a facility in Petaluma.

Other Colleges and Schools

• University of California, Berkeley. Bachelors, masters, doctorates. High admission standards. Sports, many activities. (510) 642-6000. Also, popular extension program, all sorts of classes, many vocational, for the general public. Many offered in San Francisco. Phone (510) 642-4111. Ask for catalog.

• California State University, Sonoma, Rohnert Park. Bachelor's, master's degrees. Day, evening classes. The UC schools take the top 13 percent of high school seniors, the Cal States, the top third. The UCs award doctorates, the Cal State schools stop at the master's level. Open university and extension programs allow students to take classes without pursuing degree. Phone (707) 664-2880.

• Dominican College, 1520 Grand Ave., San Rafael. Private liberal arts college. (415) 456-4440.

• Pacific Union College, located in Angwin. Private liberal arts college. (707) 965-6311.

• San Francisco Theological Seminary, 2 Kensington Road, San Anselmo. (415) 258-6500.

Directory of Private Schools

Directory information was provided by schools responding to questionnaires and phone surveys. Many schools offer family rates. Religious schools sometimes charge higher for non-members.

Marin County
Corte Madera

Allaire School, 50 El Camino Drive, Corte Madera, 94925. Phone: (415) 927-2640. Enroll: Call School, First-8th Special Ed. Fee: Call School.

Bright Beginnings, 330 Golden Hind Passage, Corte Madera, 94925. Phone: (415) 924-1677. Enroll: 135, Pre-1st. Fee: $290-$670/mo.

Lycee Francais International, 50 El Camino Drive, Corte Madera, 94925. Phone: (415) 924-1737. Enroll: 105, Pre-5th. Fee: $5,200-$6,200/yr.

Marin Country Day Elementary, 5221 Paradise Drive, Corte Madera, 94925. Phone: (415) 924-3743. Enroll: 450, K-8th. Fee: $6,650-$8,110/yr.

Marin Horizon School, 330 Golden Hind Passage, Corte Madera, 94925. Phone: (415) 924-4202. Enroll: 230, Pre-8th. Fee: $3,800-$6,000/yr.

Marin Montessori School, 5200 Paradise Dr., Corte Madera, 94925. Phone: (415) 924-5388. Enroll: 135, Pre-6th. Fee: Varies, call school.

Real School-Academics & Arts of Marin, 50 El Camino Drive, Corte Madera, 94925. Phone: (415) 927-0249. Enroll: Call school, K-8th. Fee: $4,900/yr.

Tam Creek, 50 El Camino Drive, Corte Madera, 94925. Phone: (415) 927-3336. Enroll: 35, K-3rd. Fee: $3,650-$4,450/yr.

Fairfax

Cascade Canyon School, 2626 Sir Francis Drake Blvd. P.O. Box 879, Fairfax, 94930. Phone: (415) 459-3464. Enroll: 30, K-8th. Fee: $4,000-$5,000/yr.

Saint Rita Elementary, 102 Marinda Drive, Fairfax, 94930. Phone: (415) 456-1003. Enroll: 210, K-8th. Fee: $170/mo, Catholic.

Kentfield

Marin Catholic High, 675 Sir Francis Drake Blvd., Kentfield, 94904. Phone: (415) 461-8844. Enroll: 560, Ninth-12th. Fee: $4,700/yr, Catholic.

Larkspur

Marin Primary, 20 Magnolia Ave., Larkspur, 94939. Phone: (415) 924-2608. Enroll: 235, Pre-6th . Fee: $525/mo.

Saint Patrick's Elementary, 120 King St., Larkspur, 94939. Phone: (415) 924-0501. Enroll: 260, K-8th. Fee: Call school.

Mill Valley

Albright School, 1046 Redwood Hwy, Mill Valley, 94941. Phone: (415) 383-1200. Enroll: 34-40, Pre & K. Fee: $530/mo., $450 for returning Kinder.

Mount Tamalpais School, 100 Harvard Ave., Mill Valley, 94941. Phone: (415) 383-9434. Enroll: 240, K-8th. Fee: $5,950-6,775/yr.

North Bay Marin School, 70 Lomita Drive, Mill Valley, 94941. Phone: (415) 381-3003. Enroll: 85, Sixth-12th. Fee: $5,800-6,300/yr.

Wende Kumara Day School, 540 Marin Ave., Mill Valley, 94941. Phone: (415) 388-5437. Enroll: 35-40, Pre-1st. Fee: Call school.

Novato

Christian Life School, 1370 S. Novato Blvd., Novato, 94947. Phone: (415) 892-5713. Enroll: 300, Pre-9th. Fee: $1,600-$1,900/yr, Assemblies of God.

Good Shepherd Lutheran School, 1180 Lynwood Drive, Novato, 94947. Phone: (415) 897-2510. Enroll: 226, Pre-3rd. Fee: $80-225/mo., Christian.

Kaleidoscope School, 710 Wilson Ave., Novato, 94948-0162. Phone: (415) 897-8761. Enroll: 36, Pre-1st. Fee: Call school.

Kids Korner, 799 Plaza Linda, Novato, 94947. Phone: (415) 897-0723. Enroll: 52, Pre & After School Care. Fee: $100-$385/mo.

Miss Sandie's School, 2001 Center Road, Novato, 94947. Phone: (415) 892-2712. Enroll: 200, Pre. Fee: Call school.

Montessori School of Novato, 1915 Novato Blvd., Novato, 94948-1921. Phone: (415) 892-2228. Enroll: 40, Pre & K. Fee: Varies, call school.

Novato Seventh-day Adventist School, 495 San Marin Drive, Novato, 94945. Phone: (415) 892-9166. Enroll: 16, First-8th. Fee: Call school, Seventh-day Adventist.

Our Lady of Loretto, 1811 Virginia Ave., Novato, 94945. Phone: (415) 892-8621. Enroll: 320, First-8th. Fee: Call school, Catholic.

Robin's Nest, 1990 Novato Blvd., Novato, 94947. Phone: (415) 897-1990. Enroll: 32 max, Pre-3rd. Fee: $435/mo. full-time.

Ross

Branson School, P.O. Box 887, Ross, 94957. Phone: (415) 454-3612. Enroll: 320, Ninth-12th. Fee: Call school.

San Anselmo

Child Center, 100 Shaw Drive, San Anselmo, 94960. Phone: (415) 456-0440. Enroll: 24, Third-12th Special and General Ed. Fee: $756/mo.

Saint Anselm Elementary, 40 Belle Ave., San Anselmo, 94960-2892. Phone: (415) 454-8667. Enroll: 210, K-8th. Fee: $2,200/yr, Catholic.

San Anselmo Montessori School, 100 Shaw Drive, Box 707, San Anselmo, 94960. Phone: (415) 457-3428. Enroll: 36, Pre & K. Fee: $225-437/mo.

San Domenico Lower Elementary, 1500 Butterfield Road, San Anselmo, 94960. Phone: (415) 454-0200. Enroll: 290, Pre-8th. Fee: $2,200-$3,400/yr. Pre & Kinder, $5,600/yr. 1st-8th, Catholic.

San Domenico School, 1500 Butterfield Road, San Anselmo, 94960. Phone: (415) 454-0200. Enroll: 460, PreK-12th. Fee: $2,300/yr.- $8,900 depending on grade level; $17,200/yr for boarding 9-12th students, Catholic.

Spectrum Center, 1327 Sir Francis Drake Blvd., San Anselmo, 94960. Phone: (415) 457-7646. Enroll: 14, Ungraded Special Ed. Fee: School referral.

Sunny Hills School, 300 Sunny Hills Drive,

San Anselmo, 94960. Phone: (415) 457-3200. Enroll: 40, Seventh-12th Special Ed. Fee: $115/day.

San Rafael

Brandeis-Hillel Day School, 180 N. San Pedro Road, San Rafael, 94903. Phone: (415) 472-1833. Enroll: 122, K-8th. Fee: $5,230-$5,950/yr, Jewish.

Christ Church School, 1055 Las Ovejas Ave., San Rafael, 94903. Phone: (415) 479-4900. Enroll: 110, K-8th. Fee: $125-$200/mo, Nondenominational.

Daystar Christian School, 1675 Grand Ave., San Rafael, 94901. Phone: (415) 453-0422. Enroll: 45, Pre & K. Fee: Call School, Assembly of God.

Ice Cream and Shoe, 1055 Las Ovejas, San Rafael, 94903. Phone: (415) 492-0550. Enroll: 15, Pre-K. Fee: $435/mo.

Leebil Learning Center, 1411 Lincoln Ave., San Rafael, 94901. Phone: (415) 454-6618. Enroll: 15 max, Sixth-12th Special Ed. Fee: $33/day or $5,900/yr.

Marin Academic Center, 755 Idylberry Road, San Rafael, 94903. Phone: (415) 472-7620. Enroll: Call school, Ungraded, ages 4-11. Fee: Referrals by court.

Marin Academy, 1600 Mission Ave., San Rafael, 94901. Phone: (415) 453-4550. Enroll: 280, Ninth-12th. Fee: $10,000/yr.

Marin Formative School, 2000 Las Gallinas, San Rafael, 94903. Phone: (415) 479-4140. Enroll: 110, Pre & K. Fee: Varies, call school.

Marin Waldorf School, 755 Idylberry Road, San Rafael, 94903. Phone: (415) 479-8190. Enroll: 172, Pre-8th. Fee: $4,700-$5,550/yr.

Montessori De Terra Linda, 1055 Las Ovejas , San Rafael, 94903. Phone: (415) 479-7373. Enroll: 115, Pre-7th. Fee: $3,100-$5,200/yr.

Saint Isabella's Parochial Elementary, 1 Trinity Way, San Rafael, 94903. Phone: (415) 479-3727. Enroll: 221, First-8th. Fee: $1,950-$3,950/yr.

Saint Mark's Elementary, 39 Trellis Dr., San Rafael, 94903. Phone: (415) 472-7911. Enroll: 310, K-8th. Fee: $5,200-$6,200/yr, Nondenominational.

Saint Raphael's Elementary, 1100 Fifth Ave., San Rafael, 94901. Phone: (415) 454-4455. Enroll: 225, K-8th. Fee: $1,800-$2,000/yr, Catholic.

San Rafael PreSch & Child Care Center, 121 Knight Dr., San Rafael, 94901. Phone: (415) 457-9500. Enroll: 45, PreK. Fee: Call school.

Timothy Murphy School, PO Box M, San Rafael, 94913. Phone: (415) 499-7616. Enroll: 50, K-8th Special Ed. Fee: $122/day.

Sausalito

Sparrow Creek Montessori School, 304 Caledonia St., Sausalito, 94965. Phone: (415) 332-9595. Enroll: Call school, Pre & K. Fee: Call School.

Tiburon

Children's Circle Center, 215-A Blackfield Drive, Tiburon, 94920. Phone: (415) 381-8181. Enroll: 100, Pre-5th. Fee: Varies, call school.

Saint Hilary School, 765 Hilary Drive, Tiburon, 94920. Phone: (415) 435-2224. Enroll: 200, K-8th. Fee: $2,700/yr. , Catholic.

Woodacre

West Marin Montessori School, No. 1 Garden Way, Woodacre, 94973. Phone: (415) 488-4500. Enroll: 24, Pre-K. Fee: Call School.

Napa County
American Canyon

Noah's Ark Christian School & Day Care, 2 Andrew Road, American Canyon, 94589. Phone (707) 644-6465. Enroll: 75, Ages 2.5 to 12 yrs. Fee: Call School.

Angwin

Pacific Union College Elementary School, 135 Neilsen Court, Angwin, 94508. Phone (707) 965-2459. Enroll: 150, K-8th. Fee: Call School.

Napa

Casa Montessori School, 7800 Lincoln Ave., Napa, 94558. Phone (707) 224-1944. Enroll: 73, Pre-6th. Fee: Call School.

Hopper Creek Montessori, 2141 2nd St., Napa, 94558. Phone (707) 252-8775. Enroll: 35, Pre-K. Fee: Call School.

Justin-Siena High School, 4026 Maher St., Napa, 94558. Phone (707) 255-0950. Enroll: 400, 9th-12th. Fee: $3,500/yr.

Kolbe Academy, 1600 F St., Napa, 94559. Phone (707) 255-6412. Enroll: 45, First-12th. Fee: $140-$155/mo.

Lutheran School St. John's-Missouri Synod, 3521 Linda Vista Ave., Napa, 94558. Phone (707) 226-7970. Enroll: 250, Pre-8th. Fee: Call School.

Montecito Alternative School, 1078 East Ave., Napa, 94558. Phone (707) 255-3000. Enroll: Call school, NA. Fee: Call School.

Napa Adventist Junior Academy, 2201 Pine St., Napa, 94559. Phone (707) 255-5233. Enroll: 196, K-10th. Fee: Call School.

New Horizons, 3734 Norfolk St., Napa, 94558. Phone (707) 255-5066. Enroll: 30, 2-12 yrs. Fee: Call School.

St. John The Baptist Catholic School, 983 Napa St., Napa, 94559. Phone (707) 224-8388. Enroll: 295, K-8th. Fee: Call School.

Sunrise Montessori of Napa Valley, 4149 Linda Vista Ave., Napa, 94558. Phone (707) 253-1105. Enroll: 35, Pre & K. Fee: Call School.

Sunrise Montessori of Napa Valley, 1000 Soda Canyon Road, Napa, 94558. Phone (707) 257-2392. Enroll: 60, Pre-3rd. Fee: Call School.

Young World of Learning, 2243 Redwood Road, Napa, 94559. Phone (707) 252-9330. Enroll: NA, NA. Fee: NA.

St. Helena

Montessori Family Center, 960 Dowdell Lane, St. Helena, 94574. Phone (707) 963-1614. Enroll: 36, Pre & K. Fee: Call School.

St. Helena Catholic School, 1255 Oak AVe., St. Helena, 94574. Phone (707) 963-4677. Enroll: 127, K-8th. Fee: Call School.

St. Helena Montessori School, 1328 Spring St., St. Helena, 94574. Phone (707) 963-1527. Enroll: 50-60, Pre-6th. Fee: $200/mo. Pre & K; $340/mo. K-6.

Sonoma County
Cazadero

Cazadero Academy, 20775 Fort Ross Road/ PO Box 410, Cazadero, 95421. Phone: (707) 847-3642 or 632-5127. Enroll: 13, Eighth-12th. Fee: $100/mo.

Cloverdale

Cloverdale Seventh-day Adventist School, 1085 S. Cloverdale Blvd., Cloverdale, 95425. Phone: (707) 894-5703. Enroll: 19, K-8th. Fee: $1,480/yr, Seventh-day Adventist.

Cotati

Rancho Bodega School, 8297 Old Redwood Hwy., Cotati, 94931. Phone: (707) 795-7166. Enroll: 37, First-12th. Fee: $250/mo.

Graton

Manzanita Bilingual School, 432 Brush St. South, Graton, 95444. Phone: (707) 823-5657. Enroll: 29, K-5th. Fee: $315/mo.

Pacific Christian Academy, 8877 Donald St., Graton, 95444. Phone: (707) 823-2880. Enroll: 74, Pre-12th. Fee: $150/mo, Church of Christ.

Healdsburg

Rio Lindo Adventist Academy, 3200 Rio Lindo Ave., Healdsburg, 95448. Phone: (707) 431-5100. Enroll: 210, Ninth-12th. Fee: $735/mo. tuition for church members, room & board, Seventh-day Adventist.

St. John's Elementary, 217 Fitch St., Healdsburg, 95448. Phone: (707) 433-2758. Enroll: 250, PreK-8th. Fee: $1,900/yr., Catholic.

Occidental

Russian River Christian Academy, 6250 Bohemian Hwy., Occidental, 95465. Phone: (707) 874-2381. Enroll: 33, K-12th. Fee: $99/mo., Interdenominational.

Petaluma

Calvary Life Christian School, 222 Bassett St., Petaluma, 94952. Phone: (707) 763-7604. Enroll:46, K-12th. Fee: Call school, United Pentecostal.

Happy Day Presbyterian School, 939 B St., Petaluma, 94953. Phone: (707) 762-8671. Enroll: 163, Pre & K. Fee: $84-$180/mo, Ecumenical Protestant.

Learning to Learn, 391 Maria, Petaluma, 94952. Phone: (707) 762-8570. Enroll: 100, Pre-1st. Fee: Call School.

Montessori Schools of Petaluma, 211 Springhill Road, Petaluma, 94952. Phone: (707) 763-9222. Enroll: 48, First-6th. Fee: $150-425/mo.

Montessori Schools of Petaluma, 825 Middlefield Drive, Petaluma, 94952. Phone: (707) 763-9222. Enroll: 85, Pre & K. Fee: $150-425/mo.

Petaluma Christian Academy, 705 N. Webster St., Petaluma, 94952. Phone: (707) 762-3931. Enroll: 79, K-6th. Fee: $1,606/yr. member, $1720/yr. non-member, Baptist.

Petaluma Valley Day School, P.O. Box 750549, Petaluma, 94975-0549. Phone: (707) 778-0164. Enroll: 150, K-6th. Fee: $3,200 yr. or $335/mo, Nonsectarian.

St. Vincent de Paul High School, Keokuk at Magnolia, Petaluma, 94952-0517. Phone: (707) 763-1032. Enroll: 250, Ninth-12th. Fee: $2,850/yr, Catholic.

St. Vincent's Elementary, Union & Howard Streets, Petaluma, 94952. Phone: (707) 762-6426. Enroll: 320, First-8th. Fee: Call school, Catholic.

Rohnert Park

Cross and Crown Lutheran School, 5475 Snyder Lane, Rohnert Park, 94928. Phone: (707) 795-7863. Enroll: 85, K-6th. Fee: $125-157/ yr, Lutheran.

Kinder Care Learning Center, 6150 State Farm Drive, Rohnert Park, 94928. Phone: (707) 584-0124. Enroll: 152, Pre-6th. Fee: Call School.

Learning to Learn, 1300 Medical Center Dr., Rohnert Park, 94928. Phone: (707) 584-4224. Enroll:139, Pre-K. Fee: Call School.

Redwood Country Day School, 1300 Medical Center Drive, Rohnert Park, 94928. Phone: (707) 586-0675. Enroll: 60, K-4th. Fee: $325/mo.

Snyder Lane Christian School, 4689 Snyder Lane, Rohnert Park, 94928. Phone: (707) 584-9759. Enroll: 72, Pre-5th. Fee: $800-$1,750/yr, Southern Baptist.

T's Academy, 187 South West Blvd., Rohnert Park, 94928. Phone: (707) 585-0570. Enroll: 14, Eighth-12th. Fee: Call school.

Santa Rosa

Academy of Sonoma, 180 Wikiup Dr., Santa Rosa, 95403. Phone: (707) 573-9100. Enroll: 60, Pre-6th. Fee: Call School.

Cardinal Newman High, 50 Ursuline Road, Santa Rosa, 95403. Phone: (707) 546-6470. Enroll: 420, Ninth-12th Boys. Fee: $3,550/yr, Catholic.

Center School, 1020 Center Dr., Santa Rosa, 95403. Phone: (707) 538-3967. Enroll: 22, Pre-12th. Fee: Call School.

Covenant Christian School, 1315 Pacific Ave., Santa Rosa, 95404. Phone: (707) 528-8040. Enroll: 102, K-9th . Fee: Varies, call school, Christian.

George C. Page School, 1621 Cleveland Ave., Santa Rosa, 95401. Phone: (707) 528-0721. Enroll: 50, Fourth-9th. Fee: $340/mo.

Higham Family School, 3505 Wallace Road, Santa Rosa, 95404. Phone: (707) 539-3688. Enroll: 26, K-3rd. Fee: $415/mo.

Judy's 4-R School & Tutoring Service, 605 Baker Ave., Santa Rosa, 95407. Phone: (707) 576-1608. Enroll: 21, K-12th. Fee: $200/mo.

Merryhill Country School, 4044 Mayette Ave., Santa Rosa, 95405. Phone: (707) 575-7660. Enroll: 140, Pre-4th. Fee: $416/mo.

Montessori Visions School, 1625 Franklin Ave., Santa Rosa, 95404. Phone: (707) 575-7959. Enroll: 22, K-3rd. Fee: Call school.

New Horizon School & Learning Center, 827 Third St., Santa Rosa, 95404. Phone: (707) 579-3723. Enroll: 35, Second-12th. Fee: Varies, call school.

Open Bible Christian Academy, 920 Link Lane, Santa Rosa, 95401. Phone: (707) 544-0485. Enroll: 40, K-12th. Fee: $135/mo., Pentecostal.

Plumfield School, 1485 S. Wright Road, Santa Rosa, 95407. Phone: (707) 544-1455. Enroll: 24, K-8th Boys. Fee: Call school.

Redwood Junior Academy, 385 Mark West Springs Road, Santa Rosa, 95404. Phone: (707) 545-1697. Enroll: 180, Pre-12th. Fee: $207-400/mo., Seventh-day Adventist.

Santa Rosa Christian School Inc., 950 S. Wright Road, Santa Rosa, 95407. Phone: (707) 542-6414. Enroll: 270, K-8th. Fee: $2,150/yr, Interdenominational.

Sonoma Country Day School, 50 Mark West Springs Road, Santa Rosa, 95403. Phone: (707) 575-7115. Enroll: 168, K-8th. Fee: $5,750/yr.

St. Eugene's Elementary, 300 Farmer's Lane, Santa Rosa, 95405. Phone: (707) 545-7252. Enroll: 320, K-8th. Fee: Call School, Catholic.

St. Luke Lutheran Day Elementary, 905 Mendocino Ave., Santa Rosa, 95401-4880. Phone: (707) 545-0526. Enroll: 121, Pre-8th. Fee: $88-204/mo., Lutheran.

St. Rose Elementary, 4300 Old Redwood Hwy., Santa Rosa, 95403. Phone: (707) 545-0379. Enroll: 360, K-8th. Fee: $2,000/yr., Catholic.

Stuart School, 431 Humboldt St., Santa Rosa, 95404. Phone: (707) 528-0721. Enroll: 75, Pre-3rd. Fee: $340/mo.

Summerfield Waldorf School, 155 Willowside Road, Santa Rosa, 95401. Phone: (707) 575-7194. Enroll: 350, K-12th. Fee: $3,650-4,420/yr.

Ursuline High School, 90 Ursuline Road, Santa Rosa, 95403. Phone: (707) 542-2381. Enroll: 406, Ninth-12th Girls. Fee: $3,695/yr, Catholic.

Woodside Creek School, 2323 Chanate Rd., Santa Rosa, 95404. Phone: (707) 545-0542. Enroll: 72, Pre-K. Fee: $220-374/mo.

Woodside Creek School, 2323 Chanate Road, Santa Rosa, 95404. Phone: (707) 545-0542. Enroll: 72, Pre & K. Fee: $108-$374/mo.

Woodside Towne School, 2810 Summerfield Rd., Santa Rosa, 95405. Phone: (707) 539-1414. Enroll: 62, Pre-K. Fee: $108-$374/mo.

Woodside West Primary School, 2577 Guerneville Road, Santa Rosa, 95401. Phone: (707) 528-6666. Enroll: 34, K-3rd. Fee: $320/mo.

Woodside West School, 2577 Guerneville Rd., Santa Rosa, 95401. Phone: (707) 528-6666. Enroll: 100, Pre-3rd. Fee: $108-$374/mo.

Sebastopol

Full Circle School, 13431 Green Valley Road, Sebastopol, 95473. Phone: (707) 823-9549. Enroll: 21, First-9th Boys. Fee: Call School.

Greenacre Homes Inc., 7590 Atkinson Road, Sebastopol, 95472. Phone: (707) 823-5100. Enroll: 16, First-9th. Fee: $90/day.

Journey High School, 6782-A Sebastopol Road, Sebastopol, 95472. Phone: (707) 829-8881. Enroll: 24, Seventh-12th. Fee: Referrals from public schools.

Nonesuch School, 4004 Bones Road, Sebastopol, 95472. Phone: (707) 823-6603. Enroll: 32, Ungraded. Fee: $350/mo.

Pleasant Hill Christian School, 1782 Pleasant Hill Road, Sebastopol, 95472. Phone: (707) 823-5868. Enroll: 56, K-6th. Fee: $150-$185/mo, Interdenominational.

Sebastopol Christian Home School, 7789 Healdsburg Ave., Sebastopol, 95472. Phone: (707) 823-2754. Enroll: 100, K-9th. Fee: $185-$195/mo, Assembly of God.

Sonoma

Hanna Boys Center, 17000 Arnold Drive, Sonoma, 95476. Phone: (707) 996-6767. Enroll: 84, Fourth-10th Boys. Fee: According to ability to pay, Catholic.

Montessori School of Sonoma Inc., 19675 Eighth St. East, Sonoma, 95476. Phone: (707) 996-2422. Enroll: 120, Pre-3rd. Fee: Call School.

Sonoma Adventist School, 20575 Broadway, Sonoma, 95476-7609. Phone: (707) 996-3805. Enroll: 6, Fifth-8th. Fee: Call school, Seventh-day Adventist.

Sonoma Valley Christian School, 18980 Arnold Drive, Sonoma, 95476. Phone: (707) 996-1853. Enroll: 30, K-6th. Fee: $160/mo, Interdenominational.

St. Francis Solano, 342 W. Napa St., Sonoma, 95476. Phone: (707) 996-4994. Enroll: 320, K-8th. Fee: $1,300/yr., Catholic.

Vintage Country Day School, P.O. Box 1514, Sonoma, 95476. Phone: (707) 996-6560. Enroll: 65, Pre-6th. Fee: $190-$315/mo.

Windsor

First Baptist School, 10285 Starr Road, Windsor, 95492. Phone: (707) 838-6694. Enroll: 80, K-8th. Fee: $1,800/yr, Baptist.

12/Day Care

A List to Start You on Your Search for a Care Center in Marin, Napa or Sonoma

DAY CARE OVER THE LAST 10-20 years has undergone a transformation in the Bay Region. As more mothers entered the work force, the demand for quality care rose and private enterprise moved to fill the need, followed, often begrudgingly, by public schools.

Yes, more can be done, especially in incorporating child care in work places. But compared to the 1970s, day care is much more accessible now and probably better managed. Community colleges train people who work in and run care centers. Because of well-publicized abuses in the past, many parents are more aware that day-care providers should be chosen carefully.

What Day-Care Directory Contains

Here is a list of day-care providers that serve the local towns. It is not an exhaustive list. The state licenses day-care providers according to the number of children served: over 12 children or under 12.

The following list, drawn from state sources and phone books, confines itself generally to the centers with 12 or more students.

This is not an endorsement list. McCormack's Guides does not inspect centers or in any way monitor their activities.

It is a list, as current as we could make it, to start you on your search for a day-care center.

Ask Questions

Ask plenty of questions, tour the facilities, check with other parents about the care of their children. Read a pamphlet or book on day-care centers and what to look for.

Marin County
Belvedere
Belvedere Nursery, Cove Road Pl., Belvedere. Ages: 2-6 yr. Ph: (415) 435-1661.
Bolinas
Bolinas Children's Ctr, 270 Elm Rd, Bolinas. Ages: 2-10 yr. Ph: (415) 868-2550.
Corte Madera
Bright Beginnings, 330 Golden Hind Passage, Corte Madera, 94925. Ages: 0-7 yr. Ph: (415) 924-1677.

Golden Poppy PreSch Ctr, 50 El Camino Dr., Corte Madera, 94925. Ages: 0-6 yr. Ph: (415) 924-2828.

Lycee Francais-Marin, 50 El Camino Dr., Corte Madera, 94925. Ages: 3-5 yr. Ph: (415) 927-1737.

Marin Horizon School, 330 Golden Hinde Passage, Corte Madera, 94925. Ages: 2-6 yr. Ph: (415) 924-4202.

Marin Montessori, 5200 Paradise Dr., Corte Madera, 94925. Ages: 2-0 yr. Ph: (415) 924-5388.

Paradise PreSch & DCCtr, 5461 Paradise Dr., Corte Madera, 94925. Ages: 2-6 yr. Ph: (415) 924-3033.

Sprouts Infant Center, 649 Meadowsweet, Corte Madera, 94925. Ages: 0-5 yr. Ph: (415) 924-7765.

Twin Cities CCC-Neil Cummins, 58 Mohawk Ave., Corte Madera, 94925. Ages: 3-12 yr. Ph: (415) 924-6622.

Twin Cities Co-Op, 56 Mohawk Ave., Corte Madera, 94925. Ages: 2-6 yr. Ph: (415) 924-3150.
Fairfax
Creekside After-School, 150 Oak Manor Dr., Fairfax, 94930. Ages: 5-12 yr. Ph: (415) 453-8140.

Fairfax Tiny Tots, Fairfax Pavillion, Fairfax. Ages: 18 mo.-5 yr. Ph: (415) 456-9779.
Kentfield
College of Marin Children's Ctr, Arcade Building, Kentfield, 94904. Ages: 2-7 yr. Ph: (415) 485-9468.

Kentfield After School Ctr-Bacich, 25 McAllister, Kentfield, 94904. Ages: 4.9-10 yr. Ph: (415) 454-8686.

Ross Valley Nursery, 689 Sir Francis Drake, Kentfield, 94904. Ages: 2.9-5.6 yr. Ph: (415) 461-5150.
Larkspur
Children's Cottage Co-Op, 2900 Larkspur Landing, Larkspur, 94939. Ages: 1-5 yr. Ph: (415) 461-0822.

Marin Primary, 20 Magnolia Ave., Larkspur. Ages: 2.6-10 yr. Ph: (415) 924-2608.

Marin City
Head Start-Marin City, 620 Drake Ave., Marin City, 94965. Ages: 3-5 yr. Ph: (415) 332-3460.

Manzanita Child Dev Ctr, 620 Drake Ave., Marin City, 94965. Ages: 3-14 yr. Ph: (415) 332-3460.

Marin Learning Center, St. Andrews Presbyterian Church, Marin City, 94965. Ages: 2-8 yr. Ph: (415) 332-5309.
Mill Valley
Albright School, 1046 Redwood Highway, Mill Valley, 94941. Ages: 2-6 yr. Ph: (415) 383-1200.

Extended Day Serv-Old Mill Sch, 352 Throckmorton, Mill Valley, 94941. Ages: 5-10 yr. Ph: (415) 383-1308.

Extended Day Serv-Park Sch, 360 E. Blithedale Ave., Mill Valley, 94941. Ages: 5-10 yr. Ph: (415) 388-1458.

Golden Gate Baptist Theo Sem PreSch Ctr, Strawberry Drive, Mill Valley, 94941. Ages: 2-6 yr. Ph: (415) 388-8080.

Homestead Valley CC Ctr-Homestead School, 305 Montford, Mill Valley, 94941. Ages: 4.9-12 yr. Ph: (415) 388-8767.

Kumara Day School, 540 Marin Ave., Mill Valley. Ages: 2-8 yr. Ph: (415) 388-5437.

Marin Day School-Cottage, 322 Throckmorton, Mill Valley, 94941. Ages: 2-5 yr. Ph: (415) 381-4206.

Marin Day School-Mill Valley, 10 Old Mill Rd., Mill Valley, 94941. Ages: 2-5 yr. Ph: (415) 381-3120.

Mill Valley Co-Op, 51 Shell Rd., Mill Valley. Ages: 3-4.11 yr. Ph: (415) 388-9174.

Mountain School, 117 E. Strawberry Dr., Mill Valley. Ages: 2-6 yr. Ph: (415) 388-3888.

Our School-Robin's Nest, 305 Montford Ave., Mill Valley, 94941. Ages: 2-6 yr. Ph: (415) 388-5999.

Ross Acad Montessori, 7 Thomas Dr., Mill Valley. Ages: 2-6 yr. Ph: (415) 383-5777.

Tamalpais PreSch, Camino Alto & Sycamore St., Mill Valley, 94941. Ages: 2-6 yr. Ph: (415) 388-4286.

Wee Care Child Ctr, 8 Olive St., Mill Valley. Ages: 0-4.11yr. Ph: (415) 388-2015.
Novato
All Saints Ctr, 2 San Marin, Novato, 94945. Ages: 4 mo.-12 yr. Ph: (415) 899-4202.

Execu-Tots Learning Ctr, 799 Plaza Linda, Novato, 94947. Ages: 2-10 yr. Ph: (415) 897-0723.

Extended Day Svcs-Lynwood School, 1320 Lynwood Dr., Novato, 94947. Ages: 4.9-10 yr. Ph: (415) 897-2443.

Good Shepherd Lutheran, 1180 Lynwood Dr., Novato, 94947. Ages: 2-5 yr. Ph: (415) 897-2510.

Indian Valley College, 1800 Ignacio Blvd., Novato, 94947. Ages: 2.5-6 yr. Ph: (415) 883-4034.

Kaleidoscope School, 710 Wilson Ave., Novato, 94947. Ages: 3.9-7 yr. Ph: (415) 897-8761.

Lanham Village, 84 Martin Dr., Novato, 94947. Ages: 2-12 yr. Ph: (415) 883-2039.

Marin YMCA-Loma Verde, 399 Alameda De La Loma, Novato, 94949. Ages: 4.9-12 yr. Ph: (415) 883-4681.

Merryhill Country, 1787 Grant Ave., Novato, 94945. Ages: 6 wk-5 yr. Ph: (415) 898-7007.

Miss Sandie's, 2001 Center Rd., Novato. Ages: 14 mo.-12 yr. Ph: (415) 892-2712.

Montessori School of Novato, 1915 Novato Blvd., Novato, 94948. Ages: 18 mo.-6 yr. Ph: (415) 892-2228.

Noah's Ark PreSch, 1370 South Novato Blvd., Novato, 94947. Ages: 2.9-5 yr. Ph: (415) 892-5713.

North Bay Children's Ctr, 405 Norman Dr., Novato, 94949. Ages: 3 mo.- 4 yr. Ph: (415) 883-6222.

Novato Enrichment, 629 Plum St., Novato, 94947. Ages: 4.9-12 yr. Ph: (415) 892-4111.

Novato Enrichment #2, 755 Sutro Ave., Novato, 94947. Ages: 4.9-12 yr. Ph: (415) 897-2711.

Novato Enrichment #3, Dodhe Main Gate Rd., Novato, 94945. Ages: 4.9-12 yr. Ph: (415) 897-2711.

Novato Parents Nursery, 1473 So. Novato Blvd., Novato, 94947. Ages: 2.9-6 yr. Ph: (415) 897-4498.

Novato Parks & Rec Dept, 1800 Center Rd., Novato, 94947. Ages: 5-12 yr. Ph: (415) 897-4323.

Novato State PreSch, 7th St. & Escolta Ave., Novato, 94947. Ages: 3-5 yr. Ph: (415) 883-4313.

Novato Youth Ctr, 680 Wilson Ave., Novato, 94947. Ages: 5.9-12 yr. Ph: (415) 892-1643.

St. Francis PreSch, 967 Fifth St., Novato, 94947. Ages: 2-6 yr. Ph: (415) 892-2597.

TLC PreSch, 288 San Marin Dr., Novato, 94945. Ages: 2-7 yr. Ph: (415) 892-8002.

Point Reyes Station

Papermill Creek, 503 B St., Point Reyes, 94956. Ages: 2-5 yr. Ph: (415) 663-9114.

YWCA After School, Presby. Comm. Church, Hwy 1, Point Reyes, 94956. Ages: 2.9-10 yr. Ph: (415) 663-1349.

San Anselmo

ABC Acad PreSch, 176 Tunstead Ave., San Anselmo, 94960. Ages: 2-6 yr. Ph: (415) 459-7611.

Creekside Afterschool, 116 Butterfield Rd., San Anselmo, 94960. Ages: 4.9-10 yr. Ph: (415) 459-4043.

Day Caring School, 100 Sacramento St., San Anselmo, 94960. Ages: 1-5 yr. Ph: (415) 459-6291.

Robin's Nest of San Anselmo, 100 Shaw Dr., San Anselmo, 94960. Ages: 2-5 yr. Ph: (415) 459-5355.

San Anselmo Afterschool Ctr, 115 Kensington, San Anselmo, 94960. Ages: NA. Ph: (415) 456-4699.

San Anselmo Co-Op, 24 Myrtle Lane, San Anselmo, 94960. Ages: 2.6-5 yr. Ph: (415) 454-5308.

San Anselmo Montessori, 100 Shaw Dr., San Anselmo, 94960. Ages: 2-6 yr. Ph: (415) 457-3428.

San Anselmo Parkside PreSch, 1000 Sir Francis Drake, San Anselmo, 94960. Ages: 3-8 yr. Ph: (415) 453-5329.

San Anselmo PreSch, 121 Ross Ave., San Anselmo, 94960. Ages: 2.6-5 yr. Ph: (415) 453-3181.

San Domenico Program, 1500 Butterfield Rd., San Anselmo, 94960. Ages: 2-6 yr. Ph: (415) 454-0200.

Sleepy Hollow, 1317 Butterfield Rd., San Anselmo, 94960. Ages: 2-6 yr. Ph: (415) 453-1462.

San Geronimo

San Geronimo Valley DCCtr, Sir Francis Drake Blvd., San Geronimo, 94963. Ages: 4.9-9 yr. Ph: (415) 488-9380.

San Geronimo Valley Preschool, Sir Francis Drake Blvd., San Geronimo. Ages: 2.9-6 yr. Ph: (415) 488-9344.

Valley Family PreSch Co-Op, Sir Francis Drake Blvd., San Geronimo, 94963. Ages: 2.9-6 yr. Ph: (415) 488-9344.

San Rafael

ABC Nursery, 138 N. San Pedro Rd., San Rafael, 94903. Ages: 18 mo.- 2 yr. Ph: (415) 479-9432.

Acorns to Oaks-Don Timoteo, 39 Trellis, San Rafael, 94903. Ages: 2- 11 yr. Ph: (415) 492-9669.

Canal CC Ctr, 46 Louise St., San Rafael, 94901. Ages: 2.6-8.5 yr. Ph: (415) 457-1444.

Canal Comm. Alliance, 125 Bahia Way, San Rafael, 94901. Ages: NA. Ph: (415) 454-2640.

Children's House of SR, 159 Merrydale, San Rafael, 94903. Ages: 2-8 yr. Ph: (415) 472-4777.

City of SR-Short School Ctr, 35 Marin St., San Rafael, 94901. Ages: 2-5 yr. Ph: (415) 485-3387.

Daystar Christian School, 1675 Grand Ave., San Rafael, 94901. Ages: 2.5-6 yr. Ph: (415) 453-0422.

Gallinas Village Nursery, 635 Adrian Way, San Rafael, 94903. Ages: 15 mo.-2 yr. Ph: (415) 472-2522.

Gan Israel Nursery, 1150 Idylberry Rd., San Rafael, 94903. Ages: 1-5 yr. Ph: (415) 492-1666.

Head Start-Mission, 215 Mission, San Rafael, 94901. Ages: 3-5 yr. Ph: (415) 456-4050.

Head Start-Short School, 35 Marin St., San Rafael, 94901. Ages: 3-5 yr. Ph: (415) 459-1703.

Ice Cream & Shoe, 1055 Las Ovejas Ave., San Rafael, 94903. Ages: 3-5 yr. Ph: (415) 492-0550.

Junior School, 408 Belle Ave., San Rafael, 94901. Ages: 2-6 yr. Ph: (415) 456-7363.

Learning to Learn, 16 Bayview Dr., San Rafael, 94901. Ages: 2-6 yr. Ph: (415) 457-1850.

Marin Day School-San Rafael, 1123 Court St., San Rafael, 94901. Ages: 2 mo.-5 yr. Ph: (415) 453-9822 or 381-4296.

Marin Formative, 2000 Las Gallinas Ave., San Rafael, 94903. Ages: 2-6 yr. Ph: (415) 479-4140.

Marin Waldorf, 755 Idylberry Dr., San Rafael, 94903. Ages: 3-6 yr. Ph: (415) 479-8190.

Montessori De Terra Linda, 620 Del Ganado Rd., San Rafael, 94901. Ages: 2-6 yr. Ph: (415) 457-0697.

Montessori De Terra Linda #2, 1055 Las Ovejas Ave., San Rafael, 94903. Ages: 2-6 yr. Ph: (415) 479-7373.

Montessori of Central Marin, 317 Auburn, San Rafael, 94901. Ages: 2-6 yr. Ph: (415) 456-1748.

Morning Star PreSch, 50 Los Ranchitos Rd., San Rafael, 94903. Ages: 2-6 yr. Ph: (415) 499-8663.

Oakview School, 70 Skyview Terrace, San Rafael. Ages: 2-9 yr. Ph: (415) 479-6026.

Robin's Nest of Terra Linda, 1 Wellbrock Hts., San Rafael, 94903. Ages: 2-6 yr. Ph: (415) 479-4778.

San Rafael Children's PreSch, 121 Knight Dr., San Rafael, 94901. Ages: 2-6 yr. Ph: (415) 457-9500.

Short School Ctr, 35 Marin St., San Rafael, 94915. Ages: 4.9-12 yr. Ph: (415) 485-3386.

Terra Linda Nursery, 360 Nova Albion Way, San Rafael, 94903. Ages: 2-10 yr. Ph: (415) 479-0790.

Trinity PreSch, 333 Woodland Ave., San Rafael, 94915. Ages: 2.9-5 yr. Ph: (415) 453-4526.

Twin Oaks Children's Ctr, 240 Channing Way, San Rafael, 94903. Ages: 2 mo.-6 yr. Ph: (415) 492-1444.

Sausalito

Children's Cultural Ctr, 620 Drake Ave., Sausalito, 94965. Ages: 2-6 yr. Ph: (415) 332-1044.

Iniece Bailey Ctr-MLKing School, Ebb Tide & Bridgeway, Sausalito, 94965. Ages: 0-3 yr. Ph: (415) 332-5698.

Sausalito Childcare, Bayside School, Sausalito, 94965. Ages: 3-11 yr. Ph: (415) 332-8070.

Sausalito Nursery, 625 Main St., Sausalito, 94965. Ages: 2-6 yr. Ph: (415) 332-0174.

Sparrow Creek, 304 Caledonia St., Sausalito, 94965. Ages: 2-6 yr. Ph: (415) 332-9595.

Stinson Beach

Stinson Beach Montessori, 30 Belvedere, Stinson Beach, 94970. Ages: 2-7 yr. Ph: (415) 868-0949.

Tiburon

Belvedere Tiburon CCCtr, 1185 Tiburon Blvd., Tiburon, 94920. Ages: 2-5 yr. Ph: (415) 435-4366.

Belvedere Tiburon CCCtr-Bel Aire, 277 Karen Way, Tiburon, 94920. Ages: 8-11 yr. Ph: (415) 435-4366.

Hawthorne Nursery, 145 Rock Hill Dr., Tiburon, 94920. Ages: 3-6 yr. Ph: (415) 435-9757.

Little Lambs Nursery, 9 Shepherd Way, Tiburon, 94920. Ages: 2-5 yr. Ph: (415) 435-1528.

Marin Day School-Tiburon, 445 Greenwood Beach Rd., Tiburon, 94920. Ages: 2-6 yr. Ph: (415) 381-3120.

Strawberry PreSch, 240 Tiburon Blvd., Tiburon, 94920. Ages: 2-6 yr. Ph: (415) 388-4437.

Woodare

West Marin Montessori, 1 Garden Way, Woodacre, 94972. Ages: 2.5-6 yr. Ph: (415) 488-4500.

Napa County
American Canyon
Williams PreSch-School Age, 15 Poco Way, American Canyon, 94590. Ages: 6-10 yr. Ph: (707) 644-7588.

Angwin
Discoveryland PreSch, 85 Cold Springs Rd., Angwin, 94508. Ages: 2-6 yr. Ph: (707) 965-2092.

Calistoga
Calistoga Co-Op, 1435 Oak St., Calistoga, 94515. Ages: 2-10 yr. Ph: (707) 942-0596.

Highlands Christian PreSch, 1411 4th St., Calistoga, 94515. Ages: 2-6 yr. Ph: (707) 942-5557.

Napa
A Place of My Own, 3875 Jefferson St., Napa, 94558. Ages: 2-10 yr. Ph: (707) 224-8667.

Aldea Day Treatment Pro, 2447 Old Sonoma Rd., Napa, 94558. Ages: 12-18 yr emot. dist. Ph: (707) 253-9136.

Casa Montessori, 780 Lincoln Ave., Napa, 94558. Ages: 2.6-6 yr. Ph: (707) 224-1944.

Children's World, 1625 Lincoln, Napa, 94559. Ages: 0-3 yr. Ph: (707) 224-3825.

Children's World, 600 Fourth St., Napa, 94558. Ages: 2-11 yr. Ph: (707) 224-3825.

Exer-Kids PreSch, 920 Yount St., Napa, 94558. Ages: 2-6 yr. Ph: (707) 252-0246.

Garden of Children, 605 Hunt St., Napa, 94559. Ages: 2.4-12 yr. Ph: (707) 257-2273.

Head Start-Fuller Park Ctr, Fuller Park, Laurel St., Napa, 94558. Ages: 3-6 yr. Ph: (707) 226-6749.

Head Start-Solano Ave, 2813 Solano Ave., Napa, 94559. Ages: 2.9-5.9 yr. Ph: (707) 252-1251.

Head Start-Wintun Ctr, 74 Wintun Ct., Napa, 94559. Ages: 3-5 yr. Ph: (707) 253-6862.

Head Start-Wintun II, 74 Wintun Ct., Napa, 94559. Ages: 3-5 yr. Ph: (707) 252-8931.

Hopper Creek Montessori, 2141 Second St., Napa, 94558. Ages: 2-7 yr. Ph: (707) 252-8775.

La Petite Acad, 3301 Villa Lane, Napa, 94558. Ages: 0-12 yr. Ph: (707) 257-7796.

Little Friends, 952 Napa St., Napa, 94559. Ages: 2-10 yr. Ph: (707) 252-8899.

Magic Years, 1777 Laurel St., Napa, 94558. Ages: 2.6-12 yr. Ph: (707) 253-1151.

Montecito Alternative, 1078 East Ave., Napa, 94559. Ages: 2-12 yr. Ph: (707) 255-3000.

Napa Children's Ctr, 2097 Imola Ave., Napa, 94558. Ages: 3-5 yr. Ph: (707) 253-6882.

Napa Valley Child Care, 1510 Menlo Ave., Napa, 94558. Ages: 2-6 yr. Ph: (707) 257-2844.

Napa Valley Christian, 721 Trancas, Napa, 94558. Ages: 2.6-6 yr. Ph: (707) 252-4834.

Napa Valley Co-op, 641 Randolph St., Napa, 94558. Ages: 2.9-6.6 yr. Ph: (707) 224-3319.

Napa Valley College, 2277 Napa-Vallejo Hwy, Napa, 94558. Ages: 6 mo.-5 yr. Ph: (707) 253-3046.

New Horizons I, 3734 Norfolk St., Napa, 94558. Ages: 2-12 yr. Ph: (707) 255-5066.

Petersen's Primary, 131 First St., Napa, 94559. Ages: 3.9-12 yr. Ph: (707) 255-1822.

Phillips Children's Ctr, 1210 Shelter Ave., Napa, 94559. Ages: 6-12 yr. Ph: (707) 253-3481.

Presbyterian Church, 1333 Third St., Napa, 94558. Ages: 2-5 yr. Ph: (707) 224-8693.

Salvador Activity Ctr, 1625 Salvador Ave., Napa, 94558. Ages: 2-12 yr. Ph: (707) 255-6088.

Silver Lining, 3051 Browns Valley Rd., Napa, 94558. Ages: 2-12 yr. Ph: (707) 226-5437.

Soda Canyon Nursery, 1005 Soda Canyon Rd., Napa, 94558. Ages: 2-6 yr. Ph: (707) 224-7689.

St. John's Lutheran PreSch, 3521 Linda Vista Ave., Napa, 94558. Ages: 2.9-12 yr. Ph: (707) 226-7970.

Sunrise Montessori, 4149 Linda Vista, Napa, 94558. Ages: 2-6 yr. Ph: (707) 253-1105.

Sunrise Montessori #2, 1000 Soda Canyon Rd., Napa, 94558. Ages: 3-6 yr. Ph: (707) 253-1105.

Westwood Children's Ctr, 2700 Kilburn Ave., Napa, 94558. Ages: 5-14 yr. Ph: (707) 252-5243.

Wine Country Sch, 1226 East Salvador, Napa., Ages: 2-12 yr. Ph: (707) 252-9290.

Yellow Brick Rd., 222 Spring St., Napa, 94558. Ages: 2-6 yr. Ph: (707) 255-9289.

Yellow Brick Rd. #2, 2211 First St., Napa, 94559. Ages: 2-6 yr. Ph: (707) 255-1124.

Young World of Learning, 1906 Wise Dr., Napa, 94558. Ages: 6-12 yr. Ph: (707) 252-9330.

Young World of Learning, 2243 Redwood Rd., Napa, 94558. Ages: 2-6 yr. Ph: (707) 252-9330.

Young World of Learning, 3765 Oxford St., Napa, 94558. Ages: 2-12 yr. Ph: (707) 252-9330.

Head Start-Crane Park, Crane St., Rutherford, 94574. Ages: 3-6 yr. Ph: (707) 963-4833.

Rutherford

St. Helena Co-op, Hwy 29 and Niebaum Lane, Rutherford, 94573. Ages: 2-5 yr. Ph: (707) 963-7212.

St. Helena Montessori, 1328 Spring St., Rutherford, 94574. Ages: 2-6 yr. Ph: (707) 963-1527.

St. Helena

Montessori Family Center, 960 Dowdell Lane, St. Helena, 94574. Ages: 2.5-11 yr. Ph: (707) 963-1614.

Cherrystone CC Ctr, 1310 Adams St., St. Helena, 94574. Ages: 5-9 yr. Ph: (707) 963-1051.

Harvest PreSch, 1425 Oak St., St. Helena, 94574. Ages: 2.5-7 yr. Ph: (707) 963-3822.

St. Helena Children's Ctr, 1428 Spring St., St. Helena, 94574. Ages: 3-12 yr. Ph: (707) 963-7204.

Sunrise PreSch, 1503 Tainter St., St. Helena, 94574. Ages: 2.9-6 yr. Ph: (707) 963-1250.

Yountville

Yountville Children's Ctr, 6554 Yount St., Yountville, 94559. Ages: 2-14 yr. Ph: (707) 944-8564.

Sonoma County
Bodega

Bodega Branch PreSch, 600 Salmon Creek Rd., Bodega, 94922. Ages: 2-5 yr. Ph: (707) 876-3412.

Shoreline Acres, 2255 Hwy 1, Bodega Bay, 94923. Ages: 2.9-7 yr. Ph: (707) 875-9943.

Cloverdale

Cloverdale PreSch Co-op, 450 W. 2nd St., Cloverdale, 95425. Ages: 2.9-6 yr. Ph: (707) 894-4328.

Cotati

Child's Play, 768 E. Cotati Ave., Cotati, 94928. Ages: 2.9-12 yr. Ph: (707) 792-2614.

Cotati Rohnert Park Co-op Nursery School, 150 W. Sierra Ave., Cotati, 94928. Ages: 2.9-6 yr. Ph: (707) 795-4846.

Pre-Tend PreSch, 905 E. Cotati Ave., Cotati, 94928. Ages: 2.6-6 yr. Ph: (707) 795-0803.

Rainbow Bridge Montessori, 21 William St., Cotati, 94928. Ages: 2-6 yr. Ph: (707) 795-6666.

Rainbow Bridge Montessori #2, 70 William St., Cotati, 94931. Ages: 2-4.9 yr. Ph: (707) 795-6666.

Eldridge

Rainbow Valley Sch, Dunbar Cottage-Sonoma St. Hosp., Eldridge, 95431. Ages: 0-12 yr. Ph: (707) 996-9671.

Geyserville

Geyserville Comm. Ctr, 21249 Geyserville Ave., Geyserville, 95441. Ages: 0-11 yr. Ph: (707) 857-3214.

River Valley Sch, Christian Church, Geyserville Ave., Geyserville, 95441. Ages: 2-6 yr. Ph: (707) 857-3977.

Graton

Kids Place, 8760 Bower Ave., Graton, 95472. Ages: 5-12 yr. Ph: (707) 829-8141.

Pacific Christian Acad., 8877 Donald St., Graton, 95444. Ages: 2-6 yr. Ph: (707) 823-2880.

Healdsburg

Good Beginnings Nursery, 1043 Felta Rd., Healdsburg, 95448. Ages: 2-6 yr. Ph: (707) 433-6855.

Head Start-North County, 3200 Rio Lindo Ave., Healdsburg, 95448. Ages: 3-5 yr. Ph: (707) 544-6171.

Healdsburg Child Dev Ctr, 555 North St., Healdsburg, 95448. Ages: 2.9-6 yr. Ph: (707) 433-2556.

Healdsburg Comm. Nursery, 444 First St., Healdsburg, 95448. Ages: 2.9-6 yr. Ph: (707) 433-1817.

Healdsburg Montessori, 500 Grove St., Healdsburg, 95448. Ages: 2-6 yr. Ph: (707) 431-1727.

Live Oak PreSch, 75 West Matheson, Healdsburg, 95448. Ages: 2.5-6 yr. Ph: (707) 433-1543.

Pine Street Sch, 25 Adeline Way, Healdsburg, 95448. Ages: 2-11 yr. Ph: (707) 433-8447.

St. John's School, 123 Fitch St., Healdsburg, 95448. Ages: 4-5 yr. Ph: (707) 433-2758.

Monte Rio

River Child Care, Skinner Hall, 20347 Hwy 116, Monte Rio, 95446. Ages: 3-5 yr. Ph: (707) 865-2983.

Occidental

Occidental Comm. Church, 2nd & Church

Sts., Occidental, 95464. Ages: 2.6-4.11 yr. Ph: (707) 874-3501.

Penngrove

Penngrove Montessori, 11201 Petaluma Hill Rd., Penngrove, 94951. Ages: 2-6 yr. Ph: (707) 792-9173.

Petaluma

Amerikids, 1301 Southpoint, Petaluma, 94952. Ages: 3 wk-12 yr. Ph: (707) 778-1964.

Children's Corner, 629 East D St., Petaluma, 94952. Ages: 0-5 yr. Ph: (707) 763-6191.

Children's Workshop, Arts & Crafts Bldg. Fairgrounds, Petaluma, 94952. Ages: 2.6-6 yr. Ph: (707) 763-8602.

Gan Israel PreSch, 740 Western Ave., Petaluma, 94952. Ages: 2.6-5 yr. Ph: (707) 762-0340.

Happy Day Presbyterian PreSch, 939 B St., Petaluma, 94952. Ages: 2.9-7 yr. Ph: (707) 762-8671.

Learning to Learn, 391 Maria Dr., Petaluma, 94952. Ages: 2-7 yr. Ph: (707) 762-8570.

Little Lambs, 3995 Roblar Rd., Petaluma, 94952. Ages: 2-12 yr. Ph: (707) 792-9282.

Little Shepherd, Baker & Stanley, Petaluma, 94952. Ages: 2-8 yr. Ph: (707) 769-0462.

Montessori Children's House, 825 Middlefield Dr., Petaluma, 94952. Ages: 0-6 yr. Ph: (707) 763-9222.

Old Adobe Christian PreSch, 2875 Adobe Rd., Petaluma, 94952. Ages: 2.5-6 yr. Ph: (707) 763-0646.

Pepper Kindergarten, 726 F St., Petaluma, 94952. Ages: 3.9-6 yr. Ph: (707) 762-8151.

Petaluma Child Dev Ctr, 401 S. McDowell, Petaluma, 94952. Ages: 2.9-8 yr. Ph: (707) 763-4990.

Petaluma Valley PreSch, 6 Gnoss Concourse, Petaluma, 94952. Ages: 2-5 yr. Ph: (707) 778-7230.

Shoreline Acres, 900 Burbank Lane, Petaluma, 94952. Ages: 2-5 yr. Ph: (707) 762-7913.

You and Me Children's Ctr, 450 Hayes Lane, Petaluma, 94952. Ages: 2-5 yr. Ph: (707) 762-8998.

Rohnert Park

Kinder-Care, 6150 State Farm Dr., Rohnert Park, 94928. Ages: NA. Ph: (707) 584-0124.

La Petite Acad, 1301 Medical Center Dr., Rohnert Park, 94928. Ages: 0-12 yr. Ph: (707) 585-7588.

Learning to Learn, 1300 Medical Center Dr., Rohnert Park, 94928. Ages: 0-6 yr. Ph: (707) 584-4224.

Little Friends PreSch, 5474 Snyder Lane, Rohnert Park, 94928. Ages: 2.9-7 yr. Ph: (707) 795-7863.

Little Ones Children's Ctr, 399 College View Dr., Rohnert Park, 94928. Ages: 2-10 yr. Ph: (707) 792-1620.

Pat's Playhouse, 215 Arlen Dr., Rohnert Park, 94928. Ages: 2-9 yr. Ph: (707) 795-8170.

Snyder Lane Christian, 4689 Snyder Lane, Rohnert Park, 94928. Ages: 2.9-5 yr. Ph: (707) 584-9759.

Sonoma State, 1801 East Cotati Ave., Rohnert Park, 94928. Ages: 2-5 yr. Ph: (707) 664-2230.

A Child's World, 50 Mark West Springs Rd., Santa Rosa, 95403. Ages: 2-10 yr. Ph: (707) 525-1189.

Santa Rosa

A Special Place-YWCA, 1128 Edwards Ave., Santa Rosa, 95401. Ages: 2.9-6 yr. Ph: (707) 523-4646.

Acorn Learning Ctr, 1235 W. Steele Lane, Santa Rosa, 95403. Ages: 2-10 yr. Ph: (707) 575-7486.

Bethel Children's Ctr, 1577 Guerneville Rd., Santa Rosa, 95403. Ages: 2-6 yr. Ph: (707) 527-0332.

Bethlehem Children's Ctr, 1300 St. Francis Rd., Santa Rosa, 95409. Ages: 2-6 yr. Ph: (707) 538-2266.

Brush Creek, 4657 Badger Rd., Santa Rosa, 95405. Ages: 2.9-6 yr. Ph: (707) 539-1612.

Burbank Extended CCCtr, 203 South A St., Santa Rosa, 95401. Ages: 5-14 yr. Ph: (707) 525-8344.

Childkind PreSch, 2200 Laguna Rd., Santa Rosa, 95401. Ages: 2-10 yr. Ph: (707) 823-6993.

Children's Ctr, 1835-A West Steele, Santa Rosa, 95403. Ages: 2.9-11 yr. Ph: (707) 573-9818.

Children's House Montessori, 2427 Professional Dr., Santa Rosa, 95403. Ages: NA. Ph: (707) 575-5485.

Christ Methodist, 1717 Yulupa Ave., Santa Rosa. Ages: 2-6 yr. Ph: (707) 526-0204.

Church of Divine Man, 512 Sonoma Ave., Santa Rosa, 95401. Ages: 2-6 yr. Ph: (707) 545-1869.

College Oak Montessori, 1925 West College Ave., Santa Rosa, 95401. Ages: 2-12 yr. Ph: (707) 579-5510.

Countryside PreSch I, 1592 Fulton Rd., Santa Rosa, 95401. Ages: 2.5-6 yr. Ph: (707) 526-3789.

Discoveries Rincon Valley, 6170 Montecito Blvd., Santa Rosa, 95409. Ages: 2-12 yr. Ph: (707) 539-3638.

Discoveries West, 28 Maxwell Ct., Santa Rosa, 95401. Ages: 2-12 yr. Ph: (707) 523-0454.

Franklin Park PreSch, 2095 Franklin Ave., Santa Rosa, 95404. Ages: 2.9-6 yr. Ph: (707) 546-7330.

Happy Hearts, 2260 West Steele Lane, Santa Rosa, 95401. Ages: 2-6 yr. Ph: (707) 545-8585.

Happy Time, 2233 Hoen Ave., Santa Rosa, 95404. Ages: 2-6 yr. Ph: (707) 527-9135.

Head Start-Grace Reese Ctr, 1931 Biwana Rd., Santa Rosa, 95407. Ages: 3-5 yr. Ph: (707) 544-6171.

Head Start-Wright Ctr, 3641 Stony Point Rd., Santa Rosa, 95407. Ages: 3-5 yr. Ph: (707) 585-0142.

J.X. Wilson CCCtr, 246 Brittain Lane, Santa Rosa, 95401. Ages: 5-14 yr. Ph: (707) 575-6988.

Kawana Springs Ctr, 2607 Petaluma Hill Rd., Santa Rosa, 95404. Ages: 0-3 yr. Ph: (707) 544-4653.

Kiddie Corner, 1561 Herbert St., Santa Rosa, 95401. Ages: 2-6 yr. Ph: (707) 544-0951.

La Petite Acad, 2055 Occidental Rd., Santa Rosa, 95401. Ages: 0-12 yr. Ph: (707) 573-1623.

Little Angels, 4305 Hoen Ave., Santa Rosa, 95405. Ages: 2-7 yr. Ph: (707) 579-4305.

Little Disciple, 1236 Grand Ave., Santa Rosa, 95404. Ages: 2-5 yr. Ph: (707) 546-0744.

Little Ones, 1620 Sonoma Ave., Santa Rosa, 95405. Ages: 2-6 yr. Ph: (707) 544-1620.

Little World Acad, 1363 Fulton Rd., Santa Rosa, 95401. Ages: 3-6 yr. Ph: (707) 523-1021.

Luther Burbank Ctr, 315 South A St., Santa Rosa, 95401. Ages: 2.9-6 yr. Ph: (707) 542-7570.

Merryhill Country Sch, 4044 Mayette Ave., Santa Rosa, 95405. Ages: 2-5 yr. Ph: (707) 575-7660.

Montessori Elem., 1569 Brush Creek Rd., Santa Rosa, 95404. Ages: 3-6 yr. Ph: (707) 539-7980.

Montessori PreSch, 620 McDonald Ave., Santa Rosa, 95404. Ages: 2-7 yr. Ph: (707) 544-7074.

Montessori Visions, 1625 Franklin Ave., Santa Rosa, 95404. Ages: 2-5 yr. Ph: (707) 575-7959.

Mt. Taylor Children's Center, 1451 Slater St., Santa Rosa, 95404. Ages: 2-12 yr. Ph: (707) 576-0773.

Multi-Cultural Ctr, 1650 West Third St., Santa Rosa, 95401. Ages: 3-6 yr. Ph: (707) 544-0104.

New Directions, 691-695 Russell Ave., Santa Rosa, 95401. Ages: 14-18 men. dis. Ph: (707) 545-8800.

Pep CCCtr, 2614 Paulin Dr., Santa Rosa, 95401. Ages: 2-6 yr. Ph: (707) 527-3420.

Presbyterian PreSch, 1550 Pacific Ave., Santa Rosa, 95404. Ages: 2.9-6 yr. Ph: (707) 542-7396.

Redwood Junior Acad, 385 Mark West Springs Rd., Santa Rosa, 95404. Ages: 2-6 yr. Ph: (707) 545-1697.

Rincon Valley Christian Pre-K, 4575 Badger Rd., Santa Rosa, 95409. Ages: 3.9-6 yr. Ph: (707) 538-2753.

Roseland Extended CC, 950 Sebastopol Rd., Santa Rosa, 95407. Ages: 5-12 yr. Ph: (707) 545-0100.

Santa Rosa Co-Op, 4295 Montgomery Dr., Santa Rosa, 95405. Ages: 2.9-6 yr. Ph: (707) 539-4181.

Santa Rosa Jewish Comm Ctr, 4676 Mayette Ave., Santa Rosa, 95405. Ages: 2-8 yr. Ph: (707) 578-3338.

Spring Creek, 4675 Mayette Ave., Santa Rosa, 95405. Ages: 3-5 yr. Ph: (707) 545-1771.

St. Luke Lutheran PreSch, 905 Mendocino Ave., Santa Rosa, 95401. Ages: 2.9-8 yr. Ph: (707) 545-0512.

Stuart Sch, 431 Humboldt St., Santa Rosa, 95404. Ages: 2.9-6 yr. Ph: (707) 528-0721.

Summerfield CCCtr, 1611 Dutton Ave., Santa Rosa, 95407. Ages: 2-7 yr. Ph: (707) 576-1929.

Summerfield Nursery, 4930 Newanga Ave., Santa Rosa, 95404. Ages: 2-7 yr. Ph: (707) 539-6182.

Taylor Mountain, 240 Burt St., Santa Rosa, 95407. Ages: 2-6 yr. Ph: (707) 544-3077.

West Park PreSch, 2121 Moraga Dr., Santa Rosa, 95404. Ages: 2.9-6 yr. Ph: (707) 545-4283.

Willow Creek Ctr, 2536 Marlow Rd., Santa Rosa. Ages: 2-6 yr. Ph: (707) 528-2813.

Woodside Creek, 2323 Chanate Rd., Santa Rosa. Ages: 2-6 yr. Ph: (707) 545-0542.

Woodside Towne, 2810 Summerfield Rd.,

Santa Rosa, 95405. Ages: 2-11 yr. Ph: (707) 539-1414.

Woodside West School, 2577 Guerneville Rd., Santa Rosa, 95401. Ages: 2-10 yr. Ph: (707) 528-6666.

Wright Extended, 4389 Price Ave., Santa Rosa, 95401. Ages: 5-12 yr. Ph: (707) 545-2402.

YMCA Sunshine, 2250 Mesquite Dr., Santa Rosa. Ages: 6-12 yr. Ph: (707) 575-5219.

YMCA Sunshine Co., 4580 Bennett Valley Dr., Santa Rosa, 95405. Ages: 8-12 yr. Ph: (707) 545-9622.

YWCA-A Child's Place, 786 Kawana Springs Rd., Santa Rosa, 95404. Ages: 2.9-6 yr. Ph: (707) 523-4646.

Sebastopol

Alphabet Soup, 4411 Gravenstein Hwy. No., Sebastopol, 95472. Ages: 2-10 yr. Ph: (707) 829-9460.

Ann's PreSch, 801 Hurlbut Ave., Sebastopol, 95472. Ages: 2-8 yr. Ph: (707) 823-2082.

Appleberry PreSch, 2804 Thorn Rd., Sebastopol, 95472. Ages: 2-4.9 yr. Ph: (707) 829-1210.

Bloomfield PreSch, 990 Bloomfield Rd., Sebastopol, 95472. Ages: 2.5-5 yr. Ph: (707) 829-0904.

Cricket House, 955 Gravenstein Hwy. So., Sebastopol, 95472. Ages: 3-9 yr. Ph: (707) 829-0378.

Fircrest PreSch, 1606 Gravenstein Hwy. So., Sebastopol, 95472. Ages: 2-7 yr. Ph: (707) 829-1088.

Grasshopper Green, 3790 Mount Vernon Rd., Sebastopol, 95472. Ages: 0-5 yr. Ph: (707) 829-0577.

Grasshopper Green School Age, 3790 Mount Vernon Rd., Sebastopol, 95472. Ages: NA. Ph: (707) 823-1992.

Happy Days, 1000 Gravenstein Hwy, No., Sebastopol, 95472. Ages: 2.6-6 yr. Ph: (707) 829-2814.

Montessori Children's House, 500 N. Main St., Sebastopol, 95472. Ages: 2.9-7 yr. Ph: (707) 823-1110.

Mt. Olive Lutheran, 460 Murphy Ave., Sebastopol, 95472. Ages: 2-8 yr. Ph: (707) 823-6316.

Pleasant Hill Montessori, 789 Pleasant Hill Rd., Sebastopol, 95472. Ages: 2.9-6 yr. Ph: (707) 823-6003.

Sandcastles, 8900 Bodega Hwy., Sebastopol, 95472. Ages: 2.9-12yr. Ph: (707) 823-3288.

SCC Apple Blossom, 700 Water Trough Rd.,

Sebastopol, 95472. Ages: 5-11 yr. Ph: (707) 823-1041.

Sebastopol Comm Ctr-Parkside, 7450 Bodega Ave., Sebastopol, 95472. Ages: 5-11 yr. Ph: (707) 823-1511.

Sebastopol Comm Ctr-Pinecrest, 7285 Hayden Ave., Sebastopol, 95472. Ages: 5-12 yr. Ph: (707) 823-1511.

St. Stephen's PreSch, 500 Robinson Rd., Sebastopol, 95472. Ages: 2.9-6 yr. Ph: (707) 829-0673.

Sonoma

Gingerbread House, 504 Calle Del Monte, Sonoma. Ages: 2-8. Ph: (707) 938-1102.

Little School, 1254 Broadway, Sonoma, 95476. Ages: 2-7 yr. Ph: (707) 935-3922.

Maxwell's Farm, 19209 Sonoma Hwy, Sonoma, 95476. Ages: 2.9-5 yr. Ph: (707) 996-6547.

Montessori School, 19675 8th St. East, Sonoma, 95476. Ages: 2-18 yr. Ph: (707) 996-2422.

Old Adobe School, 252 West Spain St., Sonoma, 95476. Ages: 2-5 yr. Ph: (707) 938-4510.

Sonoma Child Dev. Ctr, 620 5th St., Sonoma, 95476. Ages: 2.9-8 yr. Ph: (707) 996-3494.

Sonoma Parents, 17790 Greger Ave., Sonoma, 95476. Ages: 2.4-6 yr. Ph: (707) 996-4835.

Sunshine Nursery, 109 Patten St., Sonoma, 95476. Ages: 2-6 yr. Ph: (707) 996-2702.

Valley of the Moon, 136 Mission Terrace, Sonoma, 95476. Ages: 2.9-6 yr. Ph: (707) 938-4265.

Vintage Country, 276 E. Napa St., Sonoma, 95476. Ages: 3-6 yr. Ph: (707) 996-6560.

Westerbeke Ranch Circle Camp, 2300 Grove St., Sonoma, 95476. Ages: 2-6 yr. Ph: (707) 996-4016.

Windsor

Growing Children, 9741 Old Redwood Hwy., Windsor, 95492. Ages: 2.5-5.5 yr. Ph: (707) 838-3708.

Migrant Head Start, 9161 Starr Rd., Windsor, 95490. Ages: 2-5 yr. Ph: (707) 838-7542.

My Friends and I, 270 Mark West Station Rd., Windsor, 95492. Ages: 2-12 yr. Ph: (707) 526-5811.

Windsor Comm. Nursery, 195 Windsor River Rd., Windsor, 95492. Ages: 2.9-6 yr. Ph: (707) 838-9306.

Windsor Day Care, 8955 Conde Lane, Windsor, 95492. Ages: 5-12 yr. Ph: (707) 838-9025

13/Hospitals & Health Services

Insurance Q&A, Directory of Major Hospitals

CHOOSING A DOCTOR, a hospital or a medical provider is a formidable task. Here is an overview of what's available, how insurance usually influences choice, and some answers to frequently asked questions. Let's start with a woman, healthy and engaged. Her insurance choices:

No insurance

Being young and healthy, it is unlikely she will become seriously ill. So why pay for insurance? If she gets the flu, she goes to a local doctor and pays just to be treated for flu. She may even choose a personal doctor. But she pays only for treatments she receives. If she loses her job or has a low-paying job, she can fall back on the county-state health system, which provides medical care to the poor (along with paid care)

Pluses of no insurance: cheap, flexible (choose your doctor) and, depending on the doctor, high quality. Drawbacks: A serious illness may wipe out her bank account. Many doctors will refuse to honor the state insurance plan, forcing her to seek care at a county facility, which may be some distance off.

Some counties have their own hospitals. Sonoma does, Marin and Napa do not. They have clinics and contracts with hospitals to provide some care.

Traditional Insurance

With these plans, you choose the hospital or doctor you want. You or your employer pay the premiums or you both pay.

Often traditional insurance carries a deductible. The young woman in a year runs up medical bills totaling $3,000. She pays the first $500, the insurance company pays the rest. Many plans use a deductible and a co-payment. The

Top 25 Baby Names

Marin County		Napa County		Sonoma County	
Boys	**Girls**	**Boys**	**Girls**	**Boys**	**Girls**
Michael	Jessica	Kyle	Amanda	Michael	Ashley
Alexander	Lauren	Michael	Elizabeth	Christopher	Jessica
Christopher	Alexandra	Andrew	Jessica	Nicholas	Amanda
Nicholas	Elizabeth	Christopher	Jennifer	Matthew	Sarah
William	Nicole	Joshua	Nicole	Daniel	Nicole
James	Jennifer	David	Sarah	Anthony	Brittany
Ryan	Sarah	Eric	Lauren	David	Elizabeth
Matthew	Danielle	Jason	Michelle	Robert	Katherine
David	Hannah	Thomas	Brittany	Kyle	Megan
John	Katherine	Matthew	Emily	James	Samantha
Zachary	Michelle	Nicholas	Kayla	John	Emily
Daniel	Rebecca	Brian	Megan	Joseph	Jennifer
Adam	Stephanie	Daniel	Ashley	Andrew	Kayla
Andrew	Laura	James	Rachel	Justin	Stephanie
Jonathan	Samantha	Jordan	Danielle	Joshua	Amber
Joseph	Allison	Joseph	Laura	Ryan	Chrstina
Kevin	Ashley	Kevin	Melissa	Kevin	Melissa
Robert	Emily	Robert	Rebecca	Benjamin	Katie
Samuel	Kathryn	Tyler	Amber	William	Laura
Thomas	Rachel	Alexander	Andrea	Thomas	Alicia
Anthony	Christina	Anthony	Brianna	Jacob	Kelsey
Kyle	Kelly	Juan	Chelsea	Alexander	Kelly
Spencer	Natalie	Paul	Christina	Jonathan	Rebecca
Joshua	Caitlin	Steven	Hannah	Samuel	Alyssa
Aaron	Kayla	Benjamin	Samantha	Eric	Amy

Source: California Department of Health Services, 1989 birth records. These were the top 25 names selected by parents for newborns. In instances of ties, the names are listed in alphabetical order. In Napa County, Benjamin was tied for 25th with Brandon, Jacob, Jonathan, Justin, Ryan, Samuel and Stephen and Amber through Samantha were tied for 19th through 25th with Vanessa and Veronica. In Sonoma County, Eric was tied for 25th with Zachary and Alyssa and Amy were tied for 24th through 25th with Lauren and Michelle.

woman breaks her leg skiing. Bill $600. Insurance pays 80 percent ($480), the patient 20 percent ($120).

Pluses: Unrestricted choice of doctors and hospitals.

Drawbacks: The woman may be responsible for filing claims and paperwork. The premiums often are higher than other policies. You pay for choice.

Traditional insurance has been posting sharp increases in recent years but options — higher deductibles — are available to keep fees down.

Preferred Provider Organizations (PPO)

The insurance company approaches certain doctors and hospitals and tells

New numbers for newcomers.

To reach the switchboard call:

Upvalley .... (707) 963-3611
Downvalley .... (707) 944-8822

Dial direct for these departments:

Emergency Department–(Around the clock Service) 963-6425
Family Birthing Center & Maternity Classes 963-6354
Heart At Risk .... 963-6387 or 800-862-7575
Home Health Services .... 963-3691 or 944-8322
Hospice of Napa Valley .... 963-3691 or 944-8322
JobCare —Occupational
  Health Services 963-6491
Mental Health Services–Adolescent 963-6481
  Adult 963-6270
Pharmacy (Deer Park) 963-6453
Physical Therapy
  Deer Park (Hospital) 963-6250
  St. Helena Clinic 963-6247
  Calistoga Clinic 942-6233
Physician Referral Service .... 963-6207 or 800-540-3611

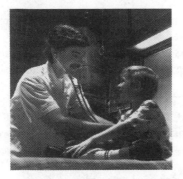

ST.
HELENA
HOSPITAL

HEALTH
CENTER

*Your access to
healthcare in the
Napa Valley.*

them: We will send patients to you but you must agree to our prices — a method of controlling costs — and our rules. The young woman chooses her doctor and hospital from the list provided by the PPO. If she goes to an "outside" doctor, she pays difference between what the PPO would pay and what the doctor charges.

Like traditional insurance, PPO insurance may charge deductibles and co-payments. Generally the higher the premium the more the policy covers.

Pluses: PPO insurance usually costs less than traditional insurance and offers freedom of choice among the affiliated doctors and hospitals. Some plans sign up many docs and hospitals. Drawback: PPOs restrict choice and they may not cover everything; for example, physical exams. Ask questions.

Health Maintenance Organization (HMO)

The insurance company and medical provider are one and the same. All or almost all medical care is given by the HMO. The woman catches the flu. She sees the HMO doctor, goes to the HMO hospital. If she becomes pregnant, she sees an HMO obstetrician at the HMO hospital and delivers her baby there.

HMOs come in different sizes and are similar to PPOs. One major difference: With HMOs you pay the complete bill if you go outside the system (with obvious exceptions; e.g., emergency care).

HMO pluses: Often the cheapest alternative. How much the HMO covers depends on the policy.

HMO hospitals are well-equipped and some have built clinics or medical offices to serve outlying areas.

Kaiser is the biggest HMO provider in California. Other HMO plans are available.

Drawback: Freedom of choice limited but clients are encouraged to pick personal doctors from within the system. If HMO facility is not close, the woman will have to drive a long distance.

Government Insurance

This comes in several forms. Medi-Cal, a state program, covers care for the poor and disabled and many uninsured people.

Theoretically, Medi-Cal patients are supposed to be able to obtain treatment from any doctor. But, according to news reports, many doctors, claiming

---

THROWING OUT THE BACK WITH THE BATH WATER

Where's the waterboy, when you really need him? In the 1991 drought some Marin residents caught the warm-up water from a shower in a bucket and used it to flush the toilet.

The result: water saved but, for some, back and neck thrown out. One therapist called the condition "bucket back."

How to see a doctor without seeing a bill.

A lot of health plans (perhaps yours) cover only 80% of a doctor's bill. Some even less. And only after you've paid the first $100 or a lot more.

With Kaiser Permanente, one low monthly payment covers virtually all your health care. Including well-baby care, lab tests, x-rays, and much more.

For more information, visit your personnel office or give us a call. In Marin, (415) 499-2139. In Sonoma County, (707) 571-4309.

For over 45 years, we've seen to the health care needs of a lot of people. But without them having to see a lot of doctor bills.

KAISER PERMANENTE

Good People. Good Medicine.

Medical centers in San Rafael and Santa Rosa. Medical offices in Napa, Novato, and Petaluma. Additional facilities located in 25 other Northern California communities.

© 1991 Kaiser Permanente

Marin County Population by Age Groups

City or Area	≤ 5	5-18	19-29	30-54	55+
Belvedere	85	288	138	797	839
Bolinas	59	200	73	617	149
Corte Madera	494	1,064	1,032	3,658	2,024
Fairfax	461	950	897	3,479	1,144
Inverness	79	211	110	644	378
Kentfield	322	958	619	1,812	1,729
Larkspur	441	1,071	1,319	4,714	3,525
Lucas Valley- Marinwood	386	1,109	608	2,514	1,365
Mill Valley	712	1,670	1,340	6,199	3,117
Novato	3,702	8,671	7,710	18,968	8,534
Ross	120	419	206	883	495
San Anselmo	732	1,642	1,364	5,592	2,413
San Rafael	2,767	6,212	8,861	19,420	11,144
Santa Venetia	218	512	403	1,404	825
Sausalito	220	429	875	4,166	1,462
Strawberry	241	474	637	2,044	981
Tiburon	336	1,093	709	3,370	2,024
Woodacre	100	255	150	772	171
Remainder	2,126	5,308	6,405	19,521	6,990
Countywide	13,601	32,536	33,456	101,164	49,339

Source: 1990 Census

payments are low and paperwork burdensome, are refusing to see Medi-Cal patients. As a result, county institutions treat many Medi-Cal patients.

If our young women were a military veteran and came down with an illness related to her service, she could be treated at a Veterans Hospital.

Through Medicare, the federal government pays the greater portion of illnesses afflicting the elderly and in some instances 100 percent of the costs. Elderly people often buy insurance to make up the difference between what the government covers and what they have to pay. Many people retain their medical benefits after they retire. It pays to find out what your employer offers.

Common Questions

The young woman is injured in a car accident and is unconscious. Where will she be taken?

Generally, she will be taken to the closest emergency room or trauma center, where her condition will be stabilized. Her doctor will then have her admitted into a hospital. Or she will be transferred to her HMO hospital or, if indigent, to a county facility.

The young woman breaks her leg. Her personal doctor is an internist and does not set fractures. What happens?

The personal doctor refers the case to a specialist. Traditional insurance pays the specialist fee.

In PPO, the woman would generally see a specialist affiliated with the PPO. In an HMO, the specialist would be employed by the HMO.

The young woman signs up for an HMO then contracts a rare disease or suffers an injury that requires treatment beyond the capability of the HMO. Will she be treated?

Often yes, but it pays to read the fine print. The HMO will contract treatment out to a facility that specializes in the needed treatment.

The young woman marries a bum or hates her job, becomes despondent and takes to drink. Will insurance pay for her rehabilitation?

Depends on her insurance. And often employer. Some may have drug and alcohol rehab plans. Some plans cover psychiatry.

The woman becomes pregnant. Her doctor, who has delivered many babies, wants her to deliver at X hospital. All the woman's friends say, Y Hospital is much better, nicer, etc. The doctor is not cleared to practice at Y Hospital. Is the woman out of luck?

With traditional insurance, the client picks the doctor and the hospital. If the woman wants her pneumonia cured at A Hospital, her bunions cut at D

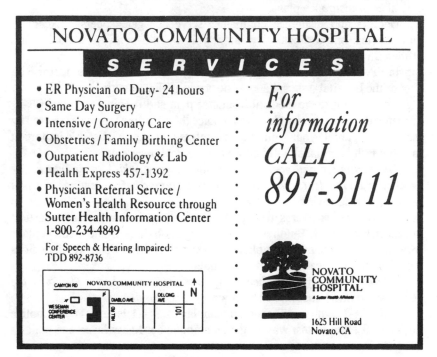

Napa County Population by Age Groups

City or Area	≤ 5	5-18	19-29	30-54	55+
American Canyon	569	1,506	1,044	2,753	1,834
Angwin	158	626	1,357	818	544
Calistoga	250	677	640	1,289	1,612
Deer Park	81	309	922	699	513
Napa	4,628	11,318	10,066	21,562	14,268
St. Helena	276	846	577	1,669	1,622
Yountville	93	261	178	696	2,031
Remainder	1,318	4,159	2,013	14,105	2,649
Countywide	7,393	19,702	16,797	43,591	25,073

Source: 1990 Census

Hospital, her baby delivered at Y Hospital, it's her choice. And she may pick her specialist. But he or she must be admitted to practice at the hospital she chooses. In certain situations, her doctor may be given courtesy practicing privileges at a hospital where the doctor does not have staff membership.

With PPOs and HMOs the woman must pick from the doctors and hospitals affiliated with the organizations. Independent hospitals often honor a number of insurance plans.

Doctors and insurance companies serve as "gatekeepers." Except in emergencies, only a doctor can admit you to a hospital. Most doctors are affiliated with only a few hospitals.

In the everyday reality of medical care, once you choose a doctor, you choose the hospital or hospitals the doctor is affiliated with.

Or you choose the medical insurance plan and it points you towards its affiliated doctors. The doctor of your choice then uses the hospitals covered by the medical plan. If your regular doctor refers you to specialist, it's important to know if the specialist will honor your medical insurance.

The young woman goes in for minor surgery, which turns into major surgery when the doctor forgets to remove a sponge before sewing up. Upon reviving, she does what?

The obvious answer is that she reaches for the phone and calls the nastiest lawyer in the county. But these days nothing is obvious. Some medical plans require clients to submit complaints to a panel of arbitrators, which decides damages, if any. Read your insurance policy.

While working in her kitchen, the woman slips, bangs her head against the stove, gets a nasty cut and becomes woozy. She should:

Call 9-1-1, which will send an ambulance. 9-1-1 is managed by police dispatch. It's the fastest way to get an ambulance. Many insurance policies cover ambulance services.

Sonoma County Population by Age Groups

City or Area	≤5	5-18	19-29	30-54	55+
Bodega Bay	51	113	111	461	391
Boyes Hot Springs	496	1,079	1,077	2,276	1,045
Cloverdale	463	1,012	741	1,646	1,062
Cotati	543	1,027	1,211	2,257	676
El Verano	287	749	506	1,402	554
Fetters Hot Spr.-Ag. Cal.	150	321	285	849	419
Forestville	156	492	277	1,107	411
Glen Ellen	8	253	113	570	167
Guerneville	119	349	244	859	395
Healdsburg	723	1,873	1,341	3,376	2,156
Monte Rio	64	181	124	480	209
Occidental	86	275	131	610	198
Petaluma	3,419	8,269	6,623	16,923	7,950
Rohnert Park	3,102	7,267	8,456	12,858	4,643
Roseland	1,001	1,873	1,834	2,876	1,195
Santa Rosa	8,116	20,362	18,570	39,675	26,590
Sebastopol	466	1,392	921	2,609	1,616
Sonoma	431	1,116	736	2,631	3,207
South Santa Rosa	359	826	670	1,512	761
Windsor	1,219	2,564	1,971	4,883	2,734
Remainder	6,980	20,863	14,793	46,768	24,534
Countywide	28,319	72,256	60,105	146,628	80,914

Source: 1990 Census

The woman marries and has children, time passes and the oldest reaches age 18. Is he covered by the family insurance?

All depends on the insurance. Some policies will cover the children while they attend college (but attendance may be defined in a certain way, full-time as opposed to part-time.)

When the woman retires, her insurance coverage may be changed.

Medical insurance in the U.S. has been evolving, sometimes changing drastically, to meet the needs of modern America. More changes are coming. Ask plenty of questions.

What's the difference between a hospital, an urgent care center and a doctor's office?

The hospital has the most services and equipment. The center has several services and a fair amount of equipment. The office, usually, has the fewest services and the smallest amount of equipment.

Hospitals have beds. If a person must have a serious operation, she goes to a hospital. Hospitals have coronary care and intensive care units, emergency care and other specialized, costly treatment units. But many hospitals also run clinics for minor ailments and provide the same services as the medical centers.

Urgent care or medical centers are sometimes located in neighborhoods, which makes them more convenient for some people. The doctors treat the minor, and often not-so-minor, ailments of patients and send them to hospitals for major surgery and serious sicknesses.

Some doctors form themselves into groups to offer the public a variety of services. Some hospitals have opened neighborhood clinics or centers to attract patients.

The doctor in his or her office treats patients for minor ailments and uses the hospital for surgeries, major illnesses. Many illnesses that required hospitalization years ago are now treated in the office or clinic.

Some hospitals offer programs outside the typical doctor-patient relationships. For example, wellness plans — advice on how to stay healthy, or control stress or quit smoking.

Where do you look?

Well, there's the phone book. There are friends who can recommend their doctors and insurance companies. Employers often offer a choice of insurance plans and allow you to switch plans (usually once a year, at a set time).

There is Physician Referral. Many hospitals have it. You call the hospital, ask for the service and get a list of doctors to choose from (see directory). The doctors will be affiliated with the hospital providing the referral. Hospitals and doctors will also tell you what insurance plans they accept for payment, and will send you brochures describing the services the hospital offers.

Directory of Hospitals & Major Medical Facilities

Marin County

Kaiser Permanente Medical Center-San Rafael, 99 Montecillo Rd., San Rafael, 94903. Phone: (415) 499-2000 or 499-2911. ICU, CCU, Obstetrics, GYN (Outpatient), Emergency Care, Psychiatric Care (Outpatient), Physicians Referral, Pediatric Services, Physical Therapy, Chemical Dependency, Alcohol Treatment (Outpatient), Radiology, Home Health Care. 120 Beds (12 ICU/CCU).

Kaiser Permanente Medical Offices-Novato, 97 San Marin Drive, Novato, 94945. Phone: (415) 899-7400. Allergy Injection, Health Education, Internal Medicine, Laboratory, Materiel Services, Obstetrics/Gynecology, Optical Services, Optometry, Pediatrics, Pharmacy, Radiology, Home Health.

Kentfield Rehabilitation Hospital & Outpatient Center, 1125 Sir Francis Drake Blvd., Kentfield, 94904. Phone: (415) 456-9680. Physical Therapy. Inpatient and outpatient medical rehab programs and services for neurological, orthopedic, pulmonary and other disabilities. 60 Beds.

Marin General Hospital, 250 Bon Air Road, Greenbrae, 94904. Phone: (415) 925-7000. ICU, CCU, Obstetrics, GYN, Emergency Care, Psychiatric Care, Physicians Referral, Pediatric Services, Physical Therapy, Cardiac Surgery, Radiology, Home Health Care, Cancer Treatment. 235 Beds.

Novato Community Hospital, 1625 Hill Rd., Novato, 94947. Phone: (415) 897-3111. ICU, CCU, Obstetrics, GYN, Emergency Care, Physicians Referral, Pediatric Services, Physical Therapy, Inpatient and Outpatient Radiology Services, Geriatric

Services, Cancer Treatment. Same day surgery available. Women's Health Line. Health Express transportation for Seniors and Disabled patients. 75 Beds.

Ross Hospital, 1111 Sir Francis Drake Blvd., Kentfield, 94904. Phone: (415) 258-6900 or toll free (800) 786-ROSS. Psychiatric Care, Alcohol & Drug Treatment. Free mental health consultation and referral service. Outpatient alcohol and drug treatment. 90 Beds.

Napa County

Queen of the Valley Hospital-Napa Valley Medical Center, 1000 Trancas, Napa, 94558. Phone: (707) 252-4411. ICU, CCU, Obstetrics, GYN, Trauma Center, Emergency Care, Physicians Referral, Pediatric Services, Physical Therapy, Skilled Nursing, Radiology, Home Health Care, Cancer Treatment, Mammography, Regional Heart Center. 180 Beds.

St. Helena Hospital & Health Center, 650 Sanitarium Road, Deer Park, 94576. Phone: (707) 963-3611. ICU, CCU, Obstetrics, Emergency Care, Adult & Adolescent Psychiatric Care, Physicians Referral, Physical Therapy, Chemical Dependency, Alcohol Treatment, Skilled Nursing,Radiology, Home Health Care. Special Challenge Course available for youth or adult groups. Call for information. Also special live-in wellness programs, such as Smoking Cessation, the McDougall Lifestyle Program, and Personalized Health. 200 Beds.

Sonoma County

Community Hospital, 3325 Chanate Road, Santa Rosa, 95404. Phone: (707) 576-4000. ICU, CCU, Obstetrics, GYN, Pediatric Services, Radiology, Intensive Care Nursery, Outpatient Services. County facility. 145 beds.

CPC Redwoods Hospital, 1287 Fulton Rd., Santa Rosa, 95401. Phone: (707) 578-4500. Physicians Referral, Psychiatric Care, Chemical Dependency, Alcohol Treament, Eating Disorders, Geriatric Services. Dual diagnosis for substance abuse with a psychiatric diagnosis. Psychiatric care for children, adolescents and adults. Inpatient and outpatient. Free psychiatric assessment service 24-hours a day. 60 Beds.

Healdsburg General Hospital, 1375 University, Healdsburg, 95448. Phone: (707) 431-6500. ICU, Obstetrics, GYN, Emergency Care, Industrial Medicine, Psychiatric Care, Physicians Referral, Pediatric Services, Physical Therapy, Chemical Dependency, Skilled Nursing, Radiology, Home Health Care, Geriatric Services, Cancer Treatment, Mammography, Same-day Surgery. 49 Beds.

Kaiser Permanente Medical Center-Santa Rosa, 401 Bicentennial Way, Santa Rosa, 95403. Phone: (707) 571-4000. ICU, CCU, Obstetrics, GYN, Emergency Care, Psychiatric Care, Physicians Referral, Pediatric Services, Physical Therapy, Chemical Dependency (outpatient), Alcohol Treatment, Skilled Nursing, Radiology, Home Health Care, Geriatric Services, Cancer Treatment, Health Education. 110 Beds.

Kaiser Permanente Medical Offices-Petaluma, 3900 Lakeville Highway, Petaluma, 94954. Phone: (707) 765-3900. Allergy Injection, Health Education, Internal Medicine, Laboratory, Materiel Services, Obstetrics, GYN, Optical Services, Optometry, Pediatrics, Pharmacy, Radiology.

Petaluma Valley Hospital, 400 N McDowell Blvd., Petaluma, 94954-2339. Phone: (707) 778-1111. ICU, CCU, Obstetrics, GYN, Emergency Care, Physicians Referral, Pediatric Services, Physical Therapy, Skilled Nursing, Radiology, Home Health Care, Geriatric Services, Cancer Treatment. Med-Surgical Department. 99 Beds.

Palm Drive Hospital, 501 Petaluma Ave., Sebastopol, 95472. Phone (707) 823-8511. ICU, CCU, Trauma Center, Emergency Care, Physicians Referral, Physical Therapy, Skilled Nursing, Radiology, Home Health Care, Cancer Treatment. 53 Beds.

Santa Rosa Memorial Hospital, 1165 Montgomery Drive, Santa Rosa, 95405. Phone: (707) 546-3210. ICU, CCU, Obstetrics, GYN, Emergency Care, Physicians Referral, Pediatric Services, Physical Therapy, Radiology, Geriatric Services, Cancer Treatment. 220 Beds.

Sonoma Valley Hospital, 347 Andrieux, Sonoma, 95476. Phone: (707) 938-4545. ICU, Obstetrics, GYN, Emergency Care, Physicians Referral, Physical Therapy, Skilled Nursing, Radiology, Home Health Care, Geriatric Services. 92 Beds.

Warrack Hospital, 2449 Summerfield Road, Santa Rosa, 95405. Phone: (707) 542-9030. ICU, CCU, GYN, Emergency Care, Physicians Referral, Physical Therapy, Radiology, Geriatric Services, Cancer Treatment. 79 Beds.

Key: ICU (Intensive Care Unit), CCU (Coronary Care Unit), OB (Obstetrics), GYN (Gynecology).

14/Fun & Games

Marin, Napa & Sonoma Parks, Museums, Arts — How to Get Info on Sports and Teams

RARE FOR SUBURBAN-RURAL counties, Marin, Napa and Sonoma attract hundreds of thousands of tourists annually, the great majority to delight in what nature has wrought — the Marin headlands, the Sonoma Coast, the mountains, the Russian River, the redwoods, the scenic countryside.

But the works of man, foremost the wineries and restaurants and miscellaneous buildings — Victorians in Petaluma, the mission at Sonoma — and public projects such as Lake Berryessa, also draw their thousands.

In some instances, the tourist spots have become, or remained, popular with local residents. Mt. Tamalpais and its trails are like second nature to Marin residents. With water, water everywhere — ocean, rivers, lakes — it's not surprising to see many garages and driveways decorated with boats.

But if a poll were done, chances are it would reveal that most local residents do not spend their time in the more obvious pursuits. In many towns, softball and gardening are probably the most popular past times. When children are young, parents often devote an enormous amount of time following or running leagues for soccer, baseball, swimming and football.

Friday-night football at the high school remains one of the big events of town life.

When trying to tap the recreational offerings of a town or region, it is perhaps best to start with ordinary and everyday.

Local Activities — The Sporting Life

Although city departments organize many activities, a great many others are sponsored by individuals or organizations with no connection to city hall.

Adult softball is often coordinated by city hall. Little League is not. Neither

Oakland A's 1992 Schedule*

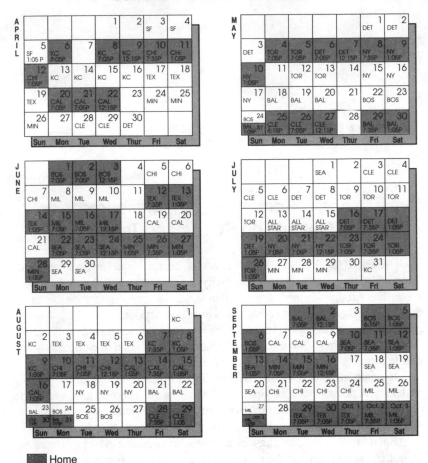

■ Home games

* Tentative schedule. Subject to change.

usually is Pop Warner football. Gymnastics shows up in many city catalogs. Swimming does not. It's usually privately sponsored. Same for soccer.

And down the line: Tennis, often public; racquetball, invariably private. Volleyball and basketball, sometimes public; boating, private.

Nurturing Mind & Body

Some of the biggest public sponsors of activities are often some of quietest in announcing their services. Many school districts offer adult classes: computers, cardiopulmonary resuscitation, aerobics. For want of money, the districts usually do one mailing of their catalogs and that's it.

San Francisco Giants 1992 Schedule*

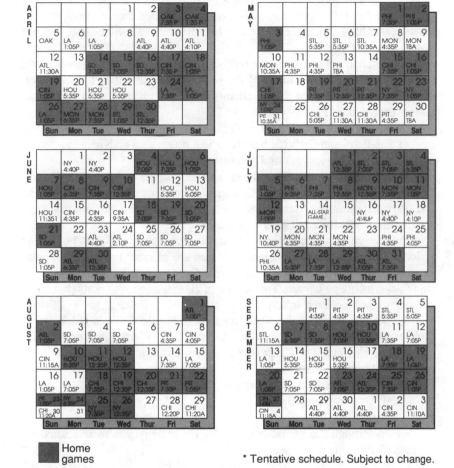

Home games

* Tentative schedule. Subject to change.

Community colleges offer conditioning and sports — tennis, swimming, etc. — for low prices and a great variety of cultural and business classes. You can take them one at a time. You don't have to enroll in programs or put yourself on a diploma track.

So Many Choices

The problem is often one of excess, not shortage. So much is offered that it's hard to track down what you really want. Some suggestions:

• Ignore city boundaries. You're a Larkspur resident. Corte Madera or San Rafael is offering something you like. Sign up. They don't care. Some places might charge a few bucks extra for outside residents.

• For community activities, get:

1) The activities calendar from city hall, if it has one. Small cities sometimes don't. Occasionally activities are organized through park and rec districts that have no connection to city hall. But city hall will be able to point you in the right direction.

2) The chamber of commerce publication for your town. This will give a list of the social clubs and many of the youth groups. If writing to a chamber, sent $5 with your request. Many chambers are run on peanuts; a few bucks speeds things along.

3)The adult school calendar. Call the local school district.

4) The Boys and Girls Club activity list, if there's a club nearby.

• For education and cultural activities, get:

1) Schedule of classes from the closest community colleges. See Chapter 11 for a list and phone numbers. Community colleges offer classes days and evenings and sometimes Saturdays. Fees run from as low as $6 for a class to a maximum of $60 for a full load — a real bargain.

2). Dominican College extension schedule. (415) 485-3255. The college is located in San Rafael. Extension classes are offered outside the regular program. You don't need transcripts, you don't need to be "accepted," you don't need a college degree. This is true of all extension programs (but some classes might be offered in sequence; Ballet I before Ballet II.)

3). Sonoma State University Extension Schedule. College is located in Rohnert Park, about 46 miles north of Golden Gate. Phone (707) 664-2880.

4) The University of California-Berkeley Extension Schedule. UC runs one of the biggest programs in the Bay Region. Many classes are offered in downtown San Francisco. Phone (510) 642-4111.

More Sources

• Flip through the phone book under the activity you're interested in. Sounds obvious but many people don't.

• Get the local paper. Almost all do a good job on "calendar of events." Business sections carry information about seminars, improvement classes, Toastmasters, etc.

• Ask the people directly involved. If you see kids kicking a soccer ball and your nipper wants to play the game, ask the kids or their coach if there's a league. If interested in little theater, call a playhouse and inquire about acting groups. Many small groups put out newsletters. Get on the mailing list.

• Ignore, in some cases, religious affiliation. The Young Men's Christian Association doesn't ask you for proof of baptism to take weight training. The Jewish Community Center near the Marin Civic Center welcomes all.

• Make an offer. Many groups would sincerely like you to use their facilities if you paid the freight and a little extra. Say you work at a place that has 10-12 tried and true basketball nuts, but there's no court nearby or the one available is always busy.

Approach the local junior high or high school and say something along the line of, we would like to rent your gym on Monday evenings or whenever it's available. We will abide by your rules, get insurance (policies are available), and not show up when you need the gym.

Places to Visit — A Marin Sampler

• **Marin Civic Center, San Rafael.** What Marin County inspired in Frank Lloyd Wright. Public building. Drop in any time. Take Civic Center Drive or San Pedro Road off of Highway 101. Tours available by arrangement. (415) 499-6104.

• **Marin Headlands,** the land just west of the bridge. Spectacular vistas of San Francisco, the Golden Gate, the Pacific. Formerly used to place artillery; fortifications still there. To reach, take Sausalito exit closest to bridge, pick up Bunker Road. Information (415) 331-1540.

• **Mt. Tamalpais.** See Farallones, Sierra, Richmond, Oakland, San Fran. Many trails to top. Rite of passage for Marin residents. Pick up Panoramic Highway off Route 1. Info at Pan Toll ranger station. (415) 388-2070.

• **Muir Woods.** Giant coast redwoods. Highway 101 to Route 1 to Panoramic Highway to Muir Woods Trail. (415) 388-2595.

• **Point Reyes.** The Pacific Coast. One big park. Lighthouse. Trails. Earthquake country, where the San Andreas Fault goes to sea. (415) 663-1092.

• **Golden Gate National Recreation Area.** The general name given the big park purchase made by the feds in the 1970s. Includes Muir Woods, Point Reyes and Headlands (but state and private groups still active in managing selected areas). Also includes parks of San Francisco coast. Info. (415) 556-0560. For trails and maps and detailed info, most bookstores carry publications about the park.

• **Golden Gate Bridge.** You can't walk across the Bay Bridge or the San Rafael. You can the Golden Gate. It's worth it.

• **Angel Island.** Off Tiburon. A park. West Coast Ellis Island. Chinese immigrants were detained here. Picnic grounds. Trails. Beaches. Views. Ferry from Tiburon. Park (415) 435-1915. Ferry (415) 546-2896.

• **Samuel P. Taylor State Park,** Redwoods, 2,576 acres. Campsites. Off Sir Francis Drake Boulevard, close to Route 1. (415) 488-9897.

• **China Camp.** State park, 1,500 acres. Chinese fishing village in last century. (415) 456-0766. Next to McNear Beach, a county park. Fishing pier, public pool, tennis courts, mile-long beach. (415) 456-1286.

• **Coast Route.** Route 1, Shoreline Highway. A pretty drive, especially in fall when fog disappears or in the spring when the hills are green. If in the mood, take it up to Russian River and beyond. Restaurants, bed and breakfast, resorts along the way.

• **Marin County Parks.** Besides McNear in San Rafael, the county maintains parks in Novato, Corte Madera and at a second location along San Pablo Bay in San Rafael. The county also is responsible for land dedicated for open space. For map, info. (415) 499-6387.

• **Bay Area Discovery Museum.** In Sausalito at old Fort Baker. Opened in 1991 and still being expanded. Kids museum that adults will find fun and interesting. Live fish, murals of Bay habitats, pretend salmon fishing, science corner, boat making, story telling, drafting table, photo dark room and more. (415) 332-7674. Wednesday through Sunday, 10-5 p.m. 557 East Fort Baker Road.

• **Bay Model Visitors' Center.** 2100 Bridgeway in Sausalito. How the rivers and estuary and currents of the Bay interact. A model. Natural history exhibits. (415) 332-3870.

• **Marin Museum of American Indian.** 2200 Novato Blvd., Novato. Artifacts, exhibits. (415) 897-4064.

• **Wildlife Center,** San Rafael, 76 Albert Park Dr. Live animals, birds, natural history. (415) 454-6961.

Places to Visit — A Napa Sampler

• **Lake Berryessa.** Lake-reservoir located in eastern part of the county, off of Highway 128. Boating, water sports. Scenic drive.

• **Marine World-Africa USA.** Located in Vallejo (Solano County) but only a few minutes drive from Napa County. Whales, dolphins, lions, tigers — big theme park. In winter, open Wednesday through Sunday, in summer, seven days. General admission $19.95, kids $14.95, seniors $16.95. Parking $3. Interstate 80 or Highway 29 to Highway 37. Phone (707) 643-6722.

• **Petrified Forest.** Located outside Calistoga. Minerals saturated ancient redwoods, turning them to stone. Daily 10-5. (707) 942-6667.

• **Robert Louis Stevenson State Park.** Located off Highway 29, in northwest section of the county, in shadow of Mt. St. Helena. His health debilitated by tuberculosis, Robert Louis Stevenson, with his bride, took up residence in miner's shack for a short time in the 1880s. In describing a mountain in "Treasure Island," Stevenson gave a detailed picture of Mt. St. Helena, his inspiration. (707) 942-4575. Nearby Calistoga has a Stevenson museum.

• **Wine Country.** In California, Napa is synonymous with wine and, over the last few decades, the wineries have gone to great lengths to welcome visitors with tours and tastings and, lately, with entertainment, such as jazz festivals.

Inspired by the wineries, many restaurants opened. And in some areas, spas that tap into mineral springs have added another element of pleasure. A little golf, a mud bath, a dip, a bottle or two of wine accompanied by an exquisite dinner — la dolce vita.

For details of wineries, pick up Napa County Guide, $4.95 at book stores or send $7 to Vintage Publications, 347-G Healdsburg Ave., Healdsburg, CA 95448.

• **Wine Train.** From Napa to St. Helena and back. Old train activated to tour the valley in style. Dine and sip (wine) on board. Features many of the local vintages. Some residents dislike train, think it an intrusion. But others tolerate and possibly like the choo-choo. Visitors have made it popular.

Twice daily on weekdays, three times daily on weekends and holidays. (800) 427-4124.

Places to Visit — A Sonoma Sampler

• **Armstrong Redwoods.** A grove of the giants. Located just outside Guerneville. Take Armstrong Woods Road from Highway 116. Info. (707) 869-2015.

• **Farm Trails.** If you want to pick what you eat straight from vine or tree, Sonoma County farmers will lay out the welcome mat. About 165 farms and wineries have formed into a "farm trails" group. For free map and details of what each offers, call (707) 586-3276.

• **Fort Ross.** What Russians built when they lived in California. A detailed restoration. Interesting. Just off Highway 1, above Jenner. State park. Info. (707) 847-3286.

• **Glen Ellen.** Where Jack London, California's favorite son, wrote and lived. Ruins of London mansion, the Wolf House. Above city of Sonoma, off Highway 12, in Sonoma Valley wine country. Jack London State Historic Park. (707) 938-5216.

• **Gravenstein-Bohemian Highways.** Back way to the Russian River, through Sebastopol, Occidental. Apples and redwoods. Take 116 off of Highway 101 near Cotati.

• **Lake Sonoma.** Park, fish hatchery, boating, waterskiing, camping, display that tells about Miwok Indians, local plants and animals. From Highway 101 at Healdsburg take Dry Creek Road. (707) 433-2200.

• **Luther Burbank Home.** Perhaps the most famous green thumb in the history of California, Burbank made everything grow. Santa Rosa and Sonoma avenues in downtown Santa Rosa. (707) 524-5445.

• **Mt. St. Helena.** Views, trails, hiking, geologically interesting. Highest mountain in the Bay Area, 4,343 feet. Looks like volcano but isn't. Take Highway 29 to Robert Louis Stevenson State Park. (707) 942-4575.

• **Petaluma Downtown.** Good collection of Victorians, some with iron fronts, an effort at fireproofing and prefabrication. Start on Petaluma Boulevard north. (707) 762-2785.

• **Russian River.** A nice drive in winter, nicer in summer, when the river is dammed to raise the level for canoeing and swimming. Canoe rentals, public beaches along river, including some in Guerneville. On Highway 101, about 5 miles above Santa Rosa you'll see the signs.

• **Sears Point International Raceway**. Sportscar, drag, motorcycle racing. Car shows. School for how to race like the pros. Highway 37 to Highway 121 near Novato. (707) 938-8448.

• **Sonoma Coast**. Highway 1. Start at Bodega Bay or Jenner. Rugged. Great views. For good view of seals, stroll beach at Goat Rock near Jenner. Restaurants, resorts along route.

• **Sonoma Mission**. Small, plain and interesting. The last mission built on El Camino Real, the King's Highway. Nicely restored. Downtown City of Sonoma. (707) 938-1519.

• **Sonoma Plaza**. Where Mariano Vallejo quartered and trained his soldiers and ran his vast estate. Bear Flag Rebellion began here. Restored barracks. Mission close by and, within a half mile, home of Vallejo. Also close by, restaurants, other historical buildings. Highway 12 to middle of City of Sonoma. (707) 938-1519.

• **Whale Watching**. Migrating south between November and February, the California Grey Whale often passes within a half mile of shore. Same on return trip in a few months. Can be seen from Bodega Head State Park, Salt Point State Park, and bluffs of state beach along Sonoma coast. (707) 847-3221.

Private chartered boats put out for closer views in March and April.

• **Wine Country**. For the quick tour, drive Highway 12 south to north, or travel the Redwood Highway north of Santa Rosa. Wineries are all along both routes. Also in Alexander and Dry Creek Valleys, the Russian River area. For details of wineries, pick up Sonoma County Guide, $4.95 at book stores or send $7 to Vintage Publications, 347-G Healdsburg Ave., Healdsburg, CA 95448.

There's more, much more, wine festivals, county fairs, ethnic festivals, church and club activities, theater. Have fun!

15/New Housing

Homes on Sale and Being Built for 1992 in Marin, Napa, Sonoma & Other NorCal Counties

SHOPPING FOR A new home? This chapter gives an overview of new housing under way in Marin, Napa, Sonoma and other nearby counties, including San Francisco and Solano. Smaller projects are generally ignored. If you know where you want to live, drive that town or ask the local planning department what's new in housing.

Prices change. Incidentals such as landscaping fees may not be included. In the 1980s, to pay for services, cities increased fees on home construction. Usually, these fees are included in the home prices but in what is known as Mello-Roos districts, the fees are often assessed like tax payments (in addition to house payments).

Nothing secret. By law developers are required to disclose all fees. But the prices listed below may not include some fees.

After rocketing in the 1980s, home prices, new and resale, stabilized and in many instances dropped. Some developers, particularly in towns with many new units, have gotten very competitive in pricing — an overdue break for buyers. This information, to the best of our knowledge, covers what's available at time of publication. For latest information, call the developers for brochures.

Marin County
Greenbrae
Marin Shores, Westworth Development, Inc., 7 Elizabeth Circle, Greenbrae. Ph: (415) 461-7774. Single-family Detached, 2-4 bedrooms, 2 plus baths, $465,000-$660,000.
Lucas Valley.
Lucas Valley Estates, Parkside Development, Lucas Valley Road to Bridgegate, Lucas Valley. Ph. (415) 491-0812. Single homes, $395,000 and up.
Novato
Hillside Park estates, Barnett-Range Corporation, Novato. Ph: (209) 951-5140. Single-family, 5 bedrooms, 3 baths, $400,000-$442,000.

San Rafael

Baypoint Lagoon, Spinnaker Development, 7 Dowitcher Way, San Rafael. Ph. (415) 258-9099. Townhouses, 3 bedrooms plus, 1,881 to 2,076 sq. ft. From $315,000 to $399,000.

Marin Lagoon, Southwest Diversified, Off McInnis Parkway at 4 Lagoon Court, San Rafael. Ph. (415) 491-1600 or 491-1400. Townhouses starting at $315,000; Estate homes from $400,000.

Regency Estates, Westworth Development, Inc., Heatherstone Lane and Heatherstone Street, San Rafael. Ph: (415) 492-8422. Single-family Detached, 4-5 bedrooms, 3 plus baths, $915,000-$945,000.

Smith Ranch, Tishman Speyer Mediq Marin, Ltd., 100 Deer Valley Road, San Rafael. Ph: (415) 491-4918. Condominium retirement community, 1-2 bedrooms, 1-2.5 baths, $240,000-$500,000.

Tiburon

Hexan Subdivision, Landvest, 15 Cibran Dr., Tiburon. Ph: (415) 457-1800. Single-family home on 0.5-acre, 4-bedroom, 3.5 bath with imported finish materials, Mt. Tam and Bay views, $1,695,000.

Monterossa, Off Red Hill Circle, Tiburon. Ph. (415) 435-7600. View condominiums. Mid $400,000 and up.

Napa County
American Canyon

Summerfield, Napa Estates Venture, 456 Canyon Creed Dr., American Canyon. Ph: (707) 553-9020. Single-family, 3-4 bedrooms, 2-2.5 baths, $157,900-$179,900.

Napa

Dry Creek, Trower Road to Dry Creek Road, turn right, Napa. Ph. (707) 258-0200. Homes, 3-4 bedroom. From $214,000.

Golden Gate Condominiums, Westworth Development, 150 Golden Gate Circle, Napa. Ph: (707) 258-6164. Condominiums, $115,000-$150,000.

The Grove at Silverado, O'Brien & Hicks-The Anden Group, 900 Augusta Circle, Napa. Ph: (707) 224-7641. Condominiums, 2-4 bedrooms, 2-4.5 baths, $650,000-$995,000.

Napa Yacht Club, Lyon Communities, Imola to Jefferson, Napa. Ph. (707) 226-1641. Executive homes, 3-5 bedrooms. Off Napa River. Boat docks or slips. From $291,000.

Rancho Las Flores, Casa Grande Co.-McBail Company, 2118 Camenson Street, Napa. Ph: (510) 226-6007. Single-family from $198,500.

Vineyard Terrace, D & K Development, 1107 Terrace Dr., Napa. Ph: (707) 224-4004. Single-family, 3-4 bedrooms, 2 baths, $195,000-$240,000.

Sonoma County
Petaluma

Adobe Creek, Frates Road off Ely, Petaluma. Ph. (707) 765-9023. Golf club estates, 3-4 bedrooms. $300,000 and up.

Cader Farms, Ryder Homes, Ely Blvd. & Rainer Circle, Petaluma. Ph: (707) 542-2030. Single-family homes from $240,000 to $300,000.

Fairway Meadows, Duffel Co., Adobe Creek off Frates Road, Petaluma. Ph. (707) 762-1833. Single homes, 3-5 bedrooms, 1,722 to 2,352 sq. ft. From $230,000 to $265,000.

Glenbrook, McBail Company, 1605 Lancaster Drive, Petaluma. Ph: (707) 762-6906. Single-family homes from $206,950.

Kings Mill, Ely Boulevard North to Kings Mill, Petaluma. Ph. (707) 763-9547. Estate homes, 3-5-bedrooms, 2,248 to 3,473 sq. ft. $300,000 and up.

Montage, Delco Builders & Developers, Ely Road, Petaluma. Ph: (510) 671-7775. Townhomes-3 bedroom, 2.5 bath, $219,950-$232,050; Single-family detached units coming in Phase II.

Park Place, Young America Homes, from Rainier to Acacia, Petaluma. Ph. (707) 769-8696. Single homes, 3-5-bedrooms, 1,705 to 2,657 sq. ft. From $252,000.

Sonoma Glen, Delco Builders & Developers, Maria Drive, Petaluma. Ph: (510) 671-7775. Single-family detached, 3-5 bedrooms, $227,950-$299,950; Condos and townhomes coming in Phase II.

Victoria, Windsor off D Street, Petaluma. Ph. (707) 765-2333. Single homes, nine floor plans, 1,528 sq. ft. to 3,100. $250,000 to $500,000.

Rohnert Park

Magnolia Park, Camino Colegio to Magnolia, Rohnert Park. Ph. (707) 792-1889. Single homes, 3-5 bedrooms. $215,950 to $249,950.

Villa Alicia, Santa Alicia Drive, Rohnert Park. Ph. 792-0265. Condos, from $96,900.

Windsong Condominiums, Westworth Development, Inc., 8201 Camino Colegio #2, Rohnert Park. Ph: (707) 664-9011. Condominiums, $89,000-$150,000.

Santa Rosa

Arbor Rose Estates, Ken Martin, developer, San Miguel to Banyon, Santa Rosa. Ph. (707) 579-1847. Single homes, 3-4 bedrooms. From $234,900.

Bradbury Place, Waltzer Road, Santa Rosa. Ph. (707) 575-4134. Single homes, 3-4 bedrooms. From $199,000.

Brittain Manor, on Brittain Lane off Occidental, Santa Rosa. Ph. (707) 525-0850. Single homes, 3-5 bedrooms. From $170,000.

Deer Meadows at Fountaingrove, take Fountaingrove and follow signs, Santa Rosa. Ph. (707) 546-3448. Single homes, 3-4-bedrooms. From mid $300,000.

Golf Course Estates, Wickiup Drive, just north of Santa Rosa. Ph. (707) 577-7965.

Park at Brush Creek, Forest Glen Way, Santa Rosa. Ph. (707) 539-3522. Single homes, from $289,500.

Parkview, West College Avenue to Eardley, Santa Rosa. Ph. (707) 545-0113. Townhouses, from $137,400.

Parktrail Estates in Bennett Valley, Christopherson Homes, 4625 Park Trail Court, Santa Rosa. Ph. (707) 537-0214. Single homes, 3-5 bedrooms. From mid $300,000.

Spring Lake Estates, Christopherson Homes, 5301 Montgomery Drive, Santa Rosa. Ph. (707) 538-2470. Single homes, 3-4-5-bedrooms. $285,950 to $409,950.

Stoney Point, Westworth Development, Sebastopol Rd to Sonoma Hwy & Stoney Pt. Road, Santa Rosa. Ph: (415) 461-6316. Townhomes from $150,000 to $170,000.

Vineyard Court, Guerneville Road south to Gamay, Santa Rosa. Ph. 579-9491. Single homes, 3-4-bedrooms. From mid $170,000.

Vintage Woods at Fountaingrove, Brenda Homes, Parker Hill Road, Santa Rosa. Ph. (707) 571-0216. Single homes, 3-4 bedrooms. $336,000 to $395,000.

Sonoma

Mission Oaks, Siesta Way at Barcelona Drive, Sonoma. Ph. (707) 939-0703. Single homes, 3-4 bedroom. From low $300,000.

Montclair Park, Newcomb off Broadway, Sonoma. Ph. (707) 939-1940. Single homes, 3-5 bedrooms. From $285,000.

Windsor

Creek Meadow, Pat Lockwood, developer, Old Redwood Highway to Deanna, Windsor. Ph. (707) 838-6282. Single homes, 3-4 bedrooms, $218,000 to $265,000.

Elsbree, Off Brooks Road, Windsor. Ph. (707) 838-8011. Single homes.

Foothill Estates, The William Lyon Company, 209 Valle Vista, Windsor. Ph: (707) 838-6300. Single-family detached, 3-5 bedrooms, 2-3 baths, low to high $200,000.

Lakewood Glen, Condiotti Developers, on Jessica, Windsor. Ph. (707) 838-3007. Single homes, 3-5 bedrooms. $189,950 to $228,950.

Lakewood Park, Condiotti Developers, on Brooks, Windsor. Ph. (707) 838-3008. Single homes, 3-4 bedrooms, $164,950 to $192,950.

Los Robles Estates, Z.A.M. Enterprises, Rio Ruso Drive, Windsor. Ph. (707) 838-7662. Single homes, 3-4 bedrooms, $178,000 to $198,000.

Oak Hill Estates, Windsor Properties, Windsor. Ph: (707) 838-9336. Half-acre to 3.5-acre homesites priced from $179,000 to $325,000.

Pleasant Pointe, Pleasant Avenue, Windsor. Ph. (707) 838-8324. Single, from $202,500.

Provence, The Gardens, Smoketree Street, Windsor. Ph. (707) 576-1448. Single homes, 3-4 bedrooms, from $180,450.

Ridgeview Estates, Covington Homes, Vinecrest Road, Windsor. Ph. (707) 838-3310. Single homes, 3-4 bedrooms, $209,950 to $234,950.

Vintage Hills, Cobblestone Developers, Foothills to Vinecrest, Windsor. Ph. (707) 838-3160. Single homes, 3-4 bedrooms. From $269,950.

San Francisco

1776 Sacramento Street, Taldan Investment Co., 1776 Sacramento St., San Francisco. Ph: (415) 923-1776. Condos, 1-3 bedrooms, 1-2 baths, from $250,000.

Nob Hill Court, Taldan Investment Co, 1045 Mason Street, San Francisco. Ph: (415) 923-1776. Luxury Condominiums, 2 & 3 bedrooms, from $450,000.

North Beach Village, Taldan Investment Co., 600-690 Chestnut Street, San Francisco. Ph: (415) 922-7800. Condominiums, 1-2 bedrooms, starting at $200,000.

Solano County
Benicia

Encore, Southampton Co., Currey Court, Benicia. Ph: (707) 745-2340. Single-family detached, 3-4 bedrooms, 2-3 baths, low to high $200,000's.

Premier Homes, Southampton Co., 819 Carsten Cr., Benicia. Ph: (707) 745-1432. Single-family detached, 3-6 bedrooms, 2-3 baths, $280,00 to mid-$300,000's.

Southampton, Southampton Co., 701 Southampton Rd., Benicia. Ph: (707) 745-2112. Townhomes, 2-3 bedroom and single-family detached, $150,000-$345,000.

Tempo Homes II, Southampton Co., 599 Rose Drive, Benicia. Ph: (707) 745-2340. Single-family detached, 3-4 bedroom, 2-2.5 baths, $210,000-$275,000.

The Villas, Southampton Co., Panorama Dr., Benicia. Ph: (707) 747-1132. Townhomes, 2-3 bedrooms, 2-2.5 baths, $150,000-low $200,000's.

Cordelia

Green Valley Lake, Fairfield Pacific-Duffel Co., Green Valley Rd. at Mangeus Blvd., Cordelia. Ph: (510) 284-9600. Single-family, 3-4 bedrooms, low to mid-$200,000's.

Dixon

Connemara, MSM Development Corp., 505 McMath Court, Dixon. Ph: (800) 334-7300. Single-family detached, 3-4 bedrooms, 2.5-3 baths, $225,000-$285,000.

Country Faire, The Housing Group-Northern California, 905 South First Street, Dixon. Ph: (510) 426-3040. Single-family, 3-4 bedrooms, 2-3 baths, $165,000-$195,000.

Dixon Heritage, Zeka International, 1930 Rehrmann Dr., Dixon. Ph: (916) 678-0888. Single-family, 3-5 bedrooms, 2-3 baths, $209,900-$219,900.

Fairfield

Diablo Vista, Miller-Sorg Group, Inc., 107 Pine Valley Court-Rancho Solano, Fairfield. Ph: (707) 428-1007. Single-family detached, 3-4 bedrooms, 2-3 baths, $272,850-$306,950.

Fairway Estates, Miller-Sorg Group, 2706 Southern Hills Court-Rancho Solano, Fairfield. Ph: (707) 428-1009. Single-family, golf, 4-5 bedrooms, 3 bath, $330,000-$395,000.

First Green at Rancho Solano, Centex Homes, 3287 Quail Hollow Drive, Fairfield. Ph: (707) 427-2922. Detached golf course homes, 3-5 bedrooms, $330,000-$425,000.

Paradise Valley, Arcadia Development Co., Fairfield. Ph: (707) 428-0311. Single-family, 3-5 bedrooms, 2-3 baths, $200,000-$300,000.

Redwood Grove, D & K Development, 1850 Blossom Ave., Fairfield. Ph: (707) 429-2929. Condominium, 2 bedrooms, 1-2.5 baths, $103,950-$119,950.

Somerset at Southbrook, A.D. Seeno Construction, 1523 Northwood Drive, Fairfield. Ph: (707) 864-0382. Single-family, 3-4 bedrooms, 2-2.5 baths, $147,000-$184,000.

Spyglass Summit, Security Owners Corp, Oliver Rd. and Waterman Blvd., Fairfield. Ph: (707) 425-2396. Single-family detached, 3-5 bedrooms, starting at $234,950.

Suisun

Heritage Park Estates, Heritage Park Estates Development Co., 910 Pepperwood, Suisun. Ph: (707) 428-5911. Single-family, 3-4 bedrooms, $135,000-$170,000.

Heritage Park Estates, Heritage Park Estates Development Co., 910 Pepperwood, Suisun. Ph: (707) 428-5911. Single-family, 3 & 4 bedrooms, $135,000-$170,000.

Lawler Montero, The Hofmann Co., 1312 Potrero Circle, Suisun. Ph: (707) 429-1179. Single-family homes, 3-4 bedrooms, from low-$190,000's.

Lawler Valencia, The Hofmann Co., 243 Seabury, Suisun. Ph: (707) 421-8012. Single-family, 2-4 bedrooms, from low-$130,000's.

Wildrose, Dasun Realty Corp., Worley Rd. & Philip Way, Suisun City. Ph: (707) 421-1201. Single-family, 3-4 bedrooms, $146,950-$181,950.

Vacaville

Foxwood, O'Brien & Hicks-The Anden Group, Nut Tree & Alamo Drive, Vacaville. Ph: (707) 447-9893. Single-family, 2-4 bedrooms, 2-2.5 baths, $129,000-$210,000.

Hidden Oaks, CNA Development, #1 Black Oak Court, Vacaville. Ph: (707) 451-1212. Single-family, 4-5 bedrooms, 2.5-3.5 baths, $250,000-$350,000.

Promenade, U.S. Home Corp., Off Vanden North of Alamo, Vacaville. Ph: (916) 927-4422. Single-family detached, 3-5 bedrooms, 2-3 baths, $187,950-$224,750.

Stonegate Estates, Estate Homes, 212 Stonegate Dr., Vacaville. Ph: (707) 449-3577. Single-family ranch and tri-level, 3-5 bedrooms, 2-3 baths, $208,450-$244,950.

The Terraces at Glen Eagle Ranch, Barnett-Range Corp., 106 Glen Eagle Wy., Vacaville. Ph: (707) 446-2397. Single-family, 3-5 bedrooms, 2-3 baths, from low $200,000.

Vallejo

Bear Ridge, Bear Forest Properties, 195 Glen Cove Marina Rd. #200, Vallejo. Ph: (707) 649-2327. Single-family executive, 4-5 bedrooms, 2.5-4.5 baths, many customized amenities included as standard features, $249,900 to $359,900.

Carriage Oaks, The Lusk Company, 513 Carousel Dr., Vallejo. Ph: (707) 557-5972. Single-family, 3 & 4 bedrooms, 2-3 baths, $165,000-$209,000.

Clearpointe, Centex Homes, 190 Outrigger-Glen Cove, Vallejo. Ph: (707) 643-7731. Duets, 2-3 bedrooms, water views, $167,000-$215,000.

Cypress Point at Northgate, Beck Development Co., Inc., Redwood Pkwy., Vallejo. Ph: (707) 557-4245. Single-family, 3-5 bedrooms, 2-3 baths, $240,000's to $270,000's.

Harbour Towne, Bear Forest Properties, 195 Glen Cove Marina Rd., Vallejo. Ph: (707) 649-2327. Single-family, 3-4 bedrooms, 2.5 baths, low $200,000 to low $300,000.

Somerset Hills, Davidon Homes, 296 Devonshire Court, Vallejo. Ph: (707) 553-1383. Single-family, 3-4 bedrooms, 2.5-3 baths, from mid-$200,000's.

Turnberry, MSM Development Corp., 15 Darlington Place, Vallejo. Ph: (800) 834-7300. Single-family detached, 3-5 bedrooms, 2-3 baths, $239,000-$309,000.

Vista Del Mar, Matrix Land & Development, 699 Glen Cove Parkway, Vallejo. Ph: (707) 553-8883. Single-family, 3-4 bedrooms, 2.5-3 baths, $264,900-$351,900.

Alameda County
Alameda

Harbor Bay Isle, The Doric Group, on San Francisco Bay, Alameda. Ph: (510) 769-5100. Single-family, townhomes, 1-5 bedrooms, 1.5-3 baths, $200,000 to $1,000,000.

Albany

Albany Hills, Landvest Fund 89, Taft & Jackson Sts., Albany. Ph: (510) 457-1800. Townhomes from high $200,000 to low $300,000.

Dublin

Torrey Pines, Standard Pacific, 7676 Tuscany Dr., Dublin. Ph: (510) 551-7777. Condominiums, 1-3 bedrooms, 1-2 baths, $140,000-$200,000.

Fremont

Capriana, A-M Homes, Ardenwood Blvd and Commerce Dr., Fremont. Ph: (800) 794-1926. Townhomes, 2-3 bedrooms, 2.5-3 baths, from low $200,000.

Laurel Heights, Signature Properties, Inc., 48960 Green Valley Road, Fremont. Ph: (510)

651-2696. Single-family, 4 bedrooms, 2-3 baths, $422,500-$499,500.

Mission Heights, Ponderosa Homes, 67 Pilgrim Loop, Fremont. Ph: (510) 651-7143. Single-family, 4-5 baths, 3-3.5 baths, bonus or media rooms, low $600,000.

The Chateaus of Chantecler, Mission Peak Development Co., Mission Blvd., Fremont. Ph: (510) 770-9877. Single-family , 4 & 5 bedrooms, from the high $600,000's.

Livermore

Amber Ridge, Pulte Home Corp., First Street at N. Mines Road, Livermore. Ph: (510) 449-1637. Single-family detached, 4 bedrooms, 2.5-3.5 baths, mid-$300,000's.

Avondale, Signature Properties, Inc., Livermore. Ph: (510) 463-1122. Single-family homes

Monticello, Standard Pacific, 624 Zurmatt St., Livermore. Ph: (510) 447-7777. Single-family detached, 3-4 bedrooms, 2-3 baths, low to high $300,000's.

Murrieta Meadows, Signature Properties, Inc., Livermore. Ph: (510) 463-1122. Single-family homes

Portola Glen Vintage Collection, Warmington Homes, 3661 Glasgow Circle, Livermore. Ph: (510) 373-1801. Executive 4-5 bedrooms, 3-car garages, from low $300,000.

Stratford Park, Signature Properties, Inc., 870 Alison Circle, Livermore. Ph: (510) 373-7002. Single-family, 3-4 bedroom, 2-3 baths, $309,500-$372,500.

The Village at Brookmeadow Park, McBail Co., 1195 Ava Street, Livermore. Ph: (510) 373-6041. Single-family homes from $209,950.

Vintage Development, Diablo Pacific Properties, Arroyo Road & Bess Ave., Livermore. Ph: (510) 373-6300. Single-family, 4-5 bedrooms, 2-3 baths, $519,000-$589,000.

Vintage Lane, Diablo Pacific Properties-Harold Smith Co., Arroyo & Bess, Livermore. Ph: (510) 376-9400. Single-family, 5 bedrooms, 3.5 baths, $519,000-$600,000.

Windmill Springs, McBail Co., 1195 Ava Street, Livermore. Ph: (510) 449-5458. Single-family detached homes from $227,000.

Newark

South Lake Estates, Sunstream Homes, Enfield Dr. in Lake District, Newark. Ph: (510) 713-3112. Single-family executive, 4 & 5 bedrooms, 2.5-3 baths, from $398,950.

Oakland

Dimond Heights, Taldan Investment Co., 2917 MacArthur Blvd., Oakland. Ph: (510) 530-5742. Condominiums, 1-2 bedrooms, from $95,000.

Dimond View Condominiums, Taldan Investment Co., 2901 MacArthur Blvd., Oakland. Ph: (510) 530-5742. Condominiums, 1-2 bedrooms, from $97,950.

Pleasanton

Country Fair II, Ponderosa Homes, 6849 Corte Munras, Pleasanton. Ph: (510) 846-0262. Single-family executive, 4 bedrooms, 2-3 baths, low $400,000's.

San Leandro

Magnolia Lane, Ryder Homes, Cheery Lane & Thornton, San Leandro. Ph: (510) 430-0133. Single-family detached homes, $230,000-$260,000.

Marina Vista, Homestead Financial Corp., 15225 Wicks Blvd., San Leandro. Ph: (510) 692-1432. Single-family, 3-4 bedrooms, 2-3 baths, to mid $300,000's.

Contra Costa County
Antioch

Almondridge, McBail Co., 2704 Almondridge Drive, Antioch. Ph: (510) 778-3246. Single-family homes from $139,900.

Brookside, Barnett-Range Corporation, Antioch. Ph: (209) 951-5140. Single-family, 2-5 bedrooms, 3 baths, 2 & 3-car garages, $228,000-$273,000.

California Country at Williamson Ranch, Kaufman & Broad, 5104 Thistlewood Court, Antioch. Ph: (510) 757-5378. Single-family, 3-4 bedrooms, $160,000-$190,000.

California Homewood at Williamson Ranch, Kaufman & Broad, 5150 Tumbleweed Ct., Antioch. Ph: (510) 754-1665. Single-family, 3-4 bedroom, $140,000's-$160,000's.

Casablanca, O'Brien & Hicks-The Anden Group, 639 Eaker Way, Antioch. Ph: (510) 778-4670. Single-family detached, 3-4 bedrooms, 2-3 baths, $168,000-$221,000.

Deerfield Heights, Ponderosa Homes, 4524 Wildcat Circle, Antioch. Ph: (510) 778-5533. Single-family, 4-5 bedrooms, 2-3 baths, bonus rooms, low $200,000 to low $300,000.

Deerfield Parc, Ponderosa Homes, 4643 Fawn Hill Way, Antioch. Ph: (510) 778-5533. Single-family, 3-5 bedrooms, 2-3 baths, high $100,000-mid $200,000.

Diablo Hills, Pacwest Development, 5059 Sundance Way, Antioch. Ph: (510) 754-1788. Single-family, 3-5 bedrooms, mid-$200,000.

Diamond Ridge Classic Collection, Warmington, 4913 Cougar Peak Way, Antioch. Ph: (510) 778-1712. Single-family, 3-4 bedrooms, 3-car garages, from $180,000's.

Diamond Ridge Vintage Collection, Warmington, 4712 Matterhorn Way, Antioch. Ph: (510) 706-1332. Executive, 4-5 bedrooms, 3-car garages from low $200,000's.

Lone Tree Estates, Davidon Homes, 2713 Joshua Court, Antioch. Ph: (510) 778-3092. Single-family, 3-5 bedrooms, 2.5-3 baths, from the $200,000's.

Mira Vista Place, Garrow & Cardinale Community Builders, Mira Vista Court, Antioch. Ph: (510) 757-3900 or 757-3770. Single-family, 3 bedrooms, 2-2.5 baths, from $169,950.

Montclair, Standard Pacific, 4513 Angel Court, Antioch. Ph: (510) 778-0220. Single-family detached, 3-4 bedrooms, 2-3 baths, low to high $200,000's.

New Horizons at Meadow Creek, Meadow Creek Estates, Inc., 4901 Chism Way, Antioch. Ph: (510) 778-0357. Executive single-family, 4 bedroom, 2-3 bath.

Sunrise Point at Meadow Creek, Meadow Creek Estates, 5109 Woodmont Wy., Antioch. Ph: (510) 754-3702. Single-family, 4-5 bedrooms, 3-car gar., $137,000-$170,000.

Brentwood

California Harvest, Kaufman & Broad, 45 Sweetgrass Drive, Brentwood. Ph: (510) 634-2230. Single-family detached 3 & 4 bedrooms, $170,000-$210,000's.

Four Seasons, Pulte Home Corp., 35 Flagstone Court, Brentwood. Ph: (510) 516-7001. Single-family detached, 3-4 bedrooms, 2-3 baths, low-$200,000's.

Golden Ridge, Homes by Renown, 535 Garland Way, Brentwood. Ph: (510) 634-4334. Single-family, 4 & 5 bedrooms, 2.5-4 baths, $325,000-$419,000.

Walnut Woods, A.D. Seeno Construction Co., Inc., 369 Madrone Place, Brentwood. Ph: (510) 516-0109. Single-family homes, 3 & 4 bedrooms, $205,000-$243,000.

Concord

Canyon Creek, Northstate Development Co., 2191 Bluerock Cr., Concord. Ph: (510) 686-5777. Executive single-family, 2-4 bedrooms, $250,000-$350,000.

Spring Ridge, North State Development Co., 2191 Bluerock Circle, Concord. Ph: (510) 686-5777. Single-family, 4 & 5 bedrooms, $275,000-$375,000.

Danville

Bas of Haskins Ranch, Bas Homes, Inc., Camino Tassajara Road, Danville. Ph: (510) 736-6616. Single-family, 3-4 bedroom, 2-3 baths, $290,000-$340,000.

Cameo Crest, The Housing Group-Northern California, One Chateau Court, Danville. Ph: (510) 736-0770. Single-family, 3-4 bedrooms, 2.5-4 baths, $450,000-$550,000.

Cimarron Hills, Davidon Homes, 105 Cimarron Court, Danville. Ph: (510) 736-5666. Single-family, 4 bedrooms, 2.5-3 baths, 4-car garages, high-$400,000's.

Crown Collection at Vista Tassajara, Standard Pacific, 110 Parkhaven Dr., Danville. Ph: (510) 736-1866. Single-family, 4-bedroom, 2.5-3 baths, $300,000's to mid $400,000.

Empire Collection at Vista Tassajara, Standard Pacific, 17 Lakefield Ct., Danville. Ph: (510) 736-1676. Single-family, 4-5 bedrooms, 2-3 baths, high $300,000's to low-$500,000's.

Heritage Park, Davidon Homes, 109 Heritage Park Dr., Danville. Ph: (510) 736-0568. Deluxe townhomes, 3 bedrooms, 2.5 baths, from mid-$200,000.

Magee Ranch, Concept II Construction, Inc., Danville. Ph: (510) 837-6484. Single-family homes, $750,000-$800,000.

Magee Ranch, Diablo Ranch Dev. Co.-W.S.I. Builders, Inc., Magee Ranch Road, Danville. Ph: (510) 837-8900. Single-family, 3-4 bedrooms, den, $600,000 up.

Meridian Hills, Signature Properties, Inc., 30 Chatsworth Court, Danville. Ph: (510) 736-6619. Single-family, 4-5 bedrooms, 3 baths, $359,500-$480,500.

Meridian Place, Signature Properties, Inc., 426 Sutton Circle, Danville. Ph: (510) 736-0353. Townhomes, 2-4 bedrooms, 2.5 baths, $226,000-$253,000.

Stone Creek, The Lusk Company, 613 Sunhill Drive, Danville. Ph: (510) 736-9114. Executive single-family, 3-5 bedrooms, 2-4.5 baths, from the $400,000's.

Hercules

Chateau at Tiffany Ridge, Sunstream Homes, Turquoise Dr., Hercules. Ph: (510) 758-2660. Single-family executive, 4-5 bedroom, 2.5-3 baths, from $359,950.

Lafayette

Pinebrook, Concept II Construction, Inc., Dewing Ave., Lafayette. Ph: (510) 837-6584. Condominiums, $265,000-$285,000.

Martinez

Elderwood Glen, Davidon Homes, 109 Woodglen Lane, Martinez. Ph: (510) 372-0506. Executive single-family, 4 bedrooms, 2.5 baths, from mid-$300,000.

Stonehurst, Security Owners Corp., Vaca Creek Rd. at Alhambra Valley Rd., Martinez. Ph: (510) 228-5872. Custom homes on 2 to 2.5 acres, lots start at $250,000.

Vinehill Estates, Altamont Development, Vinehill Way & Morello, Martinez. Ph: (510) 228-4940. Single-family, 4 & 5 bedrooms, 3 bath, 2 & 3-car garage, $350,000-$400,000.

Westaire Villas, A-M Homes, Arnold Drive and Old Orchard Rd., Martinez. Ph: (800) 794-1926. Single-family detached, 3-4 bedrooms, 2.5 baths, from the mid $200,000.

Winchester Place, Diablo Pacific Properties, Midhill & Forsythia, Martinez. Ph: (510) 376-94000. Single-family, 4 bedrooms, 2.5 baths, $300,000-$350,000.

Oakley

Fairhaven Parc, A.D. Seeno Construction Co., 910 Fairhaven Court, Oakley. Ph: (510) 625-1311. Single-family homes, 2-4 bedrooms, 2-2.5 baths, $134,000-$168,000.

Pittsburg

California Seasons, Kaufman & Broad, 4 Harmoney Court, Pittsburg. Ph: (510) 709-0121. Single-family detached, 3 & 4 bedrooms, $160,000's-$190,000's.

Marina Park, Whitecliff Homes, 140 Heron Drive-New York Landing, Pittsburg. Ph: (800) 339-9388. Waterfront Townhomes, 3-4 bedrooms, dock , $229,950-$262,950.

Oak Hills, Northstate Development Co., 5995 Woodhill Dr., Pittsburg. Ph: (510) 458-1694. Executive single-family, 3 & 4 bedrooms, $165,000-$185,000.

Oak Hills, Northstate Development Co., 5995 Woodhill Drive, Pittsburg. Ph: (510) 458-1694. Executive single-family, 3 & 4 bedrooms, $165,000-$185,000.

Point Richmond

Brickyard Landing, The Innisfree Companies, Brickyard Cove Road, Point Richmond. Ph: (510) 620-0333. Condominiums, 2-3 bedrooms, 2 baths, $210,000-$350,000.

Richmond

Breakers, A-M Homes, 580 and Marine Bay Parkway, Richmond. Ph: (510) 235-4418. Single-family detached, 3-4 bedrooms, 2.5-3 baths, from the high $200,000's.

San Ramon

Bent Creek Estates, Ponderosa Homes, 608 Helena Creek Court, San Ramon. Ph: (510) 833-9056. Single-family, 4-5 bedrooms, 2-3 baths, mid $300,000 to upper $400,000.

Bent Creek Parc, Ponderosa Homes, 201 Hat Creek Court, San Ramon. Ph: (510) 828-1311. Single-family Jr. Executive, 3-5 bedrooms, 2-3 baths, Low-mid $300,000's.

Echo Ridge, Grupe Development Co. of No. Ca., 3 Tamarron Way, San Ramon. Ph: (510) 735-1010. Single-family detached, 2-3 bedrooms, low to mid-$300,000's.

Old Ranch Estates, Davidon Homes, 1150 Timbercreek Road, San Ramon. Ph: (510) 945-8000. Single-family, 2-4 bedrooms, 2.5 baths, from mid-$300,000.

Vista Pointe, Vermillion Group, Inc., 10 Crow Canyon Ct., Suite 100, San Ramon. Ph: (510) 831-8900, Single-family duets, 2-4 bedrooms, 2.5-3 baths, start at $278,000.

Walnut Creek

Blackwood Estates, Davidon Homes, Blackward Dr. at Ward Dr., Walnut Creek. Ph: (510) 945-8000. Single-family homes, 3-4 bedrooms, 2-plus baths, from $500,000.

16/Jobs & Prices

Job Outlook by Industry in Marin, Napa, Sonoma — Salaries, Grocery Prices, Unemployment Rate

ALTHOUGH HURT by the recession, Marin, Napa and Sonoma counties are doing better than other counties, a pattern that showed up throughout the 1980s, when local unemployment rates always ran below state and national averages.

This is cold comfort to anyone who has lost a job or has suffered a loss in pay. But the strength and resiliency of the local economy offers hope for the future.

Service Sector Most Promising

In all three counties, service leads all sectors in the creation of jobs. Between 1990 and 1992, Napa is expected to add 2,100 service jobs, mostly in resort and restaurant work, Marin, 2,500 (computers, data processing, engineering, personnel), and Sonoma (health, engineering, accounting, research, management).

These predictions were made by the California Employment Development Department, using the best available data, and subject to the everyday forces of modern life. Take with grain of salt.

But they do point out the sectors where growth is expected.

Retail Trade Next

Retail trade is the second fastest growing sector, anticipating between 4,800 jobs in Sonoma, 2,000 in Marin, and 1,300 in Napa.

Commute Counties

Marin, Napa and Sonoma are commute counties, very much dependent on the jobs throughout the Bay Area.

Jobs by Industry Sector

Marin County

Job Sector	1991	1992	Change
Agriculture	400	400	0
Mining & construction	5,800	5,700	-100
Manufact. durable goods	1,700	1,500	-200
Manufact. non durable	3,100	3,000	-100
Transport & public util.	2,400	2,500	+100
Wholesale trade	5,100	5,300	+200
Retail Trade Total	21,800	23,700	+1,900
Restaurants & bars	7,400	7,600	+200
Food stores	3,100	3,300	+200
Department stores	1,900	2,300	+400
Apparel & other retail	7,400	8,400	+1,000
Finance	2,900	2,900	0
Insurance	4,300	4,200	-100
Real Estate	2,400	2,400	0
Services Total	34,600	36,400	+1,800
Bus. services	6,400	6,900	+500
Health services	6,800	6,900	+100
Pvt. education & museums	3,000	3,200	+200
Social services & membership	5,900	6,200	+300
Engr., mgmnt. & other	12,500	13,200	+700
Government Total	14,000	14,100	+100
Federal government	800	800	0
State and local	13,200	13,300	+100
All Sectors Total	98,500	102,100	+3,600

Sonoma County

Job Sector	1991	1992	Change
Agriculture	5,500	5,600	+100
Mining & construction	10,900	11,200	+300
Manufact. durable goods	13,900	14,200	+300
Lumber & wood products	1,900	2,000	+100
Mach., elect. & instruments	9,500	9,600	+100
Other durable goods	2,500	2,600	+100
Manufact. non durable	8,200	8,600	+400
Food processing	5,300	5,600	+300
Other nondurable goods	2,900	3,00	+100
Transport & public util.	6,900	7,100	+200
Wholesale trade	7,200	7,700	+500
Retail Trade Total	33,000	35,600	+2,600
Restaurants & bars	10,700	11,500	+800
Food stores	5,800	6,400	+600
Dept. & apparel stores	4,600	5,000	+400
Auto, svc. stations & other	11,900	12,700	+800
Finance, ins. & real estate	9,300	9,900	+600
Services Total	38,200	41,600	+3,400
Bus. services	5,500	6,000	+500
Health services	9,600	10,000	+400
Hotels & lodging services	2,900	3,200	+300
Engr., mgmt. & research	3,800	4,400	+600
Other services	16,400	18,000	+1,600
Government	24,500	24,700	+200
All Sectors Total	157,600	166,200	+8,600

Source: California Economic Development Department, June, 1991.

What They Earn

Position	Annual Salary
Accounting Clerk	$19,240-$27,040
Admin. Assistant	Up to $27,000
Airline, Various Positions	$12,480-$37,400
Appraiser	$26,260-$31,512
Assembler	$10,400
Auto Sales	$30,000-plus
Baker	$16,640-$24,960
Beverage Manager	$14,500-$20,800
Bookkeeper	$19,760-$27,040
Butcher	$14,560-$29,120
Canvassers	$31,200-$52,000
Carpenter	$16,640
Carpet Shampooer	$19,200
Cashier	$11,440
City Manager, Mill Valley	$83,340-$92,160
Computer Operator	$20,800-$24,960
Construction Laborer	Up to $45,760
Controller, Corporate, Assist.	$25,500-$30,000
Convention Coordinator	$27,040
Cook, Public School	$17,659
Customer Service Rep	$14,560
Dairy Farm Manager	$32,386-$35,624
Data Entry	$17,160-$24,960
Delivery Driver	$12,480
Dental Assistant	$19,670-$29,120
Dental Hygienist	$63,700
Deputy Dist. Attorney, Sonoma	$35,256-$42,852
Diesel Mechanic	$20,800-plus
Dispatcher, Santa Rosa	$27,720-$33,708
Draftsperson/Designer	$33,624-$41,208
Drug Counselor	$20,000-$23,000
Education Specialist, Public School	$34,440
Electrician, City of Santa Rosa	$34,049-$37,273
Electronics Assembler	$12,480-$14,560
Electronics Technician	$21,840-$35,360
Environmental Engineer	$53,742
Environmental Manager	$40,000-$45,000
Financial Service Rep	$30,000-plus
Firefighter, Calistoga	$21,912-$26,640
Gardener, Public School	$20,040-$23,712
Hair Stylist	$12,480-$19,760
Health Care Admin. Analyst	$31,200-$46,800
Hotel Desk Clerk	$12,480-$20,800

What They Earn

Position	Annual Salary
Housekeeper, Live-in	$14,400
Janitor	$11,960-$24,440
Lab Tester	$15,184
Legal Assistant, Paralegal	$21,600-$32,400
Legal Secretary	$26,400-$36,000
Legal Services Director	Up to $50,000
Librarian, School	$43,050-$46,599
Licensed Vocational Nurse	$24,960-$29,120
Marketing Manager	$85,000-plus
Medical Technician	$35,316-$42,528
Medical Transcriber	$24,960-$28,080
Messenger/Driver	$10,800
Office Machine Service	$18,720-$33,800
Office Manager	$30,000
Paramedic, City of Petaluma	$36,412-$44,238
Personnel Recruiter	$32,926-$39,790
Police Officer, Cotati	$28,896-$35,124
Police Officer, Santa Rosa	$34,968-$42,504
Police Officer, Sausalito	$38,136-$44,292
Principal, Petaluma Public School	$45,480-$55,284
Programmers, Computers	Up to $70,000
Public Works Supervisor, Petaluma	$37,800-$45,948
Receptionist	Up to $19,000
Registered Nurse	$33,280-$39,520
Respiratory Therapist	$29,120-$33,800
Restaurant Cook	$20,800-$29,120
Restaurant Manager	Up to $63,000
Roofer	$52,000
Sales Clerk	$14,560-$19,670
School Bus Driver	$12,480
Secretary	$16,500-$19,700
Security Guard	$11,440-$16,640
Shipping Clerk	$16,640
Short Order Cook	$12,480-$19,260
Teacher's Aide	$13,520
Telemarketer	$26,000-$52,000
Teller, Bank	$11,960-$19,240
Travel Agent	$16,000-$22,000
Truck Driver	$22,880
Warehouse Assistant	$15,600
Winery Bottling Manager	$20,800

Source: California Employment Development Department and survey of local help wanted ads, fall and summer, 1991.

Grocery Prices

Item	High	Low	Avg
Apple Juice, frozen, cheapest, 12 oz.	$1.19	$0.95	$1.04
Apple Pie, Mrs. Smith's, 26 oz.	$3.19	$2.69	$2.96
Apples, Red Delicious, 1 lb.	$0.79	$0.49	$0.62
Aspirin, cheapest, 100 pills	$1.40	$0.89	$1.08
Baby Food, Gerber, bananas, 4 oz jar	$0.38	$0.36	$0.37
Baby Food, Gerber, spinach, 4 oz jar	$0.38	$0.36	$0.37
Bacon, Armour, 1 lb.	$2.68	$1.99	$2.29
Bananas, 1 lb.	$0.39	$0.39	$0.39
Beef, chuck roast, 1 lb.	$2.89	$2.68	$2.79
Beef, ground round, 1 lb.	$2.99	$2.38	$2.79
Beer, Budweiser, 6-pack, cans	$3.89	$3.79	$3.85
Beer, Coors, 6-pack, cans	$3.89	$3.79	$3.85
Bleach, Clorox, 1 gal.	$1.23	$1.17	$1.20
Bread, sourdough, Colombo, 1 lb	$1.89	$1.67	$1.74
Bread, white, cheapest, 1 lb.	$0.59	$0.50	$0.56
Broccoli, bunch	$0.79	$0.69	$0.76
Butter, Challenge, 1 lb.	$1.99	$1.85	$1.91
Cabbage, 1 lb.	$0.33	$0.19	$0.28
Cantaloupe, 1 lb.	$0.99	$0.50	$0.76
Carrots, fresh, 1 lb.	$0.33	$0.25	$0.28
Cat food, 9 Lives, 6 oz.	$0.40	$0.34	$0.37
Charcoal, Kingsford, 10 lbs.	$3.99	$3.79	$3.89
Cheese, Swiss, 1 lb.	$3.79	$3.29	$3.59
Chicken, fryer, 1 lb.	$0.99	$0.47	$0.81
Chili, Dennison, 15 oz. can	$0.99	$0.99	$0.99
Cigarettes, Marlboro Lights, carton	$18.99	$16.99	$18.22
Coca Cola, six-pack, 12 oz. cans	$2.19	$1.99	$2.06
Coffee, Folgers, 1 lb. 10 oz.	$3.99	$3.49	$3.76
Cookies, Oreo, 1 lb.	$2.89	$2.59	$2.72
Corn Flakes, Kellogg, 18 oz.	$2.25	$1.95	$2.06
Diapers, Pampers, box of 36	$9.99	$9.39	$9.79
Dishwashing liquid, Joy, 22 oz.	$1.65	$1.19	$1.44
Dog Food, Kal Kan, 14 oz. can	$0.73	$0.63	$0.68
Eggs, large, Grade AA, doz.	$1.39	$1.35	$1.36
Flour, Gold Medal, 5 lbs.	$1.09	$0.89	$0.99
Frozen Yogurt, Dreyers, half gal.	$4.59	$4.39	$4.46
Gin, Beefeater, 750 ml.	$14.88	$13.98	$14.48
Grapefruit, 1 lb.	$0.34	$0.26	$0.31
Grapenuts, Post, 24 oz.	$3.49	$3.39	$3.46
Ham, 1.5-lb. tin	$6.99	$6.79	$6.89
Ice Cream, Store Brand, vanilla half gal.	$2.39	$2.00	$2.19
Ketchup, Del Monte, 32 oz.	$1.79	$1.49	$1.66

Grocery Prices

Item	High	Low	Avg
Ketchup, Heinz, 28 oz.	$2.09	$1.89	$1.96
Lamb, leg of, 1 lb.	$3.39	$2.78	$3.05
Laundry Detergent, Tide, 39 oz.	$2.89	$2.75	$2.84
Lettuce, Iceberg, head	$0.69	$0.59	$0.62
Margarine, Imperial, whipped, 1-lb. tub	$1.55	$1.47	$1.50
Mayonnaise, Best Foods, 1 qt.	$2.37	$2.37	$2.37
Milk, skim, half gallon	$1.11	$1.10	$1.10
Milk, whole, half gallon	$1.19	$1.17	$1.18
Mixed vegetables, frozen, 10 oz.	$0.63	$0.59	$0.60
Mushrooms, 1 lb.	$2.49	$1.39	$2.09
Olive Oil, cheapest, 1 pt.	$3.79	$2.59	$3.32
Onions, 1 lb.	$0.27	$0.20	$0.24
Orange juice, frozen, cheapest, 12 oz.	$1.09	$0.89	$0.99
Oranges, fresh, 1 lb.	$0.99	$0.59	$0.82
Peanuts, cocktail, Planter's, 12 oz.	$2.77	$2.65	$2.72
Peas, frozen, 10 oz.	$0.69	$0.59	$0.64
Pork, chops, 1 lb.	$2.88	$2.19	$2.55
Potato Chips, Eagle, 6.5 oz	$1.59	$1.29	$1.42
Potatoes, 1 lb	$0.34	$0.25	$0.31
Raisins, bulk, 1 lb.*	$1.29	$1.19	$1.24
Red Snapper, fresh, 1 lb.	$4.19	$2.98	$3.72
Rice, Hinode, 5 lbs.	$3.99	$2.29	$3.38
Seven-Up, 6-pack, cans	$2.25	$1.69	$1.98
Soap, bar, Ivory, 4-pack	$1.85	$1.55	$1.71
Soup, Campbell, Chicken Noodle, 10 oz.	$0.53	$0.51	$0.52
Soy Sauce, Kikkoman, 20 oz.	$2.85	$2.15	$2.41
Spaghetti, cheapest, 1 lb.	$0.95	$0.49	$0.78
Sugar, cheapest, 5 lbs.	$1.79	$1.69	$1.74
Toilet Tissue, 4-roll pack, cheapest	$0.99	$0.59	$0.82
Tomatoes, Beefsteak	$0.59	$0.49	$0.56
Toothpaste, Crest, 6.4 oz.	$2.25	$2.19	$2.21
Tortillas, cheapest, 14 oz.	$0.59	$0.43	$0.50
Turkey, ground, 1 lb.	$3.99	$1.78	$2.89
Turkey, whole, hen, 1 lb.*	$1.19	$0.78	$0.99
Vegetable Oil, Wesson, 24 oz.	$1.65	$1.49	$1.58
Whiskey, Cutty Sark, 750 ml.	$16.88	$15.88	$16.25
Whiskey, Johnnie Walker Red, 750 ml.	$15.99	$15.88	$15.92
Wine, Burgundy, Gallo, 1.5 liter	$4.50	$3.49	$4.06
Wine, Chablis, Gallo, 1.5 liter	$4.50	$3.49	$4.06

Source: Survey of three San Francisco Bay Area supermarkets in fall, 1991. Prices are the highest, lowest and average of those found at the three stores. Asterisk (*) items were available at only two stores during survey.

Jobs by Industry Sector

Napa County

Job Sector	1988	1993*	Change
Mining & construction	2,600	2,900	+300
Manufact. durable goods	900	900	0
Manufact. non durable**	4,200	4,900	+700
Transport & public util.	1,200	1,300	+100
Wholesale trade	1,100	1,200	+100
Retail Trade Total	7,700	9,000	+1,300
Restaurants & bars	3,200	3,800	+600
Food stores	1,300	1,400	+100
Department stores	600	700	+100
Auto dlrs. & service stations	800	900	+100
Other retail trade	1,800	2,200	+400
Finance	1,000	1,200	+200
Insurance & real estate	700	1,000	+300
Services Total	12,200	14,300	+2,100
Business services	1,100	1,400	+300
Health services	3,600	4,000	+400
Hotels & lodging	1,900	2,400	+500
Personal services	300	350	+50
Other services	5,300	6,150	+850
Government Total	8,200	8,900	+700
Federal government	300	300	0
State and local	7,900	8,600	+700
All Sectors Total	39,800	45,600	+5,800

Source: California Economic Development Department, June, 1991. *Projections. **Agriculture was combined with manufacturing projections.

Unemployment Rate

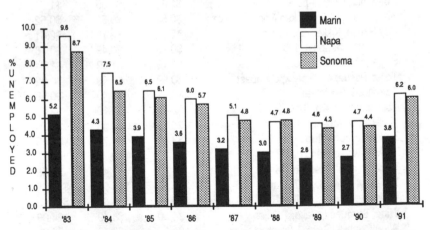

Source: U.S. Bureau of Labor Statistics, average annual unemployment rate. Average rate for 1991 calculated from January, 1991, through September, 1991. Full-year rate may vary.

17/Commuting Help

From Marin, Napa & Sonoma to San Fran — Driving Distances, Buses and Ferries

IN THE VERY SHORT LIST of drawbacks to living in the North Bay, one affliction far and away overshadows the rest: commuting.

Only one road leads directly to San Francisco. Highway 101 travels the length of Marin and Sonoma counties and feeds into the Golden Gate Bridge.

As freeways go, it's not bad, and in the 1990s, with the passage of highway spending measures, it will be improved. For people living in Sausalito and southern and central Marin, the commute, relative to what so many others go through, is pretty good. When traffic is flowing, they can make their front doors within a half hour.

Beyond, say, San Rafael, matters get dicey. And it's not so much the road as the bridge. It's a bottleneck, unable to move the traffic at freeway speeds.

Voices are raised occasionally to add a second auto deck to the Golden Gate but don't hold your breath waiting. Better access to San Francisco would mean more cars on City streets — sure to arouse San Fran opposition.

It would also mean heavier development pressures on Marin and Sonoma counties, which many residents don't want.

Napa Ways

Although some Napa County commuters probably head over to Highway 101 to get to San Francisco, Interstate 80 through Vallejo is the shorter route. It leads down the East Bay shore to the Bay Bridge, and into the City — another wearying journey.

Not only do jams develop at the Crockett-Vallejo Bridge, but at times the whole length of the East Bay stretch congests into stop-and-go.

The last 20 years have seen a great deal of development in West Contra

Mileage to Golden Gate Bridge
Traveling Highway 101

Marin County		Sonoma County	
City or Location	**Miles**	**City or Location**	**Miles**
Belverdere	10	Cotati	45
Corte Madera	9	Cloverdale	86
Fairfax	15	Guerneville	78
Kentfield	11	Healdsburg	71
Larkspur	10	Petaluma	39
Mill Valley	7	Rohnert Park	46
Novato	28	Santa Rosa	57
Ross	12	Sebastopol	64
San Anselmo	13	Sonoma	47
San Rafael	11	Sonoma Co.Airport	59
Sausalito	2	Windsor	65
Tiburon	9	**Note:** Approximate driving distances.	

Distance to Bay Bridge (Oakland)
Traveling Highway 29 & Interstate 80

Napa County

City or Location	Miles	City or Location	Miles
City or Location	**Miles**	**City or Location**	**Miles**
Calistoga	64	American Canyon	29
St. Helena	56	Crockett-Vallejo Bridge	21
Yountville	47	El Cerrito BART Station	6
Napa	38	**Note:** Approximate driving miles.	

Costa and Solano County. The freeways just have not kept up.

About the only silver lining glimmering is the Contra Costa job market. It boomed in the 1980s, creating thousands of jobs within a shorter drive for Napa residents than City jobs.

Rail Alternative-Marin & Sonoma

What's being talked up now: revamping Golden Gate Bridge to run a rail line across. One possibility: something that ties in with BART (Bay Area Rapid Transit), which serves Contra Costa, San Francisco, Alameda and San Mateo counties. For the foreseeable future, no matter how much 101 is widened and spruced up, you will still have to deal with the constricted Golden Gate. Fortunately there are some alternatives.

The 101 Grind

First, however, the nature of Highway 101. Marin commuters along 101 will, depending on the location of home and hearth, drive anywhere from 2 to 28 miles to reach the Golden Gate Bridge. Sonoma County drivers can look forward to a drive of 39 to 86 miles. See chart.

Richmond-San Rafael Bridge

The North Bay is also served by the Richmond-San Rafael Bridge, a span of 5.5 miles, usually a fast shot to the East Bay. The Miller-Knox freeway, Richmond to Interstate 80, places you on Interstate 80 at Albany, about five miles from the San Francisco-Oakland Bay Bridge, and another 8 miles from San Francisco.

If the Golden Gate is hopelessly jammed, and you must be in San Francisco with a car, or if you're jammed going north from the City, this is the alternate route. From San Rafael, it's trip of about 30 miles.

Forget the Side Roads

In almost every other county in the Bay Region, it pays to know the side roads that parallel the freeway and can get you around jams. In Marin, and to a lesser extent, Sonoma and Napa, it doesn't. Few worth knowing exist.

The frontage roads usually start, stop and curlicue off into side streets or roads that take you to the countryside. If commuting to the City, you're stuck with the freeways.

The obvious strategy: leave home early, leave work early. As much as possible, avoid the rush hours. Buy a book of toll tickets. It will save you a few bucks, and a few minutes at the bridge toll plaza.

Car Pooling

To save more time and bucks, join a car pool. The Golden Gate and San Rafael bridges have set aside a lane for pools (at least three persons per vehicle). No toll. In Marin County, parts of Highway 101 reward car poolers with their own lanes. Only two or more needed to drive these lanes.

RIDES, phone 861-POOL, will help you find a carpool in your town — no charge, in all three counties. In the typical arrangement, passengers meet at one or two spots and are dropped off at one or two destinations. The pools go all over. All that's needed are passengers and a driver.

If you want to set up a van pool, RIDES will help you find passengers and lease a van. Typically, passengers share van expenses, and driver rides free and has personal use of van.

Driving alone with a round-trip commute of 60 to 79 miles costs over $500 monthly, RIDES estimates. With a car pool, costs drop to $78-105, says RIDES.

Buses

Bus lines traverse the three counties. Yes, buses take longer and the car is handier, but the bus companies, through discounts and express buses, try to speed you along and leave some money in the pocket. The bus lines:

Golden Gate Transit District

Bus service throughout Marin to cities, hamlets, even Stinson Beach and Inverness. Expresses to San Fran. Buses also to Larkspur Landing and ferries.

Golden Gate Transit also provides San Francisco service to cities in Sonoma County, including Cotati, Petaluma, Rohnert Park, Santa Rosa and Sebastopol. Fares from downtown San Francisco, one way, range from $1.85 to $3.70, depending on distance.

Discounts of 50 percent for disabled and people over 65. Students can buy 20 tickets for $15 and commuters can buy discount coupon books. Park-and-Ride lots at some major bus stations.

For information and schedules: from southern Marin (415) 332-6600; from central and north, (415) 453-2100. From Sonoma County (707) 544-1323.

Sonoma County Transit

Local bus service to towns and cities along Highway 101 in Sonoma County. Also to City of Sonoma, Sebastopol and Russian River towns.

Sonoma Transit runs buses throughout that county and to stops where you can transfer to San Francisco buses. The company serves all the major cities along or near Highway 101, the Russian River towns and the City of Sonoma.

For schedules and more information (800) 345-7433.

Other Sonoma County Bus Lines

Five cities run local buses. For information and schedules, phone: Sebastopol, (707) 823-7863; Healdsburg, (707) 431-3309; Petaluma, (707) 778-4460; Cloverdale, (707) 894-2521; and Santa Rosa, (707) 576-5306.

Napa Buses

Napa City Buses, also known as The Vine. Service daily, except Sundays. Buses to San Francisco via BART link from Vallejo.

The Vine also serves communities up and down the valley: Calistoga, St. Helena, Rutherford, Yountville, American Canyon and Vallejo.

Fares start at 75 cents and are levied according to distance traveled. Samples: Calistoga to Vallejo, $2.50; Napa City to Vallejo, $1.50. Kids under five ride free. For info, schedule, (707) 255-7631.

BART Stations

Napa commuters to Oakland, southern Alameda County and San Francisco can pick up BART at Richmond and El Cerrito. Parking is sometimes a

problem. Arrive early, leave work early. For BART information, call (510) 236-2278.

By Ferry—Marin

From Larkspur Landing to Ferry Building in San Francisco, $2.20 weekdays, kids $1.65, seniors $1.10 First run is at 5:30 a.m., the last return trip is at 8:25 p.m. Takes 45 minutes.

From Sausalito to San Francisco Ferry Building, at foot of Market Street, $3.50 weekdays, kids $2.60, seniors, $175. First run 7:15 a.m., last return trip 8 p.m. Takes half hour.

For more info, schedules, call Golden Gate Transit District, from Marin (415) 332-6600, from Sonoma (707) 544-1323.

Red and White runs ferries from Tiburon to San Fran (415) 546-2810.

First ferry, 7:05 a.m., last from City, 7:15 p.m. Cost $4.50 each way. Discount books.

Ferry—Napa

Napa residents can board a San Francisco ferry at Mare Island Way near Vallejo City Hall. One ferry in morning, one in evening: 6:30 a.m. and 5:15 p.m. $7.50 one way. Discount books. For information, (415) 546-2810.

The Last Alternative

Lastly, if you just can't hack it any longer — buses, ferries or the Golden Gate — see if you can find a job near your home. In recent years many jobs have moved out of the City. One with your name on it might be waiting for you.

Commuting Tidbits

• All major bridges in the Bay Area, except one, charge $1 toll. The Golden Gate charges $3. All give you one way free. The toll plaza for the Golden Gate is on the San Francisco side; you pay going into the City. With the Richmond-San Rafael, you pay in Richmond going west.

Discount coupons for frequent commuters can be purchased. Carpoolers during peak hours cross toll free.

• Highway 37. If you live in Novato or many parts of Sonoma and work in Vallejo or places like Concord and Walnut Creek, it may be faster to take Highway 37 (Novato to Vallejo).

Heavily traveled both ways, no median barrier, Highway 37 is one of those ghastly two-lane roads that ask to you keep your headlights on, day or night. Some improvements are being made.

• Several years ago, the coast route, Highway 1, washed out between Stinson and Muir beaches. Repairs were to have taken three years but the state moved quickly and reopened the route in 1991.

18/Crime

Low in Marin, Napa & Sonoma, Compared to Other Regions, But Always Take Precautions

IF YOU'RE BUYING A HOUSE or choosing a neighborhood, it is important to remember that although vandals, muggers and murderers can strike anywhere, they do most of their damage in sections where the poor reside.

Which is not to say that the middle class and rich are universally good. The savings and loans swindlers, generally silvered at birth, ruined many and did the country great harm. The rich and middle class have their thieves and their murderers.

Nor is it to say that the poor are universally criminal. Many poor and low-income people obcy the law and live good lives, and in many countries the connection between poverty and crime is weak. In the years immediately following World War II, almost all Japanese were impoverished but social values kept crime low.

In this country, however, violent crime is most likely to be committed by the down-and-out, the abused, the addicted, the demented and the aimless, especially if they are young. These persons, because of their backgrounds and actions, are likely to be poor and live in low-income neighborhoods.

In its annual reports, the FBI correlates crimes by ethnicity, age, sex, kinship and friendship.

The ethnic correlation gets tricky because it it implies blame by ethnicity rather than social condition. Historically, once groups move up the social scale, crime decreases.

Women are much more peaceful than men. In homicide arrests, the chances are 8 to 1 a man will be booked, says FBI.

The old are more law-abiding than the young. The FBI reports that in 1990 persons age 12 through 29 accounted for 63 percent of all arrests.

When the violent and the criminal strike, they generally attack or rob their neighbors, often their friends and relatives, studies have shown. Many crimes are crimes of proximity and easy opportunity (which is why precautions and safeguards do help; they discourage the often easily discouraged.)

Between the rich and the poor, crime moves across a spectrum. In middle-class communities, crime rates are middling. Within these communities, the poorer sections will often be afflicted with higher crime than the others.

Washington, D.C. is notorious for its crime. Yet, according to the Washington Post, police studies show that the neighborhoods that have suffered high crime for decades are the ones that now suffer the most; and crime in middle- and upper-income neighborhoods is no more serious than it has been in times past.

(But the violence in the poorer neighborhoods has worsened, mainly because of drugs and easy access to guns. And the middle class and rich neighborhoods may be taking stronger precautions than before. It's not just location.)

The same pattern holds in the Bay Area. East Oakland, high crime; Oakland hills, low. Bayview district in San Francisco, high; Twin Peaks, Pacific Heights, low.

In Sonoma County, Roseland, an unincorporated neighborhood south of Santa Rosa, sometimes gets mentioned in the newspapers as troubled. In Marin County, Marin City, outside Sausalito, and the Canal section of San Rafael have been labeled high crime. .

High compared to what? Another problem. The combined population of Marin, Napa and Sonoma is 729,000. Homicides and non-negligent man-slaughters in 1990, the last FBI count, numbered four in Marin, five in Napa, and 12 in Sonoma, the most populous of the three counties (True numbers may be slightly higher as the FBI doesn't breakout crimes in cities under 10,000 population).

Estimated total of homicides in the three counties: 21.

San Francisco, population 724,000, recorded 101 homicides in 1990. Oakland, with about half the population, 146; Richmond, with less than 90,000 residents, 36 homicides.

So when people say crime is high in Marin City, etc., what they may really mean is crime is high according to the North Bay's expectations of crime.

Oakland and San Fran and other cities would be jubilant if they could lower their crime to anything near the North Bay's.

Incidentally, the fewer the stores, the lower the crime rate, and vice versa. Theft is the most commonly reported crime.

The Twin Cities police department in Marin County includes Larkspur and Corte Madera. Violent crime low; thefts high, 7 out of every 10 crimes reported. Corte Madera includes two of the biggest malls in Marin.

Is any town or neighborhood 100 percent safe? As long as human beings

Crime Ratings by City
Marin County

City	Population	Rate	Homicides
Mill Valley	13,038	31	0
Novato	47,585	28	0
San Anselmo	11,743	31	0
San Rafael	48,404	56	1

Napa County

City	Population	Rate	Homicides
Napa, City of	61,842	56	1

Sonoma County

City	Population	Rate	Homicides
Petaluma	43,184	37	0
Rohnert Park	36,326	44	0
Santa Rosa	113,313	59	1

Other Northern California Cities

City	Population	Rate	Homicides
Oakland	372,242	109	146
Richmond	87,425	113	36
San Francisco	753,927	88	92
San Jose	782,248	49	35

Crime in Other Cities

City	Population	Rate	Homicides
Atlanta	394,017	192	231
Boston	574,283	119	143
Dallas	1,006,877	155	447
Detroit	1,027,901	122	582
Honolulu	836,231	61	34
Miami	358,548	190	129
New York	7,322,564	97	2,245
New Orleans	496,938	124	304
Philadelphia	1,585,577	72	503
Reno	133,850	86	11
Seattle	516,259	126	53
Washington, D.C.	606,900	108	472

Source: Annual 1991 FBI crime report which uses 1990 data, including 1990 Census Bureau population estimates. **Key**: Rate is all reported crimes per 1,000 residents. Homicides cover murders and non-negligent manslaughter. The FBI does not rank unincorporated towns or cities below 10,000 population.

roam the earth, the answer is no. The "safest" place will still be prey to the random element, which in many homicides is the victim's friend or relative.

The North Bay, compared to other regions, is quite safe but some places are safer than others. It's tempting to say, pick the safest place possible. But the reality is that your income will limit your choices. We can't all live in gated communities.

Choose your address with care. Drive the streets of the neighborhood. Look for telltale signs: bars on windows, men idling at liquor stores, very low school rankings (which indicate many kids are dropping out and are likely to be prone to trouble.)

Take precautions: alarms, neighborhood watches, good locks.

19/Weather

How the Fog, Breeze and Sunshine Play Their Roles in Marin, Napa and Sonoma

NORTH BAY WEATHER, without exaggeration, can be described as delightful, with one big qualifier. If you live near the coast, you have to like fog. Otherwise, in summer, you might get depressed. For inland regions, summer nights are cool, summer days rarely excessively hot, rarely humid. Rain confines itself to the winter months, a great blessing to the vineyards, and rarely falls more than 25-30 inches a year. Winters are rarely cold.

This is a general description. On some summer days you will swelter, on some winter nights you will shiver. In some years, less than 20 inches of rain will fall, in others, more than 50. Although erratic, the weather follows broad patterns, easily understood, and worthwhile understanding. It will help you decide when to hold picnics, when to eat in, when to visit the coast.

Five actors star in the weather extravaganza: the sun, the Pacific, the Golden Gate, the Central Valley and the Mountains.

The Sun

In the spring and summer, the sun moves north bringing a mass of air called the Pacific High. The Pacific High blocks storms from the California coast and dispatches winds to the coast.

In the fall, the sun moves south, taking the Pacific High with it. The winds slough off for a while, then in bluster the storms. Toward spring, the storms abate as the Pacific High settles in.

When should you have a picnic? Rarely will the summer disappoint you with rain, and if it does, the rain will be miniscule. See chart. Incidentally, this is a big reason why vineyards thrive in Northern California. The Pacific High assures a long dry growing season.

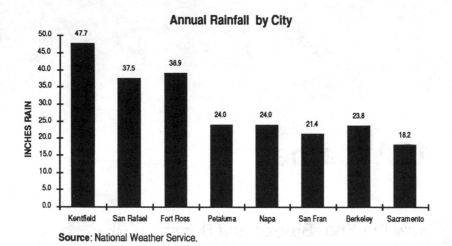

Annual Rainfall by City

Source: National Weather Service.

The Pacific

Speeding across the Pacific, the spring and summer winds pick up moisture and, approaching the coast at an angle, strip the warm water from the surface and bring up the frigid.

Cold water exposed to warm wet air makes a wonderfully thick fog. In summer, San Francisco, the coasts of San Francisco, Marin and Sonoma are often buffeted by a cold fog that blows in off the ocean. Occasionally, the fog just sits on the coast and builds into a cottony mass. When other conditions develop, the coast is clear.

The Golden Gate and the Mountains

This fog would love to scoot inland to the Bay towns and inland cities: Sausalito and San Rafael, Santa Rosa, Petaluma and Napa.

But the coastal hills and mountains stop or greatly impede its progress — except where there are openings. Of the half dozen or so major gaps, the biggest is that marvelous work of nature, the Golden Gate. The fog shoots through the Golden Gate in the spring and summer, visually delighting motorists on the Bay Bridge, bangs into the East Bay hills, and eases down toward San Jose and up

Average Monthly Temperatures

City	Ja	Fb	Mr	Ap	My	Ju	Jy	Au	Sp	Oc	No	Dc
Kentfield	47	51	53	56	60	65	67	67	66	61	53	48
San Rafael	50	53	55	58	62	66	68	68	68	64	56	45
Fort Ross	50	51	51	51	54	56	57	58	59	57	53	50
Petaluma	47	51	52	55	59	64	67	67	67	62	54	48
San Francisco	49	52	53	55	58	61	62	63	64	61	55	49

Source: National Weather Service.

to Richmond and Vallejo, where it takes the edge off the summer temperatures.

Where the mountains dip, where rivers and streams to the ocean carve gaps in the hills, the fog penetrates. The Estero Gap, just south of Bodega Bay, admits the cooling air to the Petaluma and Cotati (Santa Rosa) valleys. These towns in summer are often cooler than Cloverdale, located farther to the north and blocked by hills from the ocean influence.

Giant redwoods need fog to thrive. The Armstrong Grove near Guerneville owes much to the ocean fog that creeps up the Russian River. Muir Woods in Marin County is almost directly exposed to ocean fog.

In some areas, the hills are high enough to keep out most but not all of the fog. Sausalito fights off the bank for most of the day but in the afternoon the fog often cascades over the hills.

The Bay Area is famous for its microclimates. A slight rise in elevation, a different curve to the land can change fog and rain patterns dramatically.

In Marin County, Highway 101 north of the Waldo Tunnel often gets more fog that south of the tunnel. The blocking hills are slightly lower to the north.

The Central Valley

Also known as the San Joaquin Valley and located about 75 miles inland, the Central Valley is influenced more by continental weather than coastal. In the summer, this means heat.

Hot air rises, pulling in cold air like a vacuum. The Central Valley sucks in the coastal air through the Golden Gate and openings in the East Bay hills, foremost the Carquinez Strait, and the hills north of Vallejo until the Valley cools. Then the Valley says to the coast: no more cool air, thank you.

With the suction gone, the inland pull on the ocean fog drops off, often breaking down the fog-producing apparatus and clearing the coastline. Coast residents enjoy days of sunshine. Meanwhile, lacking the cooling air, the Valley heats up again, creating the vacuum that pulls in the fog.

This cha-cha-cha between coast and inland valley gave rise to the Bay Region's boast of "natural air conditioning." In hot weather, nature works to bring in cool air; in cool weather, it works to bring in heat.

The Mountains and Pacific Again

In the winter, great banks of tule fog often form in the Central Valley and chill the air. The Pacific in the winter holds the heat better than the land and, when not raining, often settles balmy weather along coast and Bay cities — another major reason why the Bay Area enjoys a mild climate.

Recall that cold moves toward heat, much as if heat were a suction vacuum. The Central Valley fog would like to move into the Bay but is blocked by the mountain range running up the East Bay.

Occasionally, however, Central Valley fog will penetrate through its openings, again foremost the Carquinez Strait near Vallejo, and work down

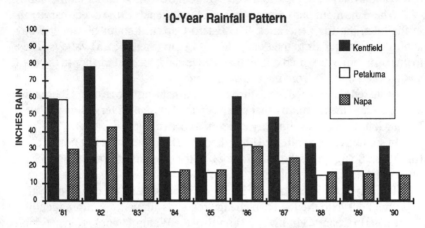

10-Year Rainfall Pattern

Sources: National Weather Service and local fire departments. *1983 rainfall data for Petaluma was not available. El Nino made 1983 an unusually wet year in California. It would be safe to assume rainfall in Petaluma in 1983 exceeded the 58 inches recorded in 1981.

into the Bay — a perilous time for shipping.

Coastal fog often forms well above the Pacific and, pushed by the wind, generally moves at a good clip. In thick coastal fog, you will have to slow down but you can see the tail lights of a car 50 to 75 yards ahead. In valley or tule fog, you can barely make out your hood ornament. This winter fog blossoms at shoe level when cold air pulls moisture from the earth. When you read of 50- and 75-car pileups in the Central Valley, tule fog is usually to blame. Another culprit: dust storms.

Within the Bay, tule fog, before radar, was often responsible for shipping accidents, including the 1901 sinking of the liner Rio de Janeiro, 130 lives lost.

On rare days, tule fog will settle over San Francisco Airport, making takeoffs and landings risky. On the ocean side of the county, Half Moon Bay Airport will be basking in the sun.

Mountains and Rain

Besides blocking the fog, the hills also greatly decide how much rain falls in a particular location. Many storms travel south to north, so a valley that opens to the south (San Lorenzo) will receive more rain than one that opens to the north (Santa Clara-San Jose.)

When storm clouds rise to pass over a hill, they cool and drop much of their rain. Some towns in the Bay Region will be deluged during a storm, while a few miles away another town will escape with showers.

In Marin County, the southerlies come up behind Mt. Tamalpais and rising, give that section a heavier dose of rain than the rest of the county. Kentfield, at the edge of the pattern, often gets a good soaking. In Napa County,

Angwin, located in the hills, will in some years get about 60 percent more rain than Napa City, which is situated on the valley floor.

Farther north the Pacific High peters out and summer storms circle around to hit the coast of Oregon and the Northwest. Occasionally, the tails of these storms will reach down into the North Bay, and the weather forecasters will announce rain north of the Golden Gate.

That basically is how the weather works in the Bay Area but, unfortunately for regularity's sake, the actors often forget their lines or are upstaged by minor stars. In some rare years, the fog doesn't develop. The Bay Area started the 1980s with heavy rains; it finished with a drought of several years.

Sunshine

Like sunshine? You are in the right place. Records show that during daylight hours the sun shines in New York City 60 percent of the time; in Boston, 57 percent; in Detroit, 53 percent; and in Seattle, 43 percent.

Atop Mt. Tamalpais the sun shines 73 percent of the year.

Redwood Drizzle

If you are planning an excursion to redwoods in the summer, bring a jacket and an umbrella. Redwoods are creatures of the fog, need it to thrive. Where you find a good redwood stand, you will, in summer, often find thick fog.

When fog passes through a redwood grove, the trees strip the moisture right out of the air. In some parts of the Bay Region redwood-fog drip has been measured at 10 inches annually.

Scorchers

Occasionally, the Pacific High loops through the northwest a mass of air that travels down the Central and inland valleys, picking up speed and losing its moisture, and blows into the Bay Region as a hot, very dry northeaster, now called a Diablo Wind. A Diablo was responsible for the great Oakland-Berkeley fire of 1991. Earlier in this century Mill Valley in Marin County and Berkeley lost whole neighborhoods to northeaster fires.

The winds are short in duration (a day or so) and would lose much of their potential for destruction if brush were cut, untreated shingles avoided and other preventive measures taken. You might check with your fire department to see what can be done to improve safety around your home.

Earthquakes

Not caused by weather but part of nature's goodie bag. The entire Bay Region is earthquake country, particularly along the coast. The San Andreas Fault runs partially through Marin.

For some sound information about what to do in an earthquake or other disaster, read the beginning of your phone book.

Subject Index